LISTENING TO RADIO,
1920–1950

LISTENING TO RADIO, 1920–1950

Ray Barfield

Foreword by M. Thomas Inge

PRAEGER

Westport, Connecticut
London

Library of Congress Cataloging-in-Publication Data

Barfield, Ray.
    Listening to radio : 1920–1950 / Ray Barfield ; foreword by M.
Thomas Inge.
      p. cm.
    Includes bibliographical references and index.
    ISBN 0–275–95492–7 (alk. paper)
    1. Radio broadcasting—United States—History. 2. Radio programs—
United States—History. I. Title.
    PN1991.3.U6B37   1996
    791.44′0973′09041—dc20   95–52706

British Library Cataloguing in Publication Data is available.

Library of Congress Catalog Card Number: 95–52706
ISBN: 0–275–95492–7

First published in 1996

Praeger Publishers, 88 Post Road West, Westport, CT 06881
An imprint of Greenwood Publishing Group, Inc.

Printed in the United States of America

The paper used in this book complies with the
Permanent Paper Standard issued by the National
Information Standards Organization (Z39.48–1984).

10 9 8 7 6 5 4 3 2 1

To my parents,
R. E. "Red" Barfield
and the late Mary W. Barfield,
who brought the 1938 Grunow console
and the 1939 child
happily together
for "Amos 'n' Andy," "Jack Benny,"
"Sam Spade," "Blondie," and all the others.

Contents

Foreword   ix

Preface   xi

Introduction: "No Radio" and No "Radio"   xv

I.   How They Listened   1

    1.   Listening in the 1920s   3

    2.   Listening in the 1930s   15

    3.   Listening in (and After) the 1940s   25

    4.   Car and Portable Radios   33

    5.   Radio Families   39

II.   What They Heard   59

    6.   Events and Commentators   61

    7.   Sportscasts   79

    8.   Cultural, Educational, and Religious Programs   87

    9.   Morning to Mid-Afternoon Programs   97

Photo essay section begins after page 106.

10. Children's Adventure Programs 107

11. Other Children's Programs 127

12. Comedy Programs 135

13. Drama Anthologies 149

14. Crime and Terror Programs 157

15. Music Programs 171

16. Audience Participation, Amateur Talent,
    and Related Programs 185

17. Radio Travels: Memory, Time, and Place 191

18. Staying Tuned: Contemporary Sources for
    Old-Time Radio 201

Bibliography 207

Contributor Index 211

General Index 215

Foreword

Those of us who grew up in the 1940s and 1950s in America, before television and the computer invaded the home, know what it was like to enjoy the special pleasures of radio listening. During the weekdays, meals and social events were arranged around the broadcast schedules so as not to miss an installment in the lives of Fibber McGee and Molly, Ma Perkins, The Great Gildersleeve, Jack Benny, Burns and Allen, or the spooky denizens of Inner Sanctum with the wonderful squeaking door. And then after school and on Saturday mornings, children had their own world of adventure opened by the likes of Jack Armstrong, Buck Rogers, The Lone Ranger, or Little Orphan Annie. The broadcasters provided the words and sound effects, but our fancies provided the rest in a marvelous drama of the imagination.

In the book you are holding, Ray Barfield has done something quite new in media studies. Rather than trace the history of radio through the usual route of the development of technology, radio stations, broadcast systems, or popular shows and programming, he has sought out a body of oral history from those who grew up with and listened to radio. He has not only collated the responses of his informants but placed their comments in a larger cultural and historical context and thus provided a kind of history from the ground up. He demonstrates thereby just how important and influential radio was in the lives of ordinary Americans. General readers and scholars alike will learn something from Barfield's engaging narrative about why radio was once such a compelling force in our culture.

M. Thomas Inge
Blackwell Professor of the Humanities
Randolph-Macon College

Preface

O pioneers! The engineers and the tinkerers, the financial backers, the performers, and others who brought radio to maturity as a major entertainment and information medium have been celebrated in epic histories of broadcasting, in analyses of program types, and in biographies and autobiographies. However, one essential figure in the shaping of early radio has been largely neglected in accounts of the medium's earliest and most interesting decades. Engineers refined their transmission methods and equipment, entrepreneurs built their networks, comedians honed their timing, sponsors contrived their messages, announcers cultivated their golden tones—all for the obvious purpose of making an impact on the home or workplace listener. And yet that auditor has been assumed to be a mute and passive lump of humanity, a dutiful buyer of every advertised product, and an eager ear for anything that programmers, performers, and creators saw fit to offer. Of course the listener was always assumed to be *there*, counted in the Hooper ratings, fulsomely greeted in program introductions, and represented in absentia by the studio audience's cued applause. Was "the unseen audience" really the passive and unvaried listenership that H. T. Webster pictured in his satirical 1940s syndicated cartoon panels? What were the individual or typical listeners' responses to a variety of program offerings in the 1920s, 1930s, 1940s, and early 1950s? What place did radio have in their lives? Where did they listen and with whom?

The purpose of this book is to let those veteran listeners speak for themselves: to describe their program choices, to recall their preferred listening places and companions, to offer their own perceptions of the special role that radio played in their daily activities during the decades before the television set assumed a major role as electronic household god.

"Remember radio?"

I have asked that question of numbers of people through newspaper columns, public radio announcements, fliers, individual letters, interviews, and other means. Responses have come from teachers and academic administrators, cryptographers, psychiatrists, engineers, business executives, homemakers, farmers and field hands, world travelers, and others. The anecdotes and comments gathered for this study have proved to be evocative, interestingly varied, often insightful, and invariably enthusiastic. These stories tell a great deal about the tone and pace of life in the United States between the end of World War I and the period of the Korean conflict.

Although I have silently regularized *some* features of punctuation, capitalization, and spelling, I have attempted to let each contributor speak as much as possible in his or her own voice, at his or her own pace. My intent is to provide a forum for veteran listeners' recollections, not to police them. In consideration of long-standing habits of mind, I have retained those "extra" capital letters that underscore especially close family relationships or other special emphases, ardent feelings, or idealizing notions. I have also recorded variants of program titles (chiefly of "Amos 'n' Andy" and of "The Grand Ole Opry") as contributors individually remember them. This is, after all, a book about the play of memory on a transient medium, and here impressions, slight misimpressions, and little asides are at least as telling as facts—and often moreso.

In a very large way this book belongs to its contributors, most of whom are named on the following pages. Regrettably, a few contributors could not be contacted for explicit permission to use their names; they have been identified in other ways. Many correspondents and interviewees led me to further sources of information and remembered experience. Still others extended a variety of courtesies. Frank Day, for instance, not only shared his own and his wife's radio experiences but also videotaped a delightful interview with two of his fellow New Englanders and prompted a letter from his former high school teacher, principal, and basketball coach. Former Dean Robert A. Waller, in addition to being a contributor and recruiting others, facilitated my having a semester's sabbatical leave from classroom duties at Clemson University; those months offered valuable time for preliminary planning of this project, and I am grateful to the university, to my college, and to my department for that opportunity.

I owe Praeger imprint advisor M. Thomas Inge a great debt for his advocacy of this study and for his steady encouragement; beyond his own immensely valuable scholarship in the popular arts, he has been a chief muse to countless explorers of such material. Nina Pearlstein has been my invariably pleasant and perceptive editor at Greenwood Publishing Group, and Maureen Melino and David Palmer have considerably eased the publication process. Frank Chorba of Washburn University and Bill Blackbeard of the San Francisco Academy of Comic Art lent their great expertise in radio studies and cartoon art, respectively. In the Clemson University Department of English, Graduate Director Martin Jacobi, Document Design Laboratory Director Tharon Howard, graduate students Laurie Brown, Mika Cantrell, Angela Craigo, Ila Fakla, Suzie Medders, Amanda Paulette and Jeannie Sullivan helped to turn typescript into presentable copy, while Judy Payne, Pearl Parker, and Mary Eberhart generously offered their secretarial assistance. Jim Farmer, El Nault, and Mary Kate Parks were splendid transcribers of a wife's, a husband's, and a mother's recollections.

For advice of many kinds I thank Sylvia Titus, Max Reed, Sterling (Skip) Eisiminger, Harold Woodell, E.P. (Ned) Willey, Ron Rash, Richard Underwood, Cecil Wardell, Gerry Rammel, James Andreas, and C.E. (Gene) Garrison. Librarians Marian Withington and Linda Ferry were patiently helpful in handling research questions, while Charlotte Cassidy, Tim Cook, Helyn Evatt, Jose (Joe) Iriarte, Jessica Otto, and Teresa Shotkoski were careful and resourceful graduate research assistants. For putting me in touch with contributors, I am indebted to Jay Cross, Beth Eckels, Ingrid Eisiminger, Jim Freeman, Jan Geist, Roy Lanford, Roy Martin, Ireland and Linda Regnier, Mr. and Mrs. H.T. Richards, and Patricia Zungoli. In "spreading the word," especially during the early days of my search for contributors, I had the essential and enormous help of Reese Fant, *Greenville News* columnist; Barbara Watkins of the *SPERDVAC Radiogram*; Jerry Pryor, editor of *The Fitzgerald Herald-Leader*; Carl Horak of *Caniffites*; the Harper family of *Pow-Wow*; Beth Jarrard, Liz Newall, and Sandra Woodward of the Clemson University news and publications services; and Alfred Turner of the South Carolina Educational Radio Network, who articulated my invitation for contributions so persuasively that one traveler pulled off a busy stretch of I-85 to copy down an address and a phone number, while another listener stayed awake for most of a night, penning his radio recollections.

For permission to draw selectively from previously published material I thank radio newsletter editors Jack French, Richard Olday, and Owens Pomeroy; Leland Burch, editor and co-publisher of *The Greer Citizen*, for Janie Lyle Black's memories of her father's pioneering as a radio retailer; Billie B. Blocker, for his privately published autobiography "B.B.: Bomber

Pilot Over Europe . . . P.O.W. in Germany"; and Jerry Pryor, editor-publisher of *The Herald Leader,* for Charles Wilson Tucker's "The Radio Fixer."

I am also grateful to John V. Cody for his original drawings and to the Library of Congress Photoduplication Service for its efficient supplying of a classic Farm Security Administration image.

For a grant to assist with illustration acquisitions I am still further in the debt of Frank Day and the Clemson University English Department.

The story of early broadcast radio can never be fully told, but a study such as this one can perhaps clarify the outlines of—or contribute evocative details to—that larger history. All of our efforts have been directed toward that goal.

Ray Barfield
Clemson University

Introduction: "No Radio" and No "Radio"

In the cityscape of the 1980s and 1990s, the "NO RADIO" sign prominently displayed above a car dashboard or in a driver's-side window has become almost as familiar a message as "Loading Zone" or "No Turns" or "Curb Your Dog." Even during a record-setting East Coast blizzard in 1994, when snow blanketed Manhattan streets up to seven feet deep, one car owner had reached his almost entirely buried vehicle to leave the message observed in passing by film scholar Richard Brown: "The owner, ever vigilant, ever a New Yorker, had scratched into the snow, below the visible glass in four-inch letters, 'No Radio.'"[1] In that notice, written in urban shorthand, the fearful car owner sought to prevent a frequent but unauthorized kind of property transfer. However, many experienced listeners might read that declaration in another sense: the kind of broadcasting that they had known and treasured had been filched away some time ago, and there is no *radio* anymore.

During recent decades the Federal Communications Commission, taking a the-more-stations-the-better stance, accelerated broadcasting's evolution by allowing the AM and FM bands to become crowded electronic platforms for "shock jocks" and long-and-loud-breathing pundits. "Urban Contemporary" joined "Top 40" as a highly favored music format, often offered by "ghost" stations without announcers, turntables, or compact disc players, but staffed by an engineer or two to supervise the importing of programs from large syndicated tape reels or from contracted satellite services. (Only the synchronized insertions of station IDs and local commercials would assure the listener that the outlet was licensed to Dover or to Dallas).

For veteran listeners, most of this contemporary radio feast is really famine. To aging ears, high fidelity stereo transmission seems only to clarify the sameness of the wallpaper music, the insistent commercials, and the yackmeister's strained efforts to startle. Radio has become what, at the cost of a few cents' worth of electricity per day, the homeowner leaves playing in an empty house as a would-be foil to would-be burglars while family members are at work, at school, and at the mall. Radio is the booming bass which marks the passing of a young driver going nowhere in particular, fast. Such uses of radio seem to be misuses in judgments of those whose ears, minds, and memories have known earlier forms and formats of the medium between the early 1920s and the 1950s and, in some places (especially on Armed Forces Radio in Europe), even later.

The pioneering decades of commercial radio fell within a period when many families, particularily in small towns and in the country, thought it unnecessary—even downright unneighborly—to lock doors and windows, and the household's taste in many things, including radio programs, was subject to easy public monitoring, especially in warm months. Before home air conditioning was available and affordable, one could stroll through Chicago, Omaha, or Baton Rouge neighborhoods at dusk and detect a unanimity of program choice as "Amos 'n' Andy" or an FDR Fireside Chat drifted from open windows in one house after another. Newspapers which today publish weekly television schedule sections once offered daily radio grids for those who wanted to choose among local "teapot" outlets and powerful clear-channel stations. Never mind that radio was then the only broadcast game in town; those were the days of radio worth hearing. Except in the memories of those now beyond the age of fifty (and in the electronic preservation of disc transcriptions and tape copies), that form of radio has melted away, like last year's snow.

NOTE

1. Reader contribution to Ron Alexander, "Metropolitan Diary," *New York Times,* February 17, 1994; 18.

I

HOW THEY LISTENED

1

Listening in the 1920s

In popular history outlines of twentieth-century events, KDKA's announcement of the 1920 presidential election results is usually listed as *the* beginning date of United States radio broadcasting. It was, instead, a significant apex in a series of apices. If there had not been scientists, inventors, and home tinkerers working out strategies and devices of "radiophonic" communication, the 1920 election returns—and much else—would have been left to the newspapers. Although non-military broadcasting had been held in check by the U.S. Navy during World War I, experimental programs had been transmitted in Detroit and elsewhere before Westinghouse's KDKA sent out its Harding-Cox presidential voting tallies from a Pittsburgh rooftop studio. A small but eager audience was prepared to receive any broadcast offered, and occasional broadcasts rapidly evolved into regularly scheduled presentations of forums, dramatic readings, church services, sports contests, and vocal and instrumental music.

The front cover of the Radio Corporation of America's 1922 "apparatus" catalog proclaimed, "Radio Enters the Home," and indeed it did, in a variety of homemade and "store bought" forms. Crystal sets, often incorporating oatmeal boxes or other handy materials, appeared on kitchen tables, and more elaborate paraphernalia came out of the attic, garage, or basement workshop and into the family living area. The monthly journal *Radio Amateur News*, which had spoken the language of the committed and technically adept wireless operator for about two years, had ceased publication in 1920, just as new uses of broadcast frequencies were emerging, but the larger radio public's needs were soon served by the weekly *Radio Digest—*

Illustrated (1922-1933), crammed with call letters, program listings, and breezy items about radio performers and listeners. "There's room on the radio bandwagon for everyone," the tone of that publication seemed to say, and its writers seldom missed an opportunity to link radio to a celebrity in any field. Photographs of three smiling young ladies graced the front page of almost every issue, while the back page usually featured humorous or novelty applications of radio, including receivers built into fringe-shaded lamps, boater hats, and ashtrays. Advertisements in newpapers and general-interest magazines showed Thorola speakers and De Forest, Zenith, Crosley, and other packaged receivers in photographs and exotic drawings depicting elegant settings, and furniture manufacturers offered stylish cabinets for hiding raw components. Radio was being domesticated quickly, and some observers misread that swiftness as a sign of yet another transient public enthusiasm, like mah-jongg or the Black Bottom.

At the age of ten, Mary Lee McCrackan left Wagener, a South Carolina town of 600, to spend the summer of 1920 with relatives in Chicago, and there she saw and heard her first radio: "It was a crystal set put together by the [owner] himself. It remained a great mystery! The only event of my life that intrigued me more [at that time] was the arrival of a baby! I had been with neighbors all day, and when I got home, there was the BABY. I asked my aunt Brit where he came from. She said that the Stork brought him. I pondered that one." Of the coming of radio to her home town, Mary Lee McCrackan remembers:

Late in the last century, and early in this one, the town of Wagener survived several world-shaking events. The Charleston earthquake was the first, and then came Sheriff Howard's bootleg whiskey raid, followed by the arrival of radio. The only station received in Wagener was "KDKA, Pittsburgh, Pennsylvania," with all its marvels and sounds. The select few who had these first radio receiver sets entertained the whole town. We had a large discarded church bench in our back yard that was moved to the porch of a neighbor who had a radio. All the spare chairs available throughout the neighborhood were collected. We would gather there in the evening to listen to all the music and talk beamed to us from Pittsburgh. The station went off the air at 11 p.m., which was the same time our street lights were extinguished. This soon changed to 11:15 p.m. to ensure our safe transit home. It was entertaining, inspiring, and full of the friendliness of our town of Wagener, South Carolina.

Born in Miami in 1917, the youngest of three girls, Helen Hunt Holmes Whitworth counted herself lucky to have a father who was skilled in the workshop. In the early 1920s, she says,

My daddy made some kind of a set that you could listen to with two sets of earphones. The little house he built was not finished inside, and some wires came down a two-by-four from the roof to where two of us could sit at a little table and eat our lunch and listen to that wonderful contraption. Naturally there was much fussing over whose turn it was each day. I think I was about six then.

One day for some reason we didn't eat lunch at the usual time. A storm came up, and lightning came down that two-by-four and ruined Daddy's little play pretty. A God's blessing none of us were sitting there then!

At about the same time another father yearned for something to enliven the Nebraska scene. An affable and widely liked natural leader, Louis Churchill was known to many as "Lou," and he was urged to run for the governorship of his state. Instead he chose to devote his energies to his family, his business interests, and his wry amusements. Not a radio builder himself, he found a means of sending his own kind of message back east, in exchange for the radio signal gratefully received on the plains. His daughter Maxine Trively tells the story:

My family moved in 1910 from a town in Eastern Nebraska to a raw cow town in Western Nebraska. We left a town with considerable culture and refinements to live in a town devoid of any sign of such. My father had bought a bank and the banker's house, which was pretty classy compared to the other residences, as we had lights (acetylene affairs), a furnace, and a bathroom (the only one in the town and probably in the county). As the result of the dearth of "culture," my father was always seeking out some "touch of civilization." Somehow he must have read about a thing called a "Radio." I'm not sure where he got the idea to have one made, but a young fellow put together a crystal set and put it in our dining room near a window. It had earphones for listening, and sometimes the crackling static made too much noise to hear a voice on the set. My father would sit hunched over the set, straining to hear something—anything. The night of magic came when he got KDKA, Pittsburgh. I believe he got a Cincinnati station too.

After listening to KDKA for some time, he wrote them a letter. He was always a great joker, and in his letter he made up a funny story. He wrote that when he turned on KDKA out in our barn on a Saturday night, all the Indians came whooping in for a big pow wow, and he sometimes had to get out his shot gun and shoot up in the air to get their attention and make them quit dancing and go home.

KDKA published this great listening event with all sincerity, not knowing any Indians or my father. But when this story hit the newsstands and began to filter west, my father heard from Chicago, Omaha, Lincoln, and a large part of western Nebraska. The headlines referred to them as "Churchill's Indians," and the coverage was most amusing. My father, being unflappable, enjoyed the whole episode and just moved on to bigger and funnier escapades.

For children, early radio broadcasts provided lessons in geography, in zoology, and in the fragility of fame. "One of my earliest memories," recalls Alice Boyd Proudfoot, "was in 1925 in Canton, Ohio, when my father called my sister and me: 'Come quickly, girls, I have Cincinnati on the crystal set!' We all crowded around, taking turns putting on earphones. We heard music from several hundred miles away!" In about the same year in Upstate New York, Allen Hilborn's father "had a tiny crystal set with headphones, and I remember listening with total fascination as station WGY in Schenectady broadcast an experimental program featuring the sounds made by animals in the city zoo. There was lots of static, but nobody cared. Two or three years later we had a larger set with a speaker—the only one in the neighborhood—and I remember the neighbors crowding into our living room to listen to a Tunney-Dempsey fight. History says Tunney won, but I was much more impressed by the 'magic' that made listening possible."

The Reverend Philip Humason Steinmetz maintained a lively involvement with radio from the early 1920s onward:

When I was eleven years old, I had one of the early crystal sets with headphones and listened to the broadcasts of Dr. Russell Conwell giving his lectures "Acres of Diamonds," which pointed to the fact that the greatest riches are right in your own backyard. It was station WOO, the Wannamaker store in Philadelphia. All through school days (I was in the Class of 1926 at Germantown Friends School) I listened to the radio with headphones and an old De Forest crystal detector radio. Then I moved to an Atwater Kent with a loudspeaker.

My father was rector of St. Paul's Episcopal Church in Elkins Park, Pennsylvania, from about 1915 to 1945. At some point about 1925 the church installed a small transmitter with the call letters WIBG, Elkins Park. It was on the air at first only on Sunday for the morning service. Later it was [sold] and it ran most of the time but continued to broadcast the Sunday service. When the amateur operator needed something for testing, I would go into the church (I was then in my teens) and play the organ or spout off some nonsense.

We had some special stamps showing our call letters which were requested by listeners who were collecting them to show how many stations they could reach. We had a lot of requests. A request had to quote something distinctive to prove that a program had been heard on the station.

In the towns, farms, and mill villages of the Deep South, radio was a welcome voice from distant cities. The region provides many illustrations of how radio's advent slaked a deep and long-felt thirst for something beyond the familiar landscape and the rituals of working and social life. Bell Mebane remembers an early educational use of radio: "I grew up in Franklin Springs, a small village in Franklin County, Georgia. My family did not own a radio for many years, but I was ten years old in 1924 when our teacher took my class to a neighbor's house to listen to President Calvin Coolidge take the oath of office. I had never even heard a radio before and still remember how it excited and thrilled the whole class to hear that ceremony." The coming of radios and airplanes created interlinked impressions of a dawning age for Florence Ward Ausburn, whose family lived near the Georgia-South Carolina state line in the mid-1920s: "My family was sharecroppers, and Charley Owens, the man who owned the land, bought a battery radio. He invited all the neighbors to come listen to the 'Grand Old Opera' on Saturday night. He lived in a big two-story house. The children would sit on the stair steps. We were thrilled and looked forward to this each week. There was lots of static, but we thought it was wonderful. I also remember the first airplane I saw. We were hoeing cotton, and we watched as far as we could see it."

Now in her early nineties, Lois Robinson recalls, "Hardly anybody had a radio when I was in high school. We lived in Greenville, Mississippi, and the first one I remember, in about 1922, was made by my brother-in-law, Howell. It wasn't in a case—just a bare sort of thing—but we all gathered around it to listen—to music mostly, sometimes with headphones." Her son George Robinson, in his early seventies, adds:

The first crystal set was at my grandmother's house. My uncle Jim built it from a kit which was ordered from a Sears Roebuck catalog. The year was 1926, and I was three years old. Almost seventy years have passed, and my memory now is quite suspect. However, certain flashes are still quite clear. The tuning mechanism was a series of interfacing half-moon-shaped plates which rotated when the knob was turned. This device, along with a collection of vacuum tubes, was in an open tray on top of a table. A vivid memory is the jolt of electricity I got when I touched the tuning plates with my hand. That happened only once and is why, even to this day, I call the repair man when anything goes wrong.

The speaker was a black inverted cone probably six inches in diameter and twelve inches tall. The sounds which came from it were truly magic to a family in Greenville, Mississippi, who thought that Memphis was somewhere on the other side of the globe. We stared at the thing, and at each other, in wonderment as we realized that the voices were actually coming through the air from KMOX in St. Louis and WLW in Cincinnati and WJR in Detroit. I can't recall what was being broadcast, which is unimportant. The all-engrossing attention was to the fact that we could pull unseen voices out of the air and into the living room from all over the world, or at least as far as the world extended to St. Louis and Detroit.

In the face of such growing radio enthusiasm, some skeptics remained. Hubert Webb remembers a man who was shown a battery-powered set and told that it would receive speech and music from hundreds of miles away. "I don't believe it," he said. Invited to sit down, put on the earphones, and hear the signal from Pittsburgh, he listened intently for more than fifteen minutes, yielded the headset to his host's hands, and declared, "I *still* don't believe it."

Janie Lyle Black remembers in very specific detail the first radio that arrived in Greer, South Carolina. It was an Atwater Kent purchased by her father, William Lyle Black, Sr., for $150 in 1922. The set was operated by dry cell and car batteries: two 45-volt B batteries, one four-volt C battery, one six-volt storage-car battery. "The antenna system," she recalls, "consisted of a short and a long line of wire antenna, often run from one tree to another tree. The radios came with a horn and also a pair of earphones." Mr. Black's purpose in ordering the "superior" Atwater Kent extended beyond his own entertainment expectations. As his daughter says,

Mr. Black put it on display in his place of business, The Electric Equipment Company on Randall Street, and people came from miles away to listen to and to see this amazing wonder! It was unbelievable that a sound could come from so far away to be picked up in Greer by a little box.

The stations that came in at that time were KDKA, Pittsburgh; PWX, Havana, Cuba (in English, too); WSM, Nashville; WGT, Schenectady; WLS, Chicago, by Sears Roebuck, "World's Largest Store." And once from as far away as Lyons, France. [The listeners] could not understand the French language, but it did not make any difference, for it was there in the air.

It was unusual how the people felt about radios; some thought they were a hoax, and others felt they were supernatural.

By appointment Mr. Black would carry the radio to one home in a community, and the neighbors would gather to hear the miracle. Sometimes the people would go so far as to crawl under the house to see if there was a hidden Victrola.

Mr. Black sold the first radio in this area to his brother-in-law, Mr. W. T. Rhodes of No. 1 Victor Avenue, manager of Victor and Monaghan Laundries—and ordered another for himself. After Mr. Rhodes bought the radio, they never lacked for company. Each night their living room was filled with curious visitors who came to listen to the programs full of whistles and static. The noises did not matter; they were expected.

Mr. Rhodes's nephew, William L. Black, Jr. (better known as Bub) wanted to hear what was going on. Bub, being timid, did not want to weave through the crowd in the front room. Since the back door was locked, he attempted to climb in the dining room window. He was careful not to make any noise as he was slipping in. One of the men saw Bub's moving reflection in a mirror over the buffet and let out a big groan, saying, "My Gawd, what in the world is that?" He jumped up and headed for the front door. The others did not know what was wrong but were not going to take any chances, and they followed suit and were ready to make tracks up the road.

After the storm finally calmed down with Mr. Rhodes's help, it was discovered that Bub was the most frightened of all, for he thought the radio had exploded and set the house on fire. He was real embarrassed and upset to know that he had caused all the commotion.

In another part of South Carolina, Rodman Lemon's father and uncle soon began to sell radios in their Barnwell grocery, hardware, and dry-goods store. Two vignettes of that venture are strong in family memory:

When the World Series began, only one man could understand what was broadcast due to the static. The postmaster, Mr. Billy Harris, was always called on to don the headphones and repeat the news as it was broadcast.

Once my uncle got in a radio that was battery operated. He took it next door to the druggist, Martin Best, who was known to be suspicious of the unknown. My uncle placed the radio on a glass counter, showed that nothing was connected to the radio, cut it on, and a man was giving the news. Mr. Best ran as if black magic would get him.

By contrast, the pharmacist in Pelzer, South Carolina, had his own crystal set, and Fred M. Dowis remembers the World Series broadcast ritual each fall: "Each day the druggist would take a ten-foot stepladder and place it out in front of the drugstore, take his crystal set, and sit on top of the ladder, put his earplug in his ear, and listen to the game, telling the group of people gathered around the play by play as the game went along." Paul Looper recalls the same pioneer listening post a few years further into the sports-avid mid-1920s: "The first broadcast I remember came from a loudspeaker hanging on the corner of Griffin's Drug Store in downtown Pelzer. It was one of Jack Dempsey's prize fights. A very large crowd had gathered in the streets and on the sidewalks, standing shoulder to shoulder. I enjoyed an RC Cola and a Moon Pie during the fight."

The arrival of a radio set in South Parsonsfield, Maine, prompted some frustration and some Yankee improvisation, according to retired high school teacher and administrator Harry Boothby:

The first radio in our family was before we had electricity. It took a six-volt battery and two other types of smaller batteries. I remember our father having problems getting them hooked up to make the radio work and in his frustration using some cuss words, and so our mother removed us from the area until the cussing subsided and there were sounds coming out of the air.

Our family was invited to the home of [trapper] Al Milliken to listen to one of the Dempsey-Tunney fights. Their radio had a speaker on a cord that made it possible to move it a short distance from the radio. The reception was poor, with squeals and loss of sound making it possible only to understand a small part of the announcer's words. In an attempt to increase the volume, the speaker was placed in a dish pan. That was believed to have made it come in louder, but still not loud enough for the circle of listeners to hear. It was decided to try a larger container, and so a washtub was used to put the speaker in, but that didn't solve the problem.

We would have made a good picture, sitting around as close as we could get to the washtub in the light of kerosene lamps.

My first memory of anything concerning radio was at about six years old. My great uncle Daniel Chellis would not believe his neighbor Everett Burnham when he was told that his new radio would enable him to hear programs from New York and Pittsburgh at the time the events were taking place. My great uncle, who had lived his life on a country farm, accepted the fact that this could be possible with the telephone, but in no way could a noise released into the air a thousand miles away be heard, even if Mr. Burnham lived on the height of land in the area. Mr. Burnham, a music lover, invited Mr. Chellis to come and listen to an opera singer, which he did. Mr. Chellis was not a lover of soprano voices. In the program, the static and squealing of the radio along with the singer's high notes convinced him to stick to his Victrola for a few years.

A different form of doubt seized Jim Chase, who lived at his daughter's home in North Parsonsfield, Maine, in the mid-1920s, when the coming of electric service made buying a radio practical for that house on a hill, the best reception point in town. According to Merrill Dunnells, his great-grandfather Chase was ninety-six years old when the radio was installed and the elderly man had his first opportunity to hear the fishing catch report, broadcast at a regular time each morning. "And when they started giving that fishing report from Boston," Merrill Dunnells says, "they would start telling how many tons of haddock, how many tons of cod, how many tons of this [had been caught], and he'd grab his ol' pipe and put in some tobacco and say, 'Oh, them Gawd-dam' LIAHS!,' and he would run for the kitchen. He didn't believe that." Mr. Dunnells recalls walking two and a half miles to his grandmother's hilltop house each day to hear a quarter-hour program featuring a cowboy singer who was sponsored by Wizard Oil. "I bought some of the stuff," he admits, "but I don't remember whether you rubbed it on ya' or poured it in ya'."

With a young man's curiosity, Nelson D. Mallary, Jr. noted the details of his family's first radio in the "early-mid-to-moderately-late 1920s" in Georgia. It "was a black box (that sat on a table) about thirty two inches long by twelve inches high by twelve inches deep. It had three large dials spaced out in the middle with a small dial on either side (o O O O o). It took the three large dials to select a station. WLW might have been '36-65-72,' while KDKA might have been '28-15-54.' The loudspeaker was on a twenty-foot heavy electric cord and looked like a giant alarm clock on a pedestal (to keep it from 'rolling'). The fabric-covered part (where the 'clock face' would have been) was fifteen inches in diameter and the whole thing eight inches thick. We kept the radio in the booknook and the loudspeaker in the living room." He adds, "It was the only radio like it I have ever seen. (I suspect it was the most expensive and the 'best' we ever owned)."

At about the same time in North Carolina, the interest of Joseph F. "Joe" Jones was caught during a family visit to Greensboro, where he discovered an early radio set in the "cluttered workshop" of his Uncle Bill, whom his mother described as a "tinkerer." The long black box had "a multitude of black knobs on it, both large and small" and had provision for four sets of heavy earphones. "Your head soon tired of wearing them," he says, adding, "Most of all I remember that most of the time we heard squawks and squeals and a lot of static. However, sometimes in between all the noise we would hear an announcer giving the news and also music. I remember my Uncle Bill tuning those many knobs back and forth and around, trying to get a clearer signal." This taste of radio listening, however tentative, inspired Joe Jones to build his own crystal set "tuned by what we called a 'cat whisker.' It was fun to listen to that home-made radio set."

As a boy of six or seven years, William A. "Bill" Buri discovered radio—and came to grief—in the late 1920s when he was taken on a visit with family friends in Philadelphia: "I danced around with the cat whisker and pulled the radio off on the floor. The people didn't appreciate that."

As the 1920s began to wane, the radio "magic" spread to more and more remote places. Corinne Holt Sawyer's father had moved his family to a mining operation in northern Minnesota, in Chisholm on the Mesabi Range, where the pioneer listener was entirely dependent on the nighttime bounce waves from Pittsburgh or New York:

When I was perhaps three to four years old, my father read several books on the subject and made a small set himself. I don't remember much about it, except that its most noticeable feature was a small cylinder wrapped in wire and that it had no speaker at all. He and Mother discovered that reception was best in our bathroom, where they attached wires from their little radio, perched on the edge of the tub, to the water pipes over the tub—pipes weren't hidden in the walls in those days, of course, but were right out in the open.

One night, Dad invited our neighbors from across the street to come over to listen to this modern marvel. The four adults jammed into the tiny bathroom, and I was there as well—to keep me from getting into mischief, I suppose, while they were occupied passing the earphones back and forth and ooooh-ing and aaaah-ing. I hadn't the least notion what they were doing.

Then suddenly my dad said, "Oh, this is something you'd like to hear, Corinne," and he put the earphones (big, black, rigid, and made of hard rubber or bakelite or something like that) on my head. It took a while for me to get even one of the phones fitted over my ear, but I can remember the wonder of the moment even today! There was a woman's voice, crackly and faint, telling the story of Little Red Riding Hood! The thrill of hearing that disembodied voice must have been something like what deaf people feel when a device allows them to hear sound for the very first time. I remember Dad saying, "Look at her grin!"

After a few moments, they took the earphones away from me to pass around the room again, and I started to cry. I was far too young to understand the concept of sharing, or to appreciate the miracle of the radio phenomenon. All I knew was they wouldn't let me hear the rest of my magical story, and I bawled till Mother had to take me away.

Our first *real* radio set—which always stood in a corner of the family living room—was acquired in the late 1920s. It had a big horn as a speaker, like the Victrola ad with the dog listening to "his master's voice."

Born in Zanesville, Ohio, in 1924, Raymond Ruland remembers, "My father bought our first radio in 1927 or '28 for the express purpose of listening to a championship prize fight. The radio was a cabinet model, an ugly thing standing on four spindly legs. The brand name was Earle, and this little one was warned, 'Don't even go near it.' Since the nearest station was KDKA, Pittsburgh, about 130 miles away, my older brothers strung an antenna from our house to the garage about forty or fifty feet away."

Owen Lyons, Jr. recalls another sports-prompted radio purchase in the winter of 1929 and 1930, when the family moved to a small village in Missouri and his father began work as a railway mail clerk for the Post Office Department:

Radio was becoming very interesting to small-towners at that time, and my dad was an avid fan of the St. Louis Baseball Cardinals. He bought an Atwater Kent console radio and two telephone poles. He installed a pole at a front and a back corner of our property, ran a wire between the two poles, with a connecting wire down to the window near the radio.

I still remember vividly his listening to the ball games every day and keeping his home-made score cards for each game. Also, during the evening meal hour every weekday it became a habit to listen to a popular fifteen-minute program called "Amos and Andy" and another daily fifteen-minute program featuring a group of brothers singing the popular songs of the day. Those young men were known as the Mills Brothers.

In those days, with Dad's antenna we could receive stations from New York City to Denver to the Rio Grande River station in Del Rio, Texas. This station was owned and operated by a man known as Dr. Brinkley, who sold his "snake-oil" medicines almost nationwide by radio. Some of the other station call signs I remember were WSM, WLW, WWL, WOR, WSB, KMOX, WREC—still strong frequencies today.

In the early 1920s, radio listening had been a largely solitary affair; the tinkerer tweaked and tuned his signal and recorded new triumphs of distance reception in his log. Then came the pass-the-headphones phase, as family members and guests awaited their turns. As speakers became more readily available and affordable, family listening became the norm, and the tableau was complete. Dad sat in his easy chair, a pipe in one hand and the newspaper in the other, his ears monitoring the radio, which he would occasionally get up to retune with a sigh that seemed to speak more of contentment and pride of possession than of complaint. Mom sat opposite, her sewing basket handy. The kids occupied the sofa or the center of the large rug, their eyes focused on the comics page but their ears attending to the doings on the radio.

In the late 1920s, Doris Baker belonged to a larger family, and radio was no less important there:

I was raised in a Masonic orphanage in Oxford, North Carolina, in the 1920s and 1930s, graduating from high school there in 1936. There were 375 children and seventy-five teachers at the orphanage. The first time I saw and heard a radio was about 1928. Our superintendent brought his radio to the auditorium and set it on the stage steps for all of us to listen. I can't remember what we heard, but we were spellbound.

We immediately decided to buy a radio for my dorm of thirty six girls, all ages. Each of us had to pay one dollar. If you just knew how hard it was for us to get up the money. We picked up acorns at three cents for a twelve-quart bucket and raked leaves for one cent for each big burlap bag that had to be stuffed until it would not hold another leaf. If we could find a mouse, we would be paid one cent, and they cut off the tail. One of my friends asked why they cut off the tail. I said, "Do you know how many times we would have sold that same mouse?" They did.

If you can imagine thirty six girls sitting in our cane-bottom chairs around that radio listening to "Grand Hotel," the Jello programs. We had two-hour study halls five nights a week. If we had been smart all week, on Friday night we might get to listen to "Amos 'n' Andy" or maybe the Jack Dempsey fights with Gene Tunney. It was a great place to be raised; it is still raising children.

Thus the first full decade of programmed radio bridged into the 1930s with all the signs of an aural institution-in-the-making. A baseball team, a prize fight or two, or a "colored" dialect program performed by two white men in Chicago and sent out on a fledgling network—each of these was reason enough for thousands to invest time in building or money in buying a radio set.

2

Listening in the 1930s

"Bringing home the radio set" and looking for "the little man who lived in the [radio] box and made the music" are recurrent motifs in listener accounts from the Depression decade. When the creation of the Rural Electrification Administration and the building of giant dams made electric power available to farms and communities in the Appalachians, in the Midwest, and in the Western states, the first family purchase was often a radio. Many families outside the cities could not wait for the power lines to be strung, however; they chose to improvise with troublesome batteries. Whether in the city or the country, the household's first radio was typically borne home like a proud trophy, a symbol of victory in the family budget wars. And not only youngsters but their grandparents too wondered how the music and the voices got into and out of "that thing." Copies of the weekly *Radio Guide* were kept near receiving instruments, which were available in an increasing variety of packagings: cathedral radios for the pious and traditional, Deco radios for the fashionable, pipe-rack radios for lounging types, and consoles and square wood veneer table sets for everyone. Near the end of the decade, a few optimistic manufacturers added a "Television" function to the row of push buttons supplementing the tuning dials of some models.

The yowler was indeed being tamed. Less and less a novelty item, the family radio seemed more and more a household necessity. Often it was the single investment in family entertainment. Calling herself "a child of the Depression," Jeanette Caler declares, "Radio was our lifeline to the world." "It was our prized possession for a long time," Juanita Capell says of the round-topped table model that her parents purchased in the early 1930s: "My Mother and Dad had nine living children, and we had trouble all of us trying to hear what we wanted to. But we managed to work it out somehow. The day we got a Radio was a great event in our lives. We enjoyed it for many years. It was all the entertainment we had." Like many other contemporary grandparents, Joe Jones still treasures a receiver which came into the family in the early Depression years: "My Dad bought us a 1933 Philco console which I believe was one of the first radio sets to have amazing 'push buttons' to tune the station. That old Philco set is today down in my basement play-room, and it still works and plays. My grandchildren have a great time with the push buttons and love to listen to the 'old' radio. It still has the big old glass tubes which came in it, but when they wear out or break, that will be the end, as I understand none of the old tubes are made any more."

When they first encountered radio in the early 1930s, some listeners had difficulty understanding its precise nature. Evelyn B. Thomason reports that her grandfather was far too early in attempting interactive communications: "Vividly I remember when my father surprised us with our first radio. It was the most beautiful and wonderful thing I had ever seen, a thing of mystery and delight. One night we took our prized possession to my grandfather's room so he could listen to the returns being broadcast from a local election—probably county; I don't remember. Anyway, everyone was intently listening when all of a sudden my grandfather held his hand up high and said in a loud, pleading voice, 'Repeat that, please!' We had a good laugh later, after explaining the situation to him, and we laugh about it to this day."

V. T. Chastain recalls,

My father, W.H. Chastain, had the first radio in the Holly Springs community ten miles north of Pickens, South Carolina. It had been a gift from friends in Michigan, and, since electricity had not yet come to our area, the radio had to be run off of a six-volt battery borrowed from the car for that purpose. At first WSM, Nashville, Tennessee, was the only station, but later we also got WFBC from Greenville. Reception was pretty good if the weather was good, but bad weather brought static. Programs consisted of country music and boxing. . . . Neighbors from all around congregated at our house to see and hear the amazing radio! One man I remember in particular really enjoyed a certain musical rendition, and he told Dad, "Make 'em play that one again, Wade." Nothing Dad could say would convince him that the musicians were in Greenville and not somewhere, somehow, inside that box!

At the age of about four, some sixty years ago, Rachel P. McKaughan was engaged in the natural childhood process of discovering the dimensions of the world, often understanding new things by analogy: "I saw [just] about the first airplane in the sky that I'd ever seen. I asked my dad how it flew, and he said there was a man in it who flew it! (A child at that age has no concept of distance and size perspective.) Later we got a radio in the home, our first. When he turned it on, I asked if that was the tiny little man who could fly an airplane! I thought someone had to be in 'the box' doing all that talking."

Trina Nochisaki was born in 1927 and dates her earliest radio recollections from about 1930. Her account pictures a family strongly committed to the medium:

We had two radios in our house. One was a magnificent Stromberg Carlson model the size of a modern day hutch with curving legs and beautiful retractable doors covering the radio part of this piece of furniture. We really didn't get to listen to it much because it was in the "parlor" and my hard-working parents had little time for sitting in this room.

The other was a Philco table model radio which was in our multi-purpose room (dining room, den). I remember my parents listening to Father Coughlin, Amos and Andy, and Fibber McGee. . . . And I can't recall how many times I tried to sneak up on the real little people I just *knew* lived in the radio—if only I could catch them unawares.

By about 1934, B. A. "Gus" Wentz was gathering the first remembrances of his life in the part of the house which his family had designated "the radio room." He says, "I remember looking into the back of the radio to try to see the 'little people' in there. The radio—an Air Castle, I think—stood on a table in the corner next to the stairs. We kids would vie for choice seats on the stairs as the family hovered around to hear the Sunday evening lineup (after church, of course). Some folks in the church would actually miss evening services to catch Fred Allen, Jack Benny, George Burns and Gracie Allen, the first time I was ever aware of a conflict between radio and 'duty to God'."

For many who were young children in the early 1930s, the receiving instruments seemed to loom very large. Paul F. Snow first encountered radio through a neighbor's Atwater Kent "powered by a wet storage battery with a monster horn speaker." "The first one that I remember," Ellen Edmonds says, "was a large cabinet that sat in the living room or 'parlor'. . . . It had a small dial that was orange when it was on. Later on, after my father passed away, we moved to the mountains of western North Carolina, near Marshall. We lived on a small farm and we owned a small 'table model' radio with a large battery. Our listening pleasure was measured by the life of the battery (we did not have electricity or inside plumbing)." For Dottie Zungoli, whose family owned the first receiver in a newly electrified Philadelphia neighborhood, the programs were delightful, but they emerged from an early combination radio-phonograph that seemed an aesthetic compromise: "It was a great big ugly thing, and on the other side of it was a Victrola."

For Mary Lee McCrackan, the listening experience was defined not by the size of the radio but by the dimensions of the house. Having known very early broadcasting in Chicago and in the Deep South, she moved to Richmond, Virginia, to live with her father, who

had remarried after being an eligible widower for fourteen years, and I came along in the deal. We lived on the third floor of the Antebellum Matthew Fontaine Maury House. It was a perfect setting for listening to such scary radio broadcasts as Sherlock Holmes and "The Hound of the Baskervilles." The description of the hounds on the radio and the associated sound effects were scary in the extreme. It was late on a cold Sunday afternoon, and the backyard shadows from the fig tree coupled with the howling wind were more than I could take. My father and mother had gone to the university to prepare for the next day's classes, but I telephoned and asked that they return home at once.

During the 1930s Bill Buri spent most of his childhood in an aunt's home in the coal-mining regions of Pennsylvania, and there he encountered the uncertainties of reception. "We would get really weird stations because it was up there in the mountains. We used to get WJZ and WOR from New York, KDKA from Pittsburgh, WBZ from Boston, and WBZA, Springfield. Sometimes if the weather was right, we'd get Canadian Broadcasting at night. We had two identical radios—I think they were Emersons— and they looked like cathedrals. In the spring when the weather got warmer, I had a little hut in the attic; they had a bed up there and a German helmet that my uncle had brought home from World War I. You could get better stations up in the top of the house." In Ardmore, Pennsylvania, George A. Walker, Jr. knew similar difficulties: "There were always frustrating periods, early on, with trying to pick up special stations or broadcasts that were beyond the capability of our radio. It got better as time went on. The stations themselves added more power, and the radios got better and better."

In those days of variable reception, a change of residence could prompt the buying of a radio. "It was a long time before we had a radio of our own," Lois Robinson says. The purchase came after her family moved in 1930 from Greenville, Mississippi, to Chicago. That new console "had a curved dial with numbers on it, and when it was turned on, the dial glowed a light orange color. Radio wasn't 'instant on' at first. It had to warm up a little before you could hear a program." The move to the city also underscored a startling contrast in listening matter: "We used to listen to the police calls late at night. In Greenville, as our funny friend Boola Woods used to say, we heard, 'Calling both cars! Calling both cars!' Greenville wasn't a very big place. But listening to police calls after we moved to Chicago was scary."

Helen J. Tidwell's memory of her family's investment in radio blends elements of humor and sacrifice:

My father traded one of his best "milk" cows for a console type radio. A beautiful piece of furniture, up on four legs, speakers covered with a fabric, dial, and four knobs, it was placed in our "parlor." The first morning after obtaining the "Squawk Box" (as [it was] sometimes referred to), my mother tuned in to a program called "Don McNeill's Breakfast Club." On that particular morning they had a cow mo-o-o-o-o-ing on the program. (Don't know if we had Elsie the Borden cow back then or not.) My mother called to my father in another room and said, "Daddy, your cow is on the radio." Being only four or five years old, I wondered how Daddy's cow got in that radio and when it would come out. It never did!

Historian Robert A. Waller tells of growing up in the mid-1930s on a farm in central Illinois: "In the days before FDR's New Deal REA brought electricity to rural America, the first radio I can remember was battery operated from a wind charger on the top of our tenant farmer's home. On becalmed days, there were sometimes limited or no evening programs when the battery had not retained or received enough of a charge to operate the system." Jim Harmon, author of *The Great Radio Heroes, Radio Mystery and Adventure and Its Appearances in Film, Television, and Other Media*, and other studies of the popular arts, says, "Our family first got electricity in the house and radio the same Christmas, when I was three. I do remember, somehow, I do. We lived in the rather rural town of Mt. Carmel, Illinois. The year was 1936. On Sundays, we all listened together to Jack Benny, Fred Allen, and the rest. I would lie on my stomach, hypnotized by the yellow eye of the dial. I've heard others say the same thing, but I know this is no false memory."

Sometimes the receiver had to be placed inconveniently because of the antenna's location. Absalom W. Snell's family experienced that problem when he was a teenager in the late 1930s: "We spent most of our time in the evenings in a bedroom with fireplace heat. The radio was located in the living room, which was not heated and seldom used, so that an antenna could be connected. One end of a multi-strand wire was connected to a high chimney and the other to a cypress pole installed for that purpose. The antenna suffered a lightning stroke, and the multi-strand wire was completely destroyed. The attached solid wire conducted the lightning to the window sill, then to the electric wire in the wall, causing damage to the wall."

Living in a city in the mid-1930s did not guarantee immediate access to a radio, as Dr. Jeanne Kenmore well knew: "In 1935 I was twelve years old. We did not have a radio! Depression days. We children saw one movie a year, but somehow—I suppose from conversations at school—we learned what we were missing. My mother, my two younger brothers and I lived in an 'upper' duplex in Minneapolis. In that city a duplex has two floors which are identical. Downstairs there was a woman with her two children about my age. So, I crouched down under a window on the front porch to try to hear the downstairs radio. When the weather was decent and a window was open, I had a perfect seat, months on end."

In Ann Chase's family, as she remarks with an unblinking directness learned from Depression-era spareness, the family radio purchase became a test of financial stability: "My father was never fired from a job—he was famous for giving them up, usually right before some big expenditure. [One day] I was playing with my friends when a large truck stopped outside our house. The driver, with his helper, dismounted and, with great authority, opened the back doors. There, surrounded by emptiness, sat an impressive floor model radio. This radio was placed in the hall below the stair, not too far away from the living room or the kitchen, so that the sound that emerged could reach the ears of either the resting or the busy."

Joan Waller grew up in the Chicago suburb of River Forest, populated by doctors', industrialists', and other professionals' families. In her home, she remembers, radio was very much a part of the children's play:

The radio occupied a prominent place at the end of the living room. Couch cushions on the floor provided seating as well as something soft to lie on while engrossed in daily radio episodes.

My father's return home from work occasioned the only brief interruption. When Dad opened the door and called, "Is anyone at home?" my two brothers, two sisters, and I would run and give him a hug, check to see if he'd brought us any presents, and then rush back to our programs.

I remember the day when a new remote control radio arrived at our house. What magic. Not only could we change programs by rotating the dial from across the room, but now we could even change the stations in our house from the house next door. While one of us took the magic box and rotated the dials from next door, the rest of us listened to the stations changing inside our house and signaled through the window to let the dial changer know it was working. We continued to change places until each of us had had our turn. Though this proved to be great fun, we soon tired of our new "toy" and returned to serious radio listening.[1]

Even if they were born into very different settings, children of the 1930s could view the arrival of the radio in similar ways. Max Salathiel was born on a farm in Central Oklahoma in 1935, and in his youth he heard members of his extended family appear on national broadcasts. "I grew up with radio," he declares. "My earliest memories are of my dad bringing in a box in late 1938 with a brand new Zenith table model receiver. It was battery operated as we didn't have electricity. We had a windcharger mounted on a windmill to charge the battery. The glass dial on the radio had a sailing ship etched on it. When you pushed a knob on the front of the radio at night, the dial would light up, displaying the frequencies and the ship." Bill Anthony recalls his early days in the city: "It all started for me in 1937, when my father came home from work with a new Zenith radio under his arm. Funny, I was only seven at the time, but I can still picture that quite clearly as though it just happened. I then started to try to tune in distant stations and even drew a picture of the dial on paper and clearly marked the numbers from the dial when I got those wonderful stations that we were not supposed to get in Pittsburgh. Every Sunday at seven, my mother would clean up after dinner, and we would all sit down to listen to Jack Benny. I remember how delighted I was that the show made my father laugh because times were tough, and he worked hard to buy that radio and [meet] all of our other needs." He adds, "The love affair with radio continues to this day, as I am an avid Old Time Radio collector (and have been for twenty five years)."

Malcolm Usrey, a children's literature scholar, weighs the value of radio in his Texas childhood:

In the 1930s and 1940s, the Texas Panhandle was not a cultural desert, but neither was it a cultural oasis. Live musical and dramatic performances were rare, with only Amarillo large enough to support serious cultural events, and for the most part, they were suspended during World War II. There was no "little" theater, though most high schools offered one dramatic performance, the annual "senior play." County fat stock shows and county fairs and the Texas Panhandle State Fair in Amarillo drew larger crowds than concerts and plays. Rural churches had their all-day Sunday singings, which lasted for two to four hours after a "dinner on the ground," leaving only those with the strongest lungs to sing the hours away into the late afternoon, time to return home and take care of farm chores—milking, feeding animals, gathering eggs. Every county seat had at least one film theater, and Amarillo may have had two or more, but the small towns and villages did not have theaters.

County seats also had small libraries, usually a small room in the court house or in a store building on the main street. Many rural people never saw the inside of a library, never read a newspaper, never read a magazine. But nearly everyone had a radio.

My family acquired its first radio in the mid-1930s, when I was about five or six years old. It was an elegant piece of furniture and an astounding piece of equipment, a large, three-feet tall Zenith with a dark mahogany finish. It had a world-wide band and was powerful enough to bring in KGNC in Amarillo about seventy five miles away, KRLD in Dallas about 300 miles away, and sometimes stations in San Antonio and New Orleans.

The author of a survey of Sherlock Holmes's appearances in several media, Gordon Kelley also feels that he was born at the right time to appreciate radio's value:

I was born in 1934, a time when the family radio was the center of most people's lives. We could only afford one radio because the Depression was still evident in the small farm town where I lived, but we really didn't need more than one because listening was a family affair.

My family lived about twenty miles south of Indianapolis, and we were fortunate in being able to get four local stations and one from Cincinnati (WLW). The reception on our large and heavy table top cathedral radio was quite good. We only had AM radio during the times I was growing up, and it was subject to all of the atmospheric disturbances that most of us today do not notice on the more prevalent FM band. There would be lots of static during the summer months when electrical storms were common, and our radio squeaked and squawked each time we changed stations. I still have this radio in working condition, and it hasn't changed at all. All the noises are still there, but there isn't much of anything to listen to.

NOTES

1. The closing paragraphs of Ed Streeter's lightly satirical *Daily Except Sundays, or What Every Commuter Should Know* (New York: Simon and Schuster, 1938; p. 144) provide an interesting contrast to Joan Waller's description of her father's return at the end of the workday. Streeter writes,

Home to the little ones. Home! The word thrills us with its deep significance. They are grouped tensely round the radio. We enter to the sound of galloping hooves. "Get that yellow cur," cries a fine baritone voice. Two pistol shots ring out. We announce ourselves with a cheery shout. From our point of view the scene calls for tossing a baby at this point.

Our little circle greets us with angry frowns. "For heaven's sake, Dad, keep quiet. Mysterious Drummond is on."

We become ourselves. We relax.

3

Listening in (and After) the 1940s

By the 1940s, the place of radio seemed fixed in the national consciousness. City dwellers were confident of good reception and a variety of station and program choices. Radio batteries could finally be set aside as the rural electrification program neared completion, and in widely separated places in the West and in the isolated valleys of Mid-Atlantic and Southern states, listeners welcomed the steady power source for their receivers. Children continued to be charmed by radio sets and favorite programs, and in "catch-up" places, their elders were, too.

On small tables beside living room chairs, copies of *Radio Mirror* shared space with issues of *Life*, *Look*, and *The Saturday Evening Post*. Listeners ritually kept copies of the daily newspaper's radio program grid handy for reference, even though experienced listeners knew by heart the days, times, and dial positions of their preferred programs. Individual and family schedules had long been adjusted to the broadcast times of favorite comedians, musical "hours" (some of which were really half-hours), and news commentators. Programs that once seemed brash and startling had grown familiar, like old friends who were expected to drop by for a daily or a weekly visit.

Ironically, the decade of the 1940s, which seemed to solidify the maturing medium's place in American popular culture, would be radio's last decade of uncontested dominance. Families and neighbors of World War II servicemen came to know world geography, joy, and grief as they tensely monitored radio reports of European and Pacific battles. In many homes, all talk and motion ceased when war bulletins interrupted regular programs.

As Edward R. Murrow reported from London and as the names of Charles Collingwood, Eric Sevareid, William L. Shirer, and others became better and better known through reports from foreign capitals and battle zones, many listeners traced the path of war by placing pins in large maps published in Sunday newspapers. For the same purpose, the George F. Cran Company of Indianapolis offered a boxed kit called "Follow the Flag to Victory," its lid featuring a photograph of a family posed in a semicircle around the console radio, the furnished map close at hand for adding victory markers. At war's end some expressed their patriotism by replacing the old cathedral table set with a Crosley "Victory" model, its red and white dial face rendered in a stylized Stars and Stripes design, with the manufacturer's name emblazoned in widely spaced letters near the top of the dial and "America" spelled out below.

At mid-decade, however, the eagerly charted victory and the return of servicemen and servicewomen brought a profound change in the temper of life in the United States. The war years had meant many kinds of restraints and confinements: not indulging in unnecessary travel in the days of gasoline rationing; submitting to the exhausting work schedules and production requirements of defense plants; obeying the "Loose Lips Sink Ships" warnings of posters and magazine public service advertisements and thus having only guarded conversations with strangers; staying at home to hear the war news while sorting the food rationing coupons or knitting for the troops. After a short and thankful catching of the national breath, reunited families wanted to get out of the house. New and redesigned appliances glittered temptingly in the postwar marketplace, and television sets were soon available in large cabinets with small screens, sometimes accompanied by a magnifying lens mounted in a floor stand. Even though radio was becoming more conveniently portable than ever before, the networks were placing their bets on television.

Radio's response to the postwar spree was to popularize quiz programs and to entrust large afternoon segments of airtime to disc jockeys. Even in the late 1940s, evening network programming offered the familiar patterns of comedy and variety shows, crime and terror dramas, and adaptations of Broadway plays and Hollywood films, but former listeners were not at home every evening. Inexpensive radios, most with limited reception range, were available in department stores and through mail order catalogues, and the centrally placed household radio was neglected as each family member acquired a set for private listening. Program rating services found that the number of people residing at one address could no longer be equated with the number of listeners to a given program at a given time.

Under these pressures, traditional radio offerings would rapidly begin to disappear in the early to mid-1950s. Although Western programs such as "The Lone Ranger," "Death Valley Days," and "Tom Mix" had established themselves as firm favorites in the 1930s, the new radio Westerns of the 1950s, including James Stewart's NBC series "The Six Shooter" (1953-1954), seemed more nearly an echo of a television fad than a fresh appeal for audiences in radio drama's waning days. Freeman Gosden and Charles Correll, having developed their blackface radio roles in the 1920s and having become the major spur to radio purchases in the early 1930s, were forced in 1954 to trade their Fresh Air Taxi Company for the proprietorship of CBS's "The Amos and Andy Music Hall," a rather restrained disc jockey program that ran until 1961, the year that the radio version of "Gunsmoke" was dropped. Fibber McGee and Molly, ratings leaders in the early war years, would leave their half-hour weekly "Johnson's Wax Program" in 1953, returning in a quarter-hour format five nights per week until 1957, and then filling five-minute segments on NBC's "Monitor," where their small-town comedy bumped against acerbic sketches by a new-style pair of radio comedians fresh from Boston, Bob Elliott and Ray Goulding, who would make a specialty of satirizing radio. Broadcasting in radio's earliest decades, the folksy Will Rogers and the zany teams of Billy Jones and Ernie Hare ("The Happiness Boys") and Col. Stoopnagle and Budd had used radio to tease radio too, but Bob and Ray had arrived near the other end of the medium's arc of dominance in American life.

In the 1940s, then, radio knew both institutional triumph and the beginnings of its major evolution, which most veteran listeners call its "decline." While they lasted, though, those radio days afforded much pleasure to old and young alike.

When Jim Fanning's family left Atlanta to visit relatives in Seattle in the summer of 1940, he worried that he would miss his favorite programs there. "But they were on," he was relieved to discover, "but at strange times for me. I did get to hear them." Although regional networks and a few dramatic series produced only for West Coast listeners added a distinct flavor to the mix, the programming of the national chains spanned the continent, a seemingly permanent fulfillment of radio's promise.

The family radio set was still an object to be explored by curious boys. H. K. Hinkley, who would become a mechanical engineer, felt such impulses:

Listening to the radio in the 1940s in southern Illinois was a nightly activity for me. My parents had a cathedral style radio they had bought second hand when they got married in 1933. It had a well-calibrated dial with a light behind that shone through a mask so that a wedge of light followed the dial pointer. The only other controls were a volume/on-off knob and a tone control. Several yards of a heavy-gauge wire were attached to the "aerial" screw on the back. The wire had been coiled and left on the table behind the set. The back of the radio was open so that the dial light and tube filaments cast an interesting pattern on the wall. I soon learned to hold a finger on the antenna screw to improve reception of distant stations. Of course, everything was distant. The nearest network stations were in St. Louis, 100 miles to the northwest.

Reception was usually good except for static induced by summer storms and the arc-welder in the service station down the block. When one station faded out, I could rapidly re-dial to another and hardly lose a word.

There was a bonus in the summer. The northern cities went to Daylight Savings Time (War Time during the early '40s) and their programming advanced an hour relative to southern Illinois and most of the South. This meant that special or favorite programs could be heard twice!

As a small boy, Paul Garrett got as close as possible to the big console. His account touches on questions that had puzzled the children of the 1930s too:

My love affair with radio started when I was two—maybe before that, but I can only remember back as far as age two. We had quite a large radio back then, large enough for me to take naps in the back of it, something I did till I was five or six. Oh how I loved looking at those large tubes, feeling the sounds of music as they poured out of the speakers.

I was continually fascinated by the metaphysical question "How did those small people get in there?" and such considerations kept me going for years.

"Mama, how do those little people get in there? Where do they get small enough guitars to get them inside the speakers?" And no matter how many times she explained that it was really large people somewhere far away making the voices, the sound effects, and the music, I knew better. They all originated right there in the radio—I knew it, because I could feel them.

As I began my school years, my love for radio waxed as strong as ever, and I added stories to what I turned to radio for. I listened to many shows every week: "Amos 'n' Andy," "Jack Benny," "The Shadow," "Gene Autry," "Roy Rogers," "Gang Busters," "Lone Ranger," "Stella Dallas," "Inner Sanctum Mysteries" with the creaking door (scared the devil out of me, I wouldn't even look out from under the covers at night after listening to it), "Fibber McGee and Molly," "Bob and Ray," "Superman," "George Burns and Gracie Allen," "The Nelson Family"—on and on.

The programs were there in the air; the problem was pulling them into one's location, as Harry Durham's family discovered in the small town of

Fort Payne, Alabama, tantalizingly close to network affiliate stations in Chattanooga (fifty miles to the north) and Birmingham (ninety miles to the south):

Fort Payne is located in a valley bordered by Lookout Mountain on the northeast and Sand Mountain on the southwest. The setting was picturesque but not conducive to good radio reception, particularly if the weather was bad. Often, when Grandmother was listening to her "pieces," static and interference would be terrible. In addition to poor radio reception, she had another problem to deal with; she was very hard of hearing. Frequently, I would see her with her ear close to the speaker on her brown table top radio, straining to catch enough of the words so that she could follow the story.

In the evenings, the rest of the family, my older brother, my parents and I, would listen to our favorite shows on a big RCA floor model which my father had bought in the late '30s or early '40s. It was a multi-band radio with electric-eye tuning and with eight buttons for pre-selected stations. I used to love to push one of the pre-select buttons and watch the tuning marker race up the dial to the next selection.

Elsewhere, the battle of the radio battery was entering its final phase. Barbara Lyon Franklin was a witness, as she recounts brightly:

I was born in December 1941, the youngest of eleven children. We lived on a farm in Virginia that was so far out that electricity did not reach our area until I was in the second grade. Therefore, our earliest radio was battery operated. That battery was ENORMOUS, at least to a small child.

Cash was a scarce commodity in our household, so everything had to be made to last as long as possible. When the battery became weak and we were unable to get clear reception, I was sat on the battery. Why that made the reception clearer, I do not know; nor do I know how the discovery was made that my sitting on it would improve the reception! This ability gave me a powerful bargaining tool when I wanted a sibling to do something for me.

After electricity came to our area and we had a radio upstairs, we children loved to sneak the radio under the covers and listen to music long after we were supposed to be asleep. One night our father heard my sister and me giggling. He told us twice to settle down. The third time he said, "I'll get some giggles" and came up the steps, belt in hand. I rolled to one edge of the bed, and my sister rolled to the other edge of the bed. Dad stood there in the dark beating the empty middle of the bed. The only thing he hit was the radio!

The place name Deep Gap, North Carolina, goes some distance in explaining why John Idol's grandparents had to wait until 1944 before purchasing their first radio from Lonzo Miller's Deep Gap Cash Store, which had a display of radios for sale and an antenna available for audition purposes. The day that the electric lines reached the Idol farm marked the decisive moment:

My dad's parents lived in an isolated hollow in the Blue Ridge Mountains and so were among the last to enjoy the marvels of electricity. When they were finally hooked up, they bought a small table-model radio. Just how they came to believe that the louder a radio was played, the more juice it would take, we never knew. But that was their conviction, and nothing we said could persuade them to play their radio above a whisper.

That belief led them to pull their chairs alongside the table, cup their ears as they leaned towards the radio, and listen to the news, the weather forecast, and the obituaries. On Sundays they would stay frozen in that position for an hour or more as they strained to hear a sermon. Their listening habits meant that we grandkids had to be quieter than church mice.

A neighboring family, the Greers, bought a splendid walnut-encased radio, a Westinghouse with a green eye and the biggest tuning dial any of us had ever seen. The Greers had their radio as loud as my grandparents had theirs soft: we could hear it as we sat on our front porch, as we hoed corn in the fields, as we waited for the school bus, or as we sawed firewood on the hill behind our house. Next to the steam whistle at the local lumberyard, it was the loudest thing in all Deep Gap, North Carolina. None of us ever felt the need to buy a portable as long as the Greers were at home, for they had their Westinghouse booming away from sunrise to near midnight.

By the 1940s, bedside radios were inexpensively and widely available in an assortment of colors and materials, and the upstairs or back-of-the-house children's room had its own set. Glen Resch remembers, "If I was sick or didn't play outside after school, I'd be listening to my table-model Silvertone with that varnished-fabric, smelly-when-it-got-hot cabinet." Elly Truebenbach got a radio of her own when she entered the eighth grade in the later 1940s: "It was a Sears model, sort of a battleship gray-green. Not all that glamorous, but sturdy. It was the best my parents could do on my father's teacher's salary. I had that radio through high school, college, and many years of marriage. It finally went to air-waves heaven after the birth of my third child. You know, I kind of miss it!"

Meantime, young Zelime "Lemie" Lentz was struggling with dinner table manners at her grandmother's home, and she often grew jealous if someone else sat by her adored grandmother. "I would cry a lot or spill something," she confesses, but she found that her punishment had its compensations: she would be sent to sit alone in her grandmother's bedroom, where she was content to listen to the red, orange, and yellow bakelite radio "with tubes that would make it glow." In a few years she heard people talking about objects called "televisions" and asked her father what they were. He explained "that television was a radio with a movie and that we would never get one because they were just for rich people." She dates that conversation at about 1951.

The crystal set, which had been many a "radio bug's" sole receiving apparatus in the 1920s, had largely become the province of Scouts seeking merit badges and of workshop hobbyists twenty or twenty-five years later. Retired postman Bob Morgan remembers of his teen years in the late 1940s,

A lot of the boys in our neighborhood had crystal radio sets. One of my friends had the first set that I had ever heard. Boy, how I wanted to be one of those to have a set that would really work in my home. Downtown in Atlanta there was a radio store, LaFayette Radio. I went to that store and bought me a Philmore crystal radio set. It was red and had a crystal with cat's whisker and a copper wire coil with a slide bar to better select the station you wanted to listen to. I also got a pair of Trim Feather-weight earphones, and all else that I needed was some wire for the aerial and a ground wire. When I got all this home and hooked up, I got my dream to come true. It worked.

Although Atlanta boasted several stations of greater power, Bob Morgan's set captured its strongest signal from 250-watt WBGE, which broadcast the Atlanta Crackers baseball games from the wooden stadium across the street from the large Sears store on Ponce de Leon Avenue. The crystal set opened up a great love of baseball: "Many nights I would listen to the game lying on the bed, and many times I went to sleep with the earphones still on my head." From the crystal set he graduated to ham radio interests and bought a Hallicrafters S-40. His printed cards identified him as a SWL (short wave listener), and he enjoyed the worldwide talk.

As a youngster in Oakland at the end of the 1940s, Larry Telles had a very specific reason for investing in a crystal set:

Since my bedtime was 9:00 in those early years, I didn't know [at first] about an excellent drama that came on from 10:00 to 10:15. It was "I Love a Mystery" that was broadcast over KFRC, a Mutual station, 610 KHZ (kilocycles in those days) from San Francisco. One night during November 1949, when the lights were out in my room, my radio was on very low when I remember hearing a wailing train whistle. The plot was centered around a railroad car. (I later figured out that it was [the sequence] "Bury Your Dead, Arizona.") I got away with hearing the ILAM program twice without getting caught. Well, now I was hooked. I decided to build a crystal set and listen to radio undetected. I bought a Philmore cat whisker/galena crystal assembly and wound a coil using an empty Quaker Oats box. Much to my disappointment, the only station I could get was KGO, 810 Kilohertz. My days of listening to "I Love a Mystery" would have to wait for a few more years.

Paul Garrett, whose early childhood explorations of radio sets and programs were recounted earlier, continued expanding his interest as the 1940s yielded to the 1950s:

As I got into my teens, the number of radios I owned escalated markedly. I'd buy old radios nobody wanted for a few cents up to a dollar, and then I'd fix them up. I remember only one radio I never got to playing, and since I equated playing music and telling stories as being life to the radio, I buried that radio somewhere behind the house by the apple tree, since it was dead. (Rest in peace, Philco, Jr. I'm sorry that those 6016s I tried to put where the 35Z5s should have gone caused most of your wiring to char.)

Many hundreds of hours I devoted to the building of and listening to crystal radios. I loved them not for their efficiency but for their primitiveness, something I knew we had in common. I rigged up an antenna that stretched from the house to the well shed, a distance of about fifty feet. The antenna was at least thirty feet in the air. Here was this little radio made out of nothing but a coil, a nail dial, a transformer and a diode, a set of headphones and a sophisticated copper wire antenna and a rather large hunk of galena crystal. All of it was free but the crystal; it cost fourteen cents at the Aug. W. Smith store in downtown Spartanburg. (I understand that the same amount of crystal these days would cost hundreds of dollars if you could get it—it's what computer chips are made from. When I got it, it was as big as a small lump of coal.)

I could pick up Radio Moscow and Radio Havana with no problem at all. I got stations from all over the world. Wasn't much I couldn't do with a radio, although I don't remember ever trying to juggle them. I listened to Nashville and Cincinnati stations easy and the signals were so strong I didn't even have to wear the headphones. I just laid them on the pillow or nearby on the bed. All this on no electricity or battery power. Those headphones, by the way, were amazing. I could put a piece of crystal on the lead-in wires and walk out by the power box and touch the wires to it and pick up a radio signal quite clearly. It was easier back then, though; there wasn't one-tenth as much atmospheric interference.

Needless to say, I loved radios. Still do. I wish they still told stories, and I wish they played better music, but I have never lost my fascination with how they get those little people inside them that can talk, tell stories, preach, give advertisements and make music. It has fascinated me for a lifetime, and frankly, I'm glad. It has made my life that much richer. There's one TV in my house and ten or twelve radios. Last time I checked, they all worked.

4

Car and Portable Radios

Like the small bedside radio and the durable crystal set, the portable radio allowed its owner a new freedom of program choices and, of course, listening places. The car radio is best remembered as a companion to the weekly ritual of the family drive. Zenith and other makers' portables had been available since the early 1920s (although their squarish bulky cases and considerable heft made for awkward carrying), and in 1924 *Radio Digest—Illustrated* had published a series of articles detailing how to place a receiver in the family Ford (with lesser attention to Chevrolet and other marques). Only in the late 1930s did radio antennas become frequent sights on passing cars, and after World War II new materials and streamlined designs made portable radios light enough for comfortable adult carrying without regret. By the late 1940s, the age of radio-on-the-go had truly arrived, and that, in turn, would accelerate changes in radio programming.

Many children born in the 1930s became accustomed to Sunday afternoon automobile drives with the radio playing above the motor's hum. Typically the Sunday drive began as soon as the midday meal was finished, and it often ran until (or even past) nightfall. Early afternoon religious and educational programs yielded to a variety of musical accompaniments for the passing miles: live symphony broadcasts were a highlight of the week for some listeners, while popular music selections were often tamed to a Sunday sense of propriety. In the late afternoon, musical programs yielded to crime dramas—with plenty of gore and mayhem, Sunday notwithstanding—and newscasts. Elton Dorval remembers the Sunday jaunt as a bridge to his family's Sunday evening ritual: "If we were out for an afternoon drive and weren't home by 4:00, we listened to 'The Shadow' on the car radio" in preparation for at-home listening to "Jack Benny," "The Phil Harris-Alice Faye Show," and "Charlie McCarthy." ("It was the only time we boys were allowed to be in the living room, but we had to sit on the floor," he adds.) For many, however, the radio-accompanied Sunday drive was a self-contained ritual with its own pace and pattern.

Then came the Sunday afternoon in late 1941 when riders and home listeners alike found their regular programs interrupted by terrible news from the Pacific. Having entered elementary school about the time of the Pearl Harbor attack, the young riding-and-listening generation faced a sudden change of routine when gas rationing curbed unnecessary travel. The husky pull of the Ford, the LaSalle, or the Studebaker through its gears no longer twined with the sounds of music and bubbly chatter spilling from passenger compartments. "The big Buicks and Pontiacs were parked in the garage," Ellen Messer Williams wistfully remembers, "and the neighborhood children got really bored listening to the grownups talking or, worse still, singing around the piano." Necessity sparked creative compensation, as she further recalls:

We would go out to the garage—winter or summer, it didn't matter—, open up the garage doors, and turn on the car radio. We listened to the "travelin' songs." In those days, all the popular songs were printed line-for-line in a song book you could buy for ten cents. We "rode" in the car, singing from our texts of "Gonna take a sentimental journey," "Chattanooga Choo Choo," and one about "spurs that jingle, jangle, jingle" as the horses carried their riders "merrily along." We still got home after dark, but we had never been anywhere but out to the garage.

While the war effort forced lifestyle changes on everyone, it also conferred new privileges on some. Every working day, for instance, Pat O'Shee's father rode the trolley to the Scottish Rite Auditorium in St. Louis (where one of the city's two symphony orchestras played for crowds who were blissfully unaware that they were seated above a top secret military operations center); he strode as casually as possible into that building on Lindell Boulevard, descended to the basement, and assumed his function as Deputy Field Director in the Office of the Field Director of Ammunition Plants for the United States. Such a position bearing such a title earned a man special compensations, including a "B" gasoline rationing sticker for the windshield of his family sedan. Thus the O'Shees rode on wartime Sundays when most families walked or stayed at home. For Patrick O'Shee, Sr., the Sunday drive was a well-earned relief from the tensions of responsibility; for young Pat O'Shee, Jr., it was a time for developing a taste for the classics: "After Sunday Dinner (noon) we would take rides in our maroon 1939 Buick four-door with its Sonomatic push-button radio. (I wish I had a push-button radio right now in my bedroom, but alas!) On Sunday rides I remember listening to the NBC Symphony on KSD, 550, St. Louis. Dr. Frank Black conducted the orchestra in Mozart's *The Marriage of Figaro* Overture, a favorite of mine since before I could read."

On a Sunday in 1944, Pat O'Shee, Jr., continuing to expand his listening repertoire, learned a firm lesson about car radios. His mother was then a patient in a St. Louis hospital that did not allow children as visitors, so while the elder O'Shee paid his wife a two-hour visit, Pat and his sister Emory were left to entertain themselves in the car parked two blocks down the street. Pleased to find that the respected Dr. Black was again on the NBC Symphony podium, Pat luxuriated in the full-length broadcast concert, which ended at about the time his father returned to find two contented offspring—and a dead car battery. "When my father traded the 1939 Buick for a 1950 Buick," Pat O'Shee observes, "he said he would 'make damned sure' that the new car would have no radio in it." And soon afterward that eager listener, entering his teens, asked for—and got—his own portable radio.

Postwar prosperity encouraged the pent-up demand for new cars, gasoline flowed freely again to civilian tanks, and the Sunday family drive was resumed, with a moderate concern for the tires (good replacements still being in short supply). Brenda Seabrooke, author of *The Bridges of Summer*, *Judy Scuppernong*, and a dozen other books about childhood and adolescence, took many of those trips in the latter half of the 1940s:

When my parents drove home on Sunday nights from my grandparents' house about sixty five miles away, they always timed our leaving to catch our favorite radio shows—"Jack Benny," "Edgar Bergen and Charlie McCarthy," and "Meet Corliss Archer." The trip took that long (three programs' worth) because of the roads. My father knew every road in south Georgia and would go out of the way to drive on stretches of paved road where there was less danger of picking up a nail dropped from a wagon and having to deal with the resulting flat tire in those inner tube days. The nights were dark, though the blackouts were over by then. The three of us all sat in the front seat, lit by the tiny radio bulb. It gave me a safe, cozy feeling as we laughed at Jack and Rochester, Bergen's ventriloquist dummies Charlie McCarthy and Mortimer Snerd, and Corliss and her boyfriend Dexter. Leaving grandparents, uncles and aunts and cousins was easier with these characters to light the way home with laughter.

The swing music enthusiasm of Marshall Ramsey, Jr. and his friends made radio listening "a big thing not only around the hearth but also in the car." He explains,

The music programs were almost always heard riding around, either with a date or with the guys. Not all cars then had radios, so the guy whose parents had a more fancy car was called on more often.

One certain group of friends of mine who shared the same enthusiasm used to do something rather unusual while listening to their favorite tunes. This is difficult to explain to people now, with the sophistication of automobiles, danger of highways, number of vehicles, but in the '40s, things were simple.

What we'd do was to tune in these programs, set the throttle on low, get out of the car, and dance alongside the moving vehicle, listening to our favorite songs. Every once in a while, someone would have to reach in the window and straighten out the wheel. No—no one was drinking, either.

As Marshall Ramsey's account suggests, having a car radio still seemed slightly novel or privileged in some families. In Niagara Falls, New York, Richard Saunders grew up in a family that drove to Hornell, about 120 miles away, to visit his paternal grandparents each Sunday. The 1941 Buick had no built-in radio. (The successor 1948 Buick would remedy that condition.) As loyal Jack Benny fans, the Saunders passengers were determined not to miss his Sunday evening show. To that end they customarily carried along a large Crosley portable, "about so big" (generous rectangular dimensions being marked off by the teller in a patch of air here). At the 7:00 starting time of "The Jack Benny Program," the Saunders car pulled off the road at any convenient stopping place, representatives of two Saunders generations piled out of the car, the portable's antenna was extended, its dial was tuned to the appropriate station, and everyone listened happily at the roadside for half an hour. (Reception was variable, and signal fading brought moans of disappointment.) With Benny's closing line, "We're a little late, folks," the Saunders travelers contentedly collapsed the antenna, packed away the portable unit, took their places in the car, and resumed their homeward journey.

An anonymous contributor (not otherwise represented in this book) has a vivid car radio recollection from his high school dating days of the late 1940s and early 1950s. His father's apple orchard near Plymouth, Michigan, made a fine private lovers' lane for this eager young man, and one Wednesday evening about dusk he drove there with a date who had been reported to be quite responsive to being gently rubbed in the lower back. After the radio was tuned to appropriate music, the recommended tactile approach was initiated. Unexpectedly, there was a protest. Looking at her watch and noting the approach of 8:30, she declared, "I want to hear 'The Great Gildersleeve'."

"But, here we are ... ," he pleaded.

"No, I want to hear 'The Great Gildersleeve'."

And, much to the handsome high school athlete's disappointment, Willard Waterman (who had recently inherited Harold Peary's radio role as Summerfield's portly and garrulous water commissioner Gildersleeve) carried the evening. "There I was alone in the middle of an apple orchard under the stars with a gal who wanted to do nothing but listen to 'The Great Gildersleeve'," the fellow says, shaking his head.

If car radios sometimes proved to be mixed blessings, portables could be less than envisioned too. Roger Rollin, today a chronicler of popular culture, recalls being freed from the family Philco table model of "truncated cathedral shape, with speakers at the top (covered by thin cloth) and, in the center, a small yellow dial shaped like a curved rectangle." About 1946 or 1947, during his high school days, he says,

I became the proud owner of my very own "portable" radio. It was about the size of a businessman's large attaché case, but in pink and grey leatherette (very modern!), with a metal carrying handle. A fold-down antenna was in the back, as was a receptacle for the cord and plug, for home use, and in the bottom a very large battery, for portability. Portability was rather limited, however, due to the size of the battery and the weight of the total package—four or five pounds, I would guess. Actually, although playing the radio anywhere, without being dependent upon electric current, seemed like a neat idea, I don't remember actually porting the radio very often, partly due to laziness, partly to the fact that reception wasn't very good anyway. What was most important about that radio was that it was my own. I could listen to the programs I wanted to hear without interfering with my parents' use of the radio—and without interference from them. It was liberation—even though I still usually listened to the same shows they did anyway.

Larry Telles describes his own portable radio, acquired in the same period, in affectionate detail:

During the years from 1945 to 1952 I listened to my own radio, which I still have in my collection of antique radios. It is a Zenith AC/DC Portable, model 6-G-601M, with a sailboat outlined in white on a black grill cloth. The battery took up the entire width of the radio and about one-half of its height. The antenna, a large U-shaped device (Wavemagnet) on a soft ribbon cable, came out of the case on the right side and had suction cups on the antenna's surface. Most of the radio shows

I listened to during those seven years came through that speaker. The yellow-tan radio's drop-down front cover made it perfect for communicating to your secret agents around the world. This radio sits in the garage today with most of its loctal tubes and parts. The drop-down front cover has been long gone. But, all the memories remain.

5

Radio Families

The typical early 1920s radio-listening vignette shows the lone hobbyist leaning across the work table or the oak home library table, headphones clamped over his ears, as he seeks to pull a broadcast signal out of an aural firmament of static and other noise. When he finds his program, he will urge others to rush in and listen before the thin voices and music fade. A quarter-century later, the post-World War II panorama shows many listeners, newly freed from rooftop or pole-mounted antennas and from huge batteries, going their separate ways with small table radios, car radios, and portables. However, especially during the large middle span of the first three radio decades—from the late 1920s through the Second World War years—listening habits centered mainly on the family set. In the daily transactions of kinship, grandparents and grandchildren listened together, husbands and wives negotiated program preferences, and children performed household tasks to earn radio listening time.

In some places, family listening encompassed more than two or three biologically connected generations living in a household; it might involve boarding houses, college or orphanage dormitories, military or WPA barracks, or mill village populations, each group depending on a single receiver. The owner of the first radio in a small town or in a city neighborhood would open his doors and windows so that a lawn or a sidewalk full of "guests" could hear the sports event, news report, or musical program. In short, radio pulled together blood-related families and created ad hoc extended families. In both the narrow and the wider senses suggested here, it is difficult to overestimate the importance of radio as a family medium. It is most frequently and most fondly remembered in that way.

It is doubtless true that, in its first thirty years, programmed radio was a boon to solitary souls—apartment and distant farmhouse dwellers, widows and widowers, those who never married, children without siblings or neighborhood companions, and youngsters left at home while one or both parents worked. Chick Meyerson of St. Louis affirms, "Radio was a great companion for an only child growing up," when he amused himself by learning station call letters and their significances. He listened for the cheerful greeting of WSB from Atlanta ("Welcome South, Brother") and knew that WGN represented *The Chicago Tribune*'s encoded claim to be the "World's Greatest Newspaper." He became proficient in finding the dial locations of KMOX, WWL, WBBM, KOA, KDKA, WBZ, WOAK, WBAP, WNBC, WSM, WJZ, WHAS, WCKY, WLW, WCAU, and WTMJ. During World War II, wives of servicemen welcomed the radio as a means of warding off an emptiness in the house. Still, most receivers were shared for much of their playing time.

Since the budgets of most homes afforded only one radio set during the medium's settling-in years, its location was "averaged out"; it was placed in the "front parlor" for formal show or in the kitchen or dining room for listening convenience. Sometimes the radio was located at the bottom of a staircase or near a heating vent so that its sounds would carry through several rooms, perhaps the entire house. Even the head of many a financially comfortable house might question the usefulness of buying a second receiver: "Who would listen to it? We already have a fine console." Thus, most families accepted the single radio as the norm. John B. Simms says of the Kentucky family of seven that he was born into, "There was no such thing as *me* listening to the radio; it was whatever Dad and Mother wanted to listen to, and we kids had no choice about the station." Juanita Capell's large family found a more democratic solution, after allowance was made for her mother's afternoon serials.

Washington Radio Conferences chaired by Secretary of Commerce Herbert Hoover in the mid-1920s and the subsequent creation of the Federal Communications Commission shaped radio as a family-safe medium. Programs would be closely governed by station, network, and FCC codes curbing raw language and "naughty" references. Lapses were rare and thereby all the more amusing to those who "got the joke." Mae West was banished from the airwaves for years after she gave a particularly sultry reading of Eve's part in a Garden of Eden sketch during a 1937 guest appearance on Edgar Bergen's program. The script had been approved by the

NBC censor, but the on-the-air intonation evoked her screen persona of rolling eyes and an open invitation to "visit" sometime. Bill Buri remembers "Can You Top This?" panelist Harry Hershfield's masterful way of leading the listener's expectation through the familiar pattern of a "dirty" joke, only to shift to a sanitized punch line that left knowing listeners in smug recognition of the unspoken "real" ending. Bob Hope and Groucho Marx were expected to play ad lib cat-and-mouse games with the control room's judge of propriety, and if the engineer's finger was not quick enough to prevent the broadcasting of the ambiguous or randy line, these "lapses of taste" were often followed by sudden program interruptions, sometimes excused as "technical difficulties." In a roomful of listeners, children were sometimes amazed by the quickness with which a comedian's throw-away remark could send the pink blush of stifled laughter to the top of Uncle Fred's bald pate. In general, though, radio seemed a "clean" medium for family listening.

Jim Farmer offers this assessment of radio's place in his boyhood home:

Radio days conjure up many warm memories. In those days, as opposed to the present, the family was the hub of all things. Within that hub was the tall walnut console with the lighted dial the size of a dinner plate. That dial was our window to the peripheral world.

[One mental] snapshot of that long ago time shows my father listening to the second Joe Louis-Billy Conn heavyweight prizefight. Dad's position in the room changed concurrently with the ebb and flow of the bout. His "neutral" position was on the extreme edge of his easy chair. When it seemed Conn, his hero, was getting the best of it, Pop's knees would hit the floor as he leaned closer to the radio in his attempt to become part of the action. When the announcer indicated Louis was in command, Dad would abruptly stand up and stalk around the room, glaring at all who dared intercept his line of vision. When the match was over (Louis won via a knockout), Dad immediately left the room. He was gone for a very long time. Mother sat quite still with that disgusted, yet tolerant, look we all knew well. It went without saying Pop had wagered more than he could afford to lose.

That tall walnut console was stationed in our home on Colgate Street in Farmington, Michigan. We moved away just prior to Christmas in 1949. Then began our direct exposure to that peripheral world. It seemed much better on the radio.

Rose Marcaccio seems not at all regretful that radio was a somewhat enforced pleasure. In fact, she vividly recalls the cycle of the family's radio week:

I was raised in Detroit with three sisters and three brothers, and our parents had definite curfew times, so we were always home to listen to the radio.

On Sunday evenings our cousins would come over and we would listen to Walter Winchell, then "Inner Sanctum," the scary show [heard at 8:30 on Sundays, from 1941 to 1943], and we would all scream, etc.

On Mondays, the best night, we would hurry to do the dishes and do our homework. My older sister would iron, my mom would sew, my dad would get his pipe, and we listened to romantic "Mr. First Nighter." We would tease each other about who would we go with if we could. I would always choose Dick Powell, my older sister would choose Clark Gable, and my middle sister loved Humphrey Bogart.

On Saturdays was "clean the house." Each girl had a part of the house, but the radio had to be on the station that had the opera on so that Dad could hear it from the garden. On Saturday nights Dad would roll up the rug in the living room, and my sister and brother John would teach us to dance to "Lucky Strike's Hit Parade."

Sometimes a single program could reset the family's evening clock. Allen Hilborn, whose father had built a crystal set in the mid-1920s, says, "By the early to mid-'30s our family schedule was dictated by 'The Amos 'n' Andy Show' from 7 to 7:15 each evening. My father refused to miss it. All activities had to be arranged for either before or after." Lois Garrison remembers that her father, afraid that he would miss the nightly "Amos 'n' Andy" broadcast, would lock up his business in a small south Georgia town, jump into the car, rush home, and bound into the house just in time to warm up the radio tubes.

Hal Higdon, born in 1931, describes the listening patterns in his family's fourth-floor apartment a few blocks from Lake Michigan, in the South Shore neighborhood in Chicago. "Our relax room was the dining room, rather than the living room of our apartment," he says. "My father had an armchair in one corner, my mother a rocking chair in the other. After Pop returned from work, he would sit around in the armchair and read, and have a Carling's Ale, and smoke, and listen to the radio. When he wasn't home, I got to occupy the armchair—and listen to the radio."

During the Depression, George Robinson's family lived at 341 South Homan Avenue "on Chicago's great west side," and radio listening was woven into other pleasures there: "Our radio was a Philco cathedral which is still being replicated in solid state and is available from K-Mart and Wal-Mart. We sat around the living room like everyone else did and listened to the same programs, while playing 500 rummy or putting together a jigsaw puzzle. When walking home in the hot summer evenings after window shopping on Madison Street, one could follow the entire progress of 'Amos and Andy' from the open windows."

In Frank Raines's family, radio enthusiasms were measured in varying degrees, but there was always a fine set available. In the late 1930s and early 1940s it was a Majestic console, its cabinet "about the size of today's 21-inch TV" and "finished like fine furniture (which it was) and standing to a height of some three and one-half feet on its own legs." In the early 1940s "we upgraded to an RCA which had a much more modern appearance in that its cabinet was encased in wood from top to bottom and the traditional wedge-shaped dial was replaced by one that was larger, rectangular, and multi-banded. The bands were BC and SW. Still much too early for FM." Listening habits changed very little as one radio replaced another: "Our radio was located in the living room and was very seldom idle, especially if either of my three sisters or I was present. We were the main users; an older brother would occasionally listen to 'The Grand Ole Opry.' My mother would listen to a few shows like 'Lum and Abner' or 'Amos and Andy' but never an entire evening. My father rarely, except for the news, would listen to programs such as 'Dr. IQ' or 'The Original Amateur Hour,' but for the most part, he had little use for the radio." Still, Frank Raines concludes, "Radio was an important facet of our lives, much more so than television is today, mainly because it was our primary source of information and entertainment."

The only listening constraints in Jim Fanning's family—"a bunch of 'radio junkies', " he calls his parents and himself—came from time spent on the job and at school. During his World War II childhood, he says,

We had the radio on all day long. My mother was an avid fan of all the daytime soap operas—"Ma Perkins," "Stella Dallas," "Backstage Wife," etc., etc. I remember coming home from school in Atlanta with my mother ironing and listening to "Stella Dallas" especially. Before my father went off to the Army, he was a devoted follower of H. V. Kaltenborn. I remember one night he got me to listen to a broadcast of Hitler. It was, of course, very scratchy and I am sure it was being analyzed in English. I didn't understand a thing, but I was sure it was important. He was also a true fan of the Metropolitan Opera Saturday afternoon broadcasts. There were no portable radios in the family then, but he would rig up the radio in the window, work outside and listen to it that way. We accused him of scaring the birds off.

Ruth F. Messer focuses her family listening memories on Sunday evenings, the family sitting at a drop-leaf table by the fireplace "while eating apples from our orchard, with the wind howling outside and snow piling up" around the wartime home in Hudson, Ohio. Dr. Ralph R. Doty, now president of Lakeland Community College in Ohio, also recalls that for family listening after the war, "Sundays were special in our home." Afternoon visits with relatives in Duluth had to be finished in time to get home for "The Shadow" at 4:00, and "Later in the day our parents patiently indulged us by allowing us to put the small radio on the kitchen counter to listen to 'Our Miss Brooks' and 'Jack Benny' while eating dinner. Woe to the person who spoke during those meals except to ask for some food to be passed down the table! And with five children at the time, keeping the kitchen quiet so we could hear the programs was a difficult task."

Having grown up in South Dakota in the 1940s, Ken Weigel claims to have experienced only "the rump end of Old Time Radio," but he nonetheless pictures a home fully involved in radio listening:

My folks appreciated the radio talent. While I don't recall much about the programs themselves, I do remember how quiet it got when Bing Crosby or Dennis Day sang, and when Elmo Tanner whistled or Larry Adler played the harmonica. Radio was our chief form of weeknight entertainment. Dad livened things up with his impersonations of Willy Lump-Lump (Red Skelton) and, removing his dental crockery, John L. C. Sivoney (Frank Fontaine). After supper we'd settle in for a round of "Twenty Questions" or mock episodes of "This Is Your Life" ("Tell us, Tommy Manville, why is it that only your odd-numbered wives can cook?")

This much I remember: daytimes at home the soap operas reigned, and evenings were filled with an assortment of nutty catch lines spoken by fabulous characters with foibles out of Frank L. Baum by Ring Lardner. Their speechways became part of our own vocabulary. "Ish Kabibble," for example, and "'Tain't funny, McGee," and "That's a joke, son!" were just as common around our house as "Time to get up," "Time for bed," and "What's taking you so long in the bathroom?"

"We were a reading family," says Malcolm Usrey. "We read books, *The Fort Worth Star-Telegram*, *The Saturday Evening Post*, *Reader's Digest*, *Life*, and half a dozen other periodicals, but it was the radio that we all listened to, magnetically and magically drawing us together, making our lives richer and fuller. Our radio played many hours of the day and night" and had done so daily since it had arrived in the mid-1930s.

In some families, however, degrees of enthusiasm for radio were measured in generational divisions. In Nashville, Tennessee, Genella Olker explains that she was "reared in the house of a Victorian grandmother, born in 1852 of a family who believed in reading and writing. I think she always scorned the radio, knowing she could get the news from a variety of British and New York newspapers we could subscribe to and purchase. Her sons, being middle-aged men, were more prone to this new form of entertainment. I remember having a radio in the house at about age eight or ten. (I was born in 1925.) I was not encouraged to listen when I could be doing better things, but I was allowed to listen to 'Little Orphan Annie' and to belong to her club. That was harmless."

In other homes, shared radio listening increased the child-grandparent bond. Dr. Gus Wentz tells of such a relationship:

My grandmother lived with us much of the time when I was in elementary school, and I was her pet grandchild, probably because I would sit and listen with her to Richard Maxwell and his "Songs of Hope and Comfort." She always wrote down the name of every song he sang and had lists of them by date, extending back to when she had started tuning in. She also subscribed to the *Radio Guide* and clipped and pasted three large scrapbooks from that and other sources. I remember that she had a nice picture of Richard Crooks, the opera singer, which she clipped from a cigarette ad on the back of a *Life* (?) magazine. Since she didn't approve of smoking, she pasted a rose over Crooks's cig.

In the 1930s and 1940s, grandsons were often both awed and bemused by their grandmothers' radio customs. Tony Harper remembers watching his grandmother's ritual preparation for listening, and he especially recalls that during her favorite afternoon programs she was "not at home" to callers in Greenville, South Carolina. John Simms observed the same cloistering when "Our Gal Sunday" and an adjacent program were on the air just before noon in Springfield, Kentucky: "She wouldn't answer the door or the telephone. But it was the same for all the other women up and down the street."

During the mid-1940s, Erma Harden Parks lived down the street from her maternal grandparents in Watkinsville, Georgia, and she visited them almost every day, smelling "the wonderful aroma of my grandmother's cooking coming from the kitchen" and finding "my grandfather, whom all the grandchildren called 'Daddy Jim,' listening to the radio in the living room. It was a big radio sitting on his desk. Daddy Jim loved to have his hair combed while he listened to the news on the radio. (One of his favorites was H. V. Kaltenborn.) The grandchildren enjoyed being asked to comb his hair because he would give us either a Mounds, an Almond Joy, or a nickel. He would reach in his desk drawer and bring out the surprise." If more than one grandchild were present, competition for the grooming privilege and the reward could be intense.

Clergyman Paul M. Youse remembers that he and his grandfather became so intrigued by one broadcast that they precipitated a family crisis:

In the late '30s or early '40s my grandfather and I, a teenager, were glued to the radio. Our ears were close to the large round speaker sitting on the receiver whose metal cases were always painted gold. The story was suspense unlimited; never mind that my great aunt had to leave momentarily to catch the Reading Railroad excursion to go home to Jenkintown. Grandmother and great aunt Lil had gone out to the 1929 Chevrolet (reported to be the first six cylinder in Lebanon County), to go to the train station; we would be out shortly.

In the program, a murderer, strapped in the electric chair, was to be executed, but there was a problem. He claimed to have swallowed some TNT, and if the executioner pulled the switch to electrocute him, the TNT would blow up the whole prison and everyone in it.

Grandmother came back into the house once to tell us it was time to leave. Yes, we would be out shortly, but we just couldn't.

The prison officials were checking the convict's story to learn whether he had swallowed TNT. He had said he used a great amount of butter to get it down. The guard who gave him his supper was called.

Grandmother came into the house a second time. Yes, we would be there immediately, but we just could not leave the set. The prisoner was very belligerent, roaring with laughter; he was going to watch his eyes pop out of his head, as they pulled the switch. The guard then reported, yes, he had requested more butter for the evening meal.

Now my grandmother along with my great aunt came in. It was urgent; there was not a moment to spare. If we did not leave that instant, Aunt Lil would miss the train. There was nothing to do but to turn off the radio and drive Aunt Lil to the station.

We never did learn what happened at the prison. I am rather glad we didn't. Had we learned of the outcome, surely I never would have remembered the incident. Now, with it unresolved, I can go back in memory to my grandparents' comfortable home and touch—in a simple and more quiet time—dear, dear people and places which are long gone.

Parent-child bonds were often strengthened or defined by shared radio listening, too. For Jane A. Kobler, Friday evenings meant a special privilege:

Dad would let me stay up late to listen to the Friday night fights. We would be in the kitchen now, the little radio on top of the brick mantle, a combination coal stove and gas stove set in the fireplace. Dad would be in his rocker by the stove, his snacks of cheese and crackers and celery on the kitchen table. I would sit at the table, treat myself to some of his snacks, while hearing great names in boxing going their rounds with champ Joe Louis. Names I remember are Maxie Baer, Max Schmeling, Jack Dempsey, Jimmy Braddock, etc.

George A. Walker, Jr., also found special meaning in listening to boxing matches with his father: "My mum and dad, who were both exceptional individuals, separated during the late 1930s. He would purposely come by and get me to listen to the Gillette Razor Blade-sponsored boxing matches, especially the championship bouts. We would park in his car or go to his apartment to listen. We heard most all of Joe Louis's fights from about '38 through '44. It was our thing."

Sometimes young ears were useful for correcting the perceptions of older ones. An anonymous contributor ("because my sisters would probably shoot me") cannot resist sharing an incident: "It was in the 1930s, and a world title heavyweight fight was on. My dad was a great fight fan, but he was almost stone deaf. We were all eight children huddled around the radio with my dad. The announcer said, 'A right to the jaw, a stiff upper cut, a left to the head. . . . Now they are in a *clinch.*' My dad jumped up and shouted, 'How in the devil did he pinch him with them big gloves on?' It may not be funny to you, but when it happened, we thought it was hilarious."

On the other hand, Norma Brown Hanrahan discovered the usefulness of having a parent with a larger knowledge of the world than her own. "My mother listened to the Briarhoppers on WBT in Charlotte," she says, "and at the age of about six I was enchanted by a sponsoring product called (to my ears) COLOR BAG. A bag of color, how nice to think of. Of course it was 'Color Back'—a hair dye. A few years later there was 'My Dear Mr. Shane,' which of course was 'Bei Mir Bist Du Schoen'." Later she also learned deference to parental listening choices: "There were the sports broadcasts my father listened to, and in those days of one radio per family (for us, anyway) I was very much upset in my early teens when I couldn't listen to an opera because my father was listening to a football game. I overcompensated—now a radio in each room."

Shared radio listening had a special meaning across the generations for Tom H. Newman:

I didn't get to know my father very well. He died of heart problems when I was only ten. I do remember that he was a sensitive person, and I can visualize him laying on the floor relaxing in front of the radio with his three kids, listening to the shows of the late 1940s.

My dad was not very big, and he worked heavy construction, so I think it felt good for him to lay out flat on the rug while he enjoyed the programs. It was also a family time for us kids to pile down there together and enjoy his company and listen too.

I also remember that my father had been a real Texas cowboy in his youth and that he loved the old-fashioned country and Western music. In the Oakland, California, area they had an afternoon radio show called the "Cactus Jack Show," and, boy, that was real "cowboy music." I can still hear the theme song, as we usually listened to it in the late afternoon as we waited for Dad to come home from work, and he listened to the "old-home" music as he got cleaned up for supper. Thank goodness we didn't have TV to watch, so we got to watch each other, even while we listened to the radio.

After he passed away, there would be times in the late afternoon when my mother would turn on the radio to the "Cactus Jack Show." My response was to perk up a bit, as it brought back pleasant memories, but it always made my mother cry a little.

Pat O'Shee's recollection of his father's listening place, after a move to Birmingham in 1946, is a quiet image in chiaroscuro tones: "I can remember the shaded lamp hanging on the wall over my father's bed, illuminating my father's head and the radio. The rest of the room was in semi-darkness. The overhead wall lamp is still there, still illuminating a small part of my late father's bedroom. Later in life he listened to basketball games on that radio in the evenings."

In times of permanent or temporary family breakup and in relocations dictated by professional responsibilities or wartime living conditions, radio was a helpful constant, part of the listener's sense of "family." Frank W. Bell, now running an engineering consulting business in Hobbs, New Mexico, traces his sustained use of the Silvertone table radio that his parents had purchased about 1937:

I grew up during the war years, as an only child, living in rural Tennessee, listening to radio station WSM in all of its 50 K watt, clear-channel glory. My situation resulted in radio being a very big part of my everyday life.

My father was a Methodist minister, which necessitated a move every four years, thereby making friends a scarcity. Radio was there always to be a companion. The early '40s found me living in the country, attending a small rural school, and while the area in which I lived offered all the modern conveniences of the time, some of the kids in school came out of a hollow which didn't have electricity, much less radio. This knowledge offered me somewhat of a feeling of superiority. I wasn't superior in class work or in any other way, but the ability to discuss events of the escalating war, pop music, and current events in general helped the ego. Later, with the beginning of high school, this particular area was supplied with electricity, and the same kids were now listening to and discussing the "Grand Old Opry." I was definitely into "Big Band," and I felt more superior.

That unifying thread of radio in early life experiences can also be seen in the reminiscences of Raymond Nault, Jr., as recorded by his wife, El.

These recollections center on 1946 or 1947, when Ray Nault was about eight or nine years old:

Each Sunday [he] visited with "Pip" and "Mim," his paternal grandparents (Joe and Vina Nault), and his Aunt Betty Lou at 315 Vine Street in Ishpeming, Michigan. Today he does not remember where his parents were [on those days]. Ray, his grandparents, and his aunt would go to the store after church and purchase a sundae or soda and bring home a newspaper and comic book. Since they had their large meal in the evening, this time would be spent just visiting and waiting for dinner. It was during this time that Ray fondly recalls listening to the radio.

Highlights of the Sunday afternoon radio time included the adventure show "Green Hornet" and the scary voice that said, "Who knows what evil lurks in the hearts of men? The Shadow knows. Ha ha ha."

Ray noted that this ritual on Sunday was such a special time for him. I later learned that his mother and father divorced, and Ray nostalgically regards the Sunday activities as family unity and stability.

In Philadelphia, Dottie Zungoli, whose father owned the neighborhood's first radio, chose a "second family" down the block, where the Bennetts soon acquired the second radio in the vicinity and thus made alternate program choices available. She especially remembers Pop Bennett's emotional involvement in "Myrt and Marge," an early serial dramatizing the difficult relationship of a mother and her daughter: "He would cry and cry. He was a bald-headed little fat old guy, but we just loved him."

Harriet Burt thinks of radio's winter holiday programs and kinfolk gathered at the family residence: "Whole families sat around the tree to hear 'A Christmas Carol' (probably read by Basil Rathbone). Children listened to Guy Lombardo on New Year's Eve and wondered about a glamorous grownup world in far-away places. Then, in Knoxville, there was the biggest radio day of all—New Year's. That was always spent at my aunts', where there were three different radios in three different rooms and a different game on each. Except on Bowl Day (Rose Bowl Day!), 1940, when we concentrated on one station as a star-bedazzled University of Tennessee team lost to Southern Cal."

Children's after-supper study times often involved both family relationships and radio listening. From the 1940s, Susan Taylor remembers "scenes in the living room when my father helped me labor over my Latin homework and how we'd stop and eat oranges when Henry Aldrich came on!" (Ironically Henry Aldrich's callow disregard of Latin grammar was the basis of a recurrent joke on "The Aldrich Family".) A decade earlier Jane A.

Kobler had enjoyed her older brother's companionship in the evening when he was doing his homework:

His work was big time stuff now; he was in First Year High School. He would set the small radio right on the dining room table, his books and papers spread out. I would sit there with him, listening first to the strains of "Poor Butterfly," indicating the next episode of "Myrt and Marge" was about to begin. Emotions ran the gamut from low to high on that one. Then "Mr. Keen, Tracer of Lost Persons," a lot of suspense. The musical theme of that one was "Someday I'll Find You."

At a later hour "Eno Crime Clues," one of the really scary ones. Mom and Dad would be in bed. They didn't realize I was staying up late while my brother was doing this serious studying.

Living in a maiden aunt's home and having become a somewhat whimsical violin student (especially at practice time), Bill Buri recalls, "Lowell Thomas came on at about a quarter to 7. At 25 of 7 I would practice. Sometimes if I didn't feel like it, I would get a book to read on the bed and I would hook the bow in my toe and go 'hee-haw, hee-haw' until she said, 'Stop that racket; Lowell Thomas is on'."

In James L. Sender's home, a strict balance was maintained between school preparation and radio privileges: "Being in grammar school until '38, I was relegated to the kitchen and homework assignments after dinner. The big, beautifully carved upright radio was, of course, in the 'parlor.' Before dinner, however, from 4:30 until 6 p.m., and only if my school work was up to par, I was allowed to use the parlor and listen to my favorite shows for children."

Listening was often measured by rituals of children's preparing for bed. Marjorie Hunter recalls the early 1930s, when radio's most popular fifteen-minute program was heard six nights a week: "Some of my fondest memories of my happy childhood days are the Saturday nights that we listened to the Radio. After the Saturday night baths and the Sunday clothing preparations were completed, we were all assembled in the Living Room where we listened to 'Amos and Andy' and if our eyes were able to stay open we listened to the 'Grand Ole Opery.' We were a large family and this was the highlight of the week for family entertainment." A few years later, Margie R. Crowley knew a special bedtime ritual once a week: "As a young child, I went to sleep listening to 'Fibber McGee and Molly.' I *lived* to hear everything fall out of their closet! Once *that* happened, I could fall asleep!"

Having a mild childhood illness was another matter; it gave the school-child an opportunity to share in the listening rituals of a mother or another attending relative. In his younger years, George Walker, Jr. often missed school because of chronic sinus problems, and he joined his mother in her morning listening: "She tuned in to 'The Farm and Home Hour' on those days that they featured the Navy, Marine Corps, or other service bands. She would have me line up all my soldiers to pass in review, as I later actually did [after enlisting in the Marine Corps in 1946]. These were good times of warmth and contentment with my mum and the lead soldiers." In fact, sympathetic companionship could turn almost any program into interesting fare.

Ed Roper remembers how a community of ordinarily prompt diners turned into a group of ardent listeners, disrupting the routine of his mother's boarding house in the early 1930s, when "Amos 'n' Andy" reached a peak of popularity. Conflicting with the established starting time of the evening meal, the serialized quarter-hour broadcast became particularly absorbing when a murder trial or a domestic crisis had been building for several days. One anticipated event, for which a "name the baby" contest created further excitement, was the birth of a child to Ruby and Amos Jones. "Listeners were all concerned about what the baby's name would be," Ed Roper recalls, "and many guests would be late for dinner in order to listen to the program." His mother was forced to abandon the politely firm "please be on time" tradition of the served boarding house meal, instead offering "a buffet dinner so people wouldn't miss the announcement or interfere with dinner." However, Mrs. Roper was not alone in having an established schedule scuttled by the skilfully measured plotting of "Amos 'n' Andy." Department stores, fearing that potential customers would stay beside their radios at home, carried the program on their public address systems, and movie houses piped the early evening broadcast into their auditoriums. During that quarter of an hour the "talking pictures," like dinner for the boarding house denizens, could wait.

Experimenters found "unofficial" ways of using the new communications media. For instance, in the early 1930s George Cartwright had a

brother-in-law who was handy with electronics and who lived in rural West Texas, where everyone was on a party phone line. He was able to connect the family radio to the telephone, and whenever the phone rang, he would turn on the radio and the whole family could sit back in their chairs and listen to both of the people talking on the phone. Occasionally when any of the neighbors came by, they too were given the "treat" of hearing others communicate over the radio. Unfortunately, before long the word got around, and people complained to the phone company, [which] threatened to remove the phone from my father-in-law's house if the "telephone program" on the radio did not cease. That program was off the air permanently.

Today it would be called a Speakerphone, available with the telephone company's blessing at "a modest extra charge."

Still another kind of listening family was created in Southern farming communities and mill villages where income was low, where long working hours involved constant danger from proximity to heavy or fast-moving machinery, and where radio promised a release from the demands and rituals of labor. In *Like a Family: The Making of a Southern Cotton Mill World*, Jacquelyn Dowd Hall, James Leloudis, Robert Korstad, Mary Murphy, Lu Ann Jones, and Christopher B. Daly gather oral history materials into a compelling picture of self-sufficient and physically isolated textile mill communities with their own subculture.[1] Much of everyday routine in these Piedmont villages was organized around company rules, company housing, the company store, mandated working hours, and the like. Almost all activities that a visitor might observe there—work, worship, recreation, schooling, holiday festivities—carried the stamp of community identification or company backing. In their chapter that takes its title from the popular gospel song "Turn Your Radio On,"[2] the chroniclers have shown the primacy of radio as an instrument for shaping the cotton mill subculture. Hillbilly bands and gospel quartets journeyed from the mill villages to perform on nearby radio stations, graduating, if they were good enough, to WBT in Charlotte or WSB in Atlanta, and in turn the performers' neighbors were pleased to find something of their own brought back over the airwaves. This study also shows the great impact of radio preachers in the mill villages. At least the workers' and their families' souls and their popular culture were their own, in a living situation otherwise largely controlled by often autocratic mill-owner families and their hired managers. Radio crystallized the mill hands' independence of spirit.[3]

Laura H. Edwards sums up the role of radio on the freest night of the week in a mill village:

In 1929 listening to the radio wasn't just the thing to do; it was the only thing.

Picture, if you can, a typical summer Saturday night on a cotton mill village street in Rock Hill, South Carolina. The street lights show you yards full of people as neighbors visit each other while their children build sand castles at the edge of an unpaved road. Of course there were a few fights to break up before the "Grand Ole Opry" came on. Was this place a million miles away??

Widow Morris had placed her cherished radio in an open window to share with friends who could not afford one. There was dancing, singing, mimicking until we'd hear the Opry signing off with "Little Jimmy" [Dickens] singing "The Lord's Prayer." He had an angelic voice.

Then we'd fall into our beds with visions of being singing stars on a station so far away.

Years later, Laura Edwards adds, she traveled to Ryman Auditorium in Nashville and "got to touch" the source of "this magic of our radio on Morgan Street."

In the 1930s, the textile mill and farm communities roughly triangulated by the cities of Greenville, Spartanburg, and Anderson, South Carolina, were especially fertile ground for the springing up of "community" or "grapevine" radio systems, run by small-scale entrepreneurs.[4] Broadly seeming to anticipate today's cable television companies, each radio "grapevine" was operated from a powerful receiver centrally located in a farmhouse or a crossroads general store and connected by wire to subscribers' homes along the village street or country lane. According to Robert B. Glazner, a single wire was run along fenceposts, stranded through chinaberries and other trees and bushes, and grounded at the end of its route.

The grapevine radio's owner collected a monthly fee and in exchange relayed programming all day long, every day, whether or not the would-be listeners were at home. Subscribers had no control of program choice, operating times, or speaker volume; the programs could not be switched on or off except at the receiver location. Thus Frances N. Sutherland remembers her first girlhood experience with radio: "We had a wire with a speaker on it. It played all the time. I guess it stopped when the people who operated it cut off the radio. We enjoyed it very much. We kept it in a central location in the house" in the Shady Grove Community near Belton, "not too far from 'Possum Kingdom'."

Joe Harris provides both an overview of the grapevine radio's significance and an amusing account of its sometimes unexpected effects:

A look at rural South Carolina in the early part of the century shows many areas of isolation that are hard to imagine today. During the Great Depression, mass communication was scarce.

And then, along came what was known as "grapevine radio." The two that I remember were near my home. One was operated from Chandler's Store at the Ware Place in lower Greenville County. The other was at Ellison's Store about a mile out the Anderson highway from Williamston, South Carolina (now S.C. 20).

The set-up was this: there was a radio at the store which picked up the broadcast signals from stations on the air. To get the broadcasts out, a single wire was run through the community, strung from pole to pole. At each house to be served, a wire was run from the pole to the house and connected to a small speaker. A ground wire was attached to the speaker, allowing the broadcasts received at the store to be heard on all the speakers attached to it. As the cost was only about ten cents per week, it was a real bargain even then.

The speaker usually stayed on all the time because it required no power and it was a break in the monotony of rural life. Any news of events from around the rest of the nation was welcome.

Another facet of "grapevine radio" was that programs could originate from the store where the "grapevine" was based. A corner of the store would be adapted to use as a studio. From time to time, musical groups would perform for the "grapevine" listeners. Religious services were conducted on a regular basis, which was a benefit to the elderly and those shut-ins unable to attend church.

My father was a member of the Welborn Quartet, sponsored by the Welborn Mortuary in West Pelzer. They sang many times at one or the other of the "grapevines" around Anderson and Greenville counties. Some of the first advertising, done through sponsorship of these programs, was done on the "grapevines."

The "grapevine" was usually cut on about 6:00 a.m. because everyone in the community would already have been up at 4:00 a.m., have the milking done, and be back in the house for breakfast by 6:00.

One former "grapevine" customer that I met years later told me about an experience that shook him up quite a bit. As stated earlier, the speaker was left on all the time. The hours of broadcasting fit the families' lifestyle, and the speaker used no power, so there was no need to cut it off. He said that he and his wife woke up shortly before 6:00 one morning. They were engaged in a moment of passion, when suddenly a voice at the foot of the bed said, "GOOD MORNING, FOLKS!!!" By the time that he realized it was only the "grapevine" speaker starting its broadcast day, he had leaped over the foot of the bed. The "grapevine" came to life at a bad moment for him.

With the isolation of the country folks, the "grapevine" was sometimes used for emergencies. Anytime there was a need to locate medical assistance, the message might be spread by the "grapevine": "IF ANYONE SEES DR. DENDY, TELL HIM THAT MRS. SMITH ON THE AUGUSTA ROAD IS IN LABOR. HE KNOWS WHERE TO GO." It was a simple system, but it benefitted many in the community.

All of these community radio systems operated in the same general way, but each "grapevine" made its own adaptation to the area that it served. Paul F. Snow recounts the excitement of the time when installation of a grapevine radio brought a steady source of programming to his location in the mid-1930s:

No one in the country had electric power, and an enterprising young man in Mauldin, South Carolina, who I believe was an electrical engineer, rigged up a powerful tuner. He assisted the farm families to build lines all through the countryside, to which a family could acquire a speaker only and hook up to his wire for, as I recall, a twenty-five cents per month fee. Many families did subscribe to this service, mine included. There were many miles of lines over a great portion of mid- to lower Greenville County.

The disadvantage to such a system was that those of us with the service had no choice of listening to any program save what they selected on the master tuner in his residence. Anyway, we had "arrived" and were at last in touch with the outside world.

Not suited to every region or clime, grapevine radio sprang up where it was needed and helped to swell the national radio family. Overall, listeners were quite willing to endure the system's limitations; most of them lacked the money, time, and technical knowledge needed to set up their own radio sets and antennas. Grapevine linkages proved to be the most viable means of satisfying the widespread yearning to share in the radio phenomenon.

In some places these wired systems continued to function well into the 1940s, and even after full rural electrification allowed each family to have its own radio, the grapevine legacy of community-wide program prefer- ence, initially imposed by system owners, remained. Now a family physi- cian, Dr. William E. "Bill" Dukes, Sr. remembers walking home from movies in the South Carolina town of Honea Path on Saturday evenings in the 1940s listening to "practically the whole 'Grand Ole Opry'" program emerg- ing each week from the houses along his way back to his family's mill village home. Well before the hour for dressing to go to church, he went each Sunday morning to milk cows in barns bordering the mill village, and he could follow the voices of local gospel quartets singing in nearby Ander- son studios and received on radios turned up to high volume in every home, as if to prime every resident and passer-by for the Sabbath's activities.

A growing nation of radio listeners created a demand for skilled radio installers and repairers. Big city radio retailers maintained service staffs, and many small towns had at least one "electric shop" with a journeyman jack-of-all-trades. Matchbook covers promised comfortable incomes to those who completed by-mail radio repair courses. From that Depression era Charles Wilson Tucker remembers a gypsy-like figure who passed through his home town, Fitzgerald, Georgia, which had a railway round- house and repair shop near the city limits:

In addition to the booming business of moving passengers and freight for nominal fees, the rail terminal also attracted hordes of non-paying passengers identified as hoboes.

Year around, the hoboes converged on the small town from trains out of the North, taking refuge in the hobo jungle east of town. There they waited, sometimes for several days, before catching another freight train to Thomasville, which seemed to be the gateway to Florida, the destination of them all. Eagerly accepting any type of employment to earn a few cents or perhaps a meal, these men of varied backgrounds and nationalities, language and culture would sweep yards, beat rugs, chop firewood, and do anything else to keep from going hungry.

Radio was considered the modern miracle of those times. With few other luxuries affordable, somehow many homes had radios. Local furniture and appliance stores offered the latest Philco, Atwater Kent, and RCA radios installed in the home, including an impressive outdoor antenna of copper wire strung between two wooden poles, all on an easy-pay plan. Some of the large hotels in Jacksonville and Atlanta boasted that each of their hundred or so rooms came equipped with its own radio.

Frank's Radio Service was one of many in the United States capitalizing on this lucrative market. This skill was not for everyone. It required a certain amount of investment for parts and test equipment and a suitable shop. Foremost, it required some special technical training, usually acquired by enrolling in a radio repair course by mail, as offered by NRI, De Forest, and others.

Frank had been in business several years and had a younger man assisting him. He had built up a good clientele and, considering the Depression, he was doing well.

Shortly after the door was opened for business one day, a man entered and asked if he could do any work for them. Frank and his helper looked at the man dressed in the long sleeve shirt, old overalls, and brogan shoes, holding his sweat-stained felt hat in his hands. It was obvious that the man had just alighted from the freight train or had walked over from the hobo jungle. The shop floor had already been swept, but more or less to humor the man, Frank asked, "What kind of work do you do?"

With a serious face, the man replied, "I am a radio fixer."

Now it was Frank's turn to force a straight face. He had never heard that term used in the occupation of radio repairman or technician. Momentarily thinking of a polite way to get rid of him, Frank's thoughts turned to the ten or so radios hidden in the back of the shop that had stumped him and his helper over the past several months and seemed to defy all efforts to get them working properly.

Out of curiosity and the possibility of a good laugh, Frank consented to let the "radio fixer" try his hand at the "dogs" he could not repair. As a place at the workbench was provided for him with tools, parts, and test equipment, it was agreed that the man would receive fifty cents for each radio set repaired.

Soon, the "radio fixer" had expertly removed the radio chassis from the cabinet, began to test and analyze, snipping defective condensers and resistors, quickly replacing them with the smoking soldering iron and turning on the recently dead radio for final adjustments to a fully operational, beautifully toned masterpiece.

The only break the "radio fixer" took all day was when Frank brought him a Coke and hamburger for lunch. By day's end the "radio fixer" had repaired all ten of the "dogs."

As Frank counted out the five dollars and placed them in the "radio fixer's" hand, he hinted strongly that they could use a man of his abilities full time. The "fixer" expressed his thanks but politely declined the job offer, stating that he was on his way to Florida and that he would be on his way.

Within three decades' span, radio grew from being the subject of hobbyists' and engineers' experiments into being a dominant medium: vox humana electrified, sometimes supported by sound effects and musical instruments, and increasingly depended upon for news and educational features, sports coverage, drama, and variety entertainment. The novelty item of the 1920s became the household fixture, almost taken for granted, in the 1940s. Investors and manufacturers, announcers, entertainers, sponsors, producers, repairers, and listeners shared in the growth of the United States as a nation culturally bound together by radio. Not everyone saw Carole Lombard's or Jimmy Stewart's latest motion picture, and not everyone read *The Boston Globe* or *The San Francisco Examiner*, but nearly everyone knew when and where to tune in H. V. Kaltenborn's commentary, "The Romance of Helen Trent," "The Lone Ranger," a dance band remote, "The Bob Hope Show," "The Railroad Hour," or "The Quiz Kids."

NOTES

1. Chapel Hill and London: University of North Carolina Press, 1987.

2. Hall et al.; pp. 237-288.

3. Ibid., passim.

4. Ironically, the systems that served these low-income rural areas were essentially the same as those which entertained the guests of New York's Waldorf and other "ritzy" major-city hotels. Susan K. Opt explains the workings of this system in "The Development of Rural Wired Radio Systems in Upstate South Carolina," *Journal of Radio Studies* 1 (1992); 71-81.

II

WHAT THEY HEARD

6

Events and Commentators

While KDKA's broadcasting of the 1920 presidential election returns proved that a significant event could be covered in a few hours of airtime for a limited listenership, radio's second attempt at reporting the race for the White House showed a phenomenal growth in the medium's reach. Priming listener interest in the early summer of 1924, receiver and speaker manufacturers, distributors, and retailers placed hundreds of newspaper advertisements urging radio owners to upgrade their equipment in time to hear the full coverage of the Democratic and Republican nominating conventions. In November, hotels in many cities promoted "radio election parties," where the usual mid-1920s night life would be mixed with a dash of election returns heard until that late (or early) hour when the last vote had been counted and the last drink had been consumed. Thus the 1924 election year demonstrated that broadcasting was able to chronicle the full campaign as much of the nation listened to a variety of stations. It was an early proof that radio might survive the novelty stage and challenge the print media in news gathering and dissemination. That is not to deny that on ordinary days the news items might be read by the studio engineer or any other available person, but the medium's potential had been shown.

In the 1920s, radio caught whatever events and persons it could, when it could, as illustrated in Roger Rollin's repeating of "an oft-told family story" of "radio's crystal set days":

My grandfather and grandmother lived on a small farm in the country, near Lincoln Place, Pennsylvania, south of Pittsburgh. It had been a tradition for the family—my mother and dad, and her three brothers and their wives—to gather every week for a big family dinner. On one Sunday in particular everyone was excited because one of America's most famous men, Thomas A. Edison, was to speak over the radio. Edison, born in 1847, was then in his eighties (he would die in 1931), and everyone knew this was likely their only chance to hear, live, the voice of America's greatest inventor. After dinner the family gathered around the crystal set in the parlor, with the coal stove blazing merrily, waiting to hear the voice of the Great Man. Finally the announcer proclaimed, "Thomas A. Edison will now speak," and everyone leaned closer to the crystal set to hang upon his every word. Everyone, that is, except my grandmother, who unaccountably had seized just that moment to shake the ashes down in the coal stove. Her clattering and banging completely drowned out the radio, Edison, and the shouts for her to stop. She finished, and so did Edison, who was able to get out only a few words. Words, alas, that my family never heard. But from then on, when any loud noises were made around our household, someone would always say, "Thomas A. Edison will now speak!"

On the other hand, Percy M. Matthews discovered a real advantage in monitoring his family's first radio:

One of my highlights was to stay up until midnight on Saturday nights to listen to a program when they would attempt to contact Admiral Richard E. Byrd and his expedition there at the South Pole. Short wave was in its infancy then, so sometimes they were not able to make contact.

One night they told that Admiral Byrd had gone to an advance base—alone—from the main camp. In a couple of days they were not able to contact him by radio and rushed to the advance camp and found the admiral overcome by carbon monoxide from his gas stove, and saved his life. A few hours later would have been too late. I reported this to my English class the following Monday, even before the newspapers had this story. In those days it was a real thrill to hear someone talk from the South Pole—scratchy as reception was some of the time, a real marvel in those days.

Of course the radio news and discussion programs often hit home in unpleasant ways. Mary Lee McCrackan remembers of the 1928 national elections: "The Al Smith-Herbert Hoover presidential campaign shook Virginia to the roots. There may have been a projection of how it would turn out, but the reporting was so much slower than today's TV, and everyone was kept in suspense. Today, the TV has the President elected before the polls close in California." Lois Garrison recalls that a close friend's father, who owned an independent grocery store in the early 1930s, would come home and listen solemnly "for hours" to radio talks about how chain groceries were expected to put "private" grocers out of business.

With the formation of NBC in 1926 and CBS the following year, listeners began to become familiar with some radio reporters' and commentators' names and intonations. In 1927, Lowell Thomas was one of the radio reporters who broadcast sightings of Charles Lindbergh's plane during the solo transatlantic flight to Paris, and by 1930 Thomas had earned a regularly scheduled newscasting time. (Late in his career, the reporter-adventurer quipped that his own epitaph should read, "Here lies the body of a man who was heard by millions of people . . . who were waiting to hear 'Amos 'n' Andy'.") H. V. Kaltenborn, "dean of radio commentators" (according to his daily introducer), had gone on the air for the Columbia Broadcasting System in its inaugural year, and after a shift to NBC in 1940 he would experience the wrath of President Harry Truman, who mocked the newscaster's lilting delivery of an erroneous report that Thomas E. Dewey had won the 1948 election; Kaltenborn survived the presidential mimicking before the newsreel cameras, and he remained on the air until 1955, when many other radio fixtures were rapidly disappearing.

From March 6, 1931 until the end of World War II, CBS cooperated with *Time*, Henry Luce's weekly newsmagazine, in presenting thundering dramatizations of events, narrated most memorably by Westbrook Van Voorhis ("Time—marches—on!"), with newsreel-style music by the network's musical director, Howard Barlow. By 1938, Fulton Lewis, Jr. was listed in radio schedules as Mutual's resident "Washington news commentator," and Cesar Saerchinger was reporting "The Story Behind the Headlines" for NBC Blue. In the latter half of the isolationist 1930s, American radio listeners began to hear increasingly frequent transatlantic accounts of political machinations and social unrest in Europe. Voicing these reports were earnest-toned young correspondents such as William L. Shirer, George Hicks, and Edward R. Murrow.

During the Depression decade, radio earned increasing credibility in covering domestic events. To be sure, Billie Blocker's mid-1930s experience as a public school student in Nash, Texas, might be typical of those who found themselves at one remove from the larger world: "A newspaper that came by rural mail delivery couldn't be all that current," and it was primarily useful for tracing the careers of Joe Palooka, Dick Tracy, Li'l Abner, and Davey O'Brien, "the little guy with the big hands who could accurately throw a football a country mile, down at Texas Christian University." Likewise, "radio was for listening to Amos and Andy and Fibber McGee and Molly . . . not for news." Elsewhere, however, radio reporting quickly bridged time, natural barriers, and the drawn borders of states and nations. Dottie Zungoli remembers rushing home from school in Philadelphia to hear reports from the Lindbergh baby kidnaping trial of Bruno R. Hauptmann as well as the court inquiry into the sinking of the S.S. *Morro Castle* off the New Jersey coast in 1934. No listener ever forgot the emotional strain on Chicago station WLS's Herbert Morrison when his general interest report of the dirigible *Hindenburg*'s arrival and docking at Lakehurst, New Jersey, on May 6, 1937 suddenly became a breathless account of explosion, fire, and mass incineration. Morrison's pained and stumbling "Oh, this is one of the worst catastrophes" and his sobbed phrase "Oh, the humanity" brought an immediacy that even the largest-type headlines could not match.

Families and whole communities developed their own patterns of listening to regularly scheduled newscasts. Ted Norrgard says, "In the small town in northern Minnesota where I grew up, there was only one station where we could get good reception, and that was WCCO, a CBS affiliate. The most listened-to program was the 10:00 news with Cedric Adams. Some old timers still claim that the lights dimmed at 10 when the news came on. You could also see the lights go out at 10:15, when the program ended. Most people turned on the news with their guests' agreement when visiting back and forth." In Gordon Kelley's home near Indianapolis, "There was local and national news at noon and at 6:00. Gilbert Forbes kept us up to date on the happenings around Indianapolis, while Fulton Lewis, Jr. and Gabriel Heatter did the same with national occurrences." Doris Swehla adds, "We listened to Academy Awards presentations and to political conventions and got more involved in them than I ever have since I can watch them on TV. No matter how late the hour, we didn't really go to sleep until we heard the final results."

As radio's reporting voices grew more and more persuasive, listeners found intonations and political leanings that suited their own tastes. While some commentators sounded tweedy and could be imagined to be speaking not from studios but from libraries with backdrops of leather-bound books, the field correspondents, often recruited from newspaper staffs, spoke in unaffected tones that held traces of North Carolinian or Midwestern roots. Listeners could trust them.

Living in Richmond, Virginia, in the 1930s, Mary Lee McCrackan was bemused by the contrasting delivery styles of H. V. Kaltenborn and local newscaster Dr. Douglas Southall Freeman, the son of a Confederate general and the author of a three-volume life of Robert E. Lee, a project "finally finished after nineteen years of labor." Dr. Freeman provided commentary and did some general announcing on Richmond's WRVA. "While speaking on the radio," she remembers, "he utilized an affected Southern drawl and could easily take twenty minutes to say what Mr. Kaltenborn could effectively cover in three minutes. When asked what he thought about Margaret Mitchell's *Gone with the Wind*, he remarked that he thought it was accurate but awfully drawn out. This after nineteen years and three volumes of *Robert E. Lee!*"

John B. Simms's grandfather, who "turned Republican when Roosevelt ran for the third time," did not like H. V. Kaltenborn (whose views were sympathetic to the Democratic administration) but still listened to him. "My grandfather did not use profanity," John Simms adds, "but he would sit there and smoke his pipe and scowl. When Kaltenborn delivered a slanted statement, my grandfather would say 'Yes-s-s' in a mocking tone of voice." For Bill Buri, on the other hand, Kaltenborn's daily program sounded "kind of like God talking." "As WWII came closer," James L. Sender says, "we listened to H. V. Kaltenborn, the news journalist, and to Robert St. John—'This is Robert St. John reporting from London'—, although we all wondered where he got his British accent, as he was a product of Oak Park High School in Oak Park, Illinois, my own alma mater, ha ha. Ernest Hemingway also graduated from Oak Park High, in 1917, and *he* never picked up an accent. Ha ha."

Gabriel Heatter often began his newscasts with the greeting "Ladies and gentlemen, there's good news tonight," but in the late 1940s and early 1950s he found more and more news to be bad. Brenda Seabrooke remembers him in the twilight of his career as a "voice of doom ranting about Communism" in the years in which national attention began to shift from Charlie McCarthy to Senator Joseph McCarthy.

Roger Rollin evokes the anticipation of the evening news in his Pittsburgh home from the late 1930s onward:

When 6:00 came, the "Children's Hour" was over. The volume on the Philco in the living room (no one had more than one radio, of course, and it was invariably located in a place of honor in the parlor) was turned up, and we heard news of the great world from H. V. Kaltenborn, Gabriel Heatter, or our family favorite, Lowell Thomas. Like the other famous newscasters, Thomas had an authoritative as well as agreeable voice that made it clear that whatever he said was The Truth. Unlike the others, however, he had a sense of humor, and my parents and I lived for the occasions when, after reading a humorous news item or making one of his rare "fluffs," Thomas would begin to lose it, would begin actually to break up on the air. Another favorite was Walter Winchell, with his machine-gun delivery, which I heard spew expletives when, coincidentally, at a Manhattan street corner he and I were almost run down by the same taxi.

Bill Buri carries Roger Rollin's comment about newscasters and "The Truth" a degree further as he speaks of Lowell Thomas, H. V. Kaltenborn, and the other network commentators: "You didn't expect them to lie to you in those days. Maybe there was a lot more naiveté around, but you expected that these people were going to give you the facts. And you're not always sure nowadays." In his text for the catalog to the 1994 National Portrait Gallery exhibit "Reporting the War: The Journalistic Coverage of World War II," Frederick S. Voss notes that network correspondents' reports from Europe in the late 1930s established a new credibility for and demonstrated the power of immediacy in broadcast news, and the newspaper "extra" edition quickly lost its usefulness in portraying sudden or significantly evolving events. The gallery's resident historian also observes, "Whereas poll studies of 1938 indicated that a majority of Americans still regarded their daily newspaper as their main source of news, polls taken three years later showed that radio had emerged as America's news medium of preference."[1] Photography critic Vicki Goldberg extends Voss's remarks, saying that radio "may have created then what television apparently has now: a class of people who do not read very much daily and may not have access to good newspapers yet are up to date on the headlines."[2]

Despite the tie to print journalism that Walter Winchell's program format noisily proclaimed in its tabloid-style opening ("Good evening, Mr. and Mrs. North and South America and all ships at sea. Let's go to press! . . . Flash! In Berlin today . . ."), radio news departments began to feel increasingly self-sufficient in their efforts, and network promotional departments were ready to declare broadcast news a mature and reliable service to the public. Backed by the technical, financial, and New Deal-friendly resources of the Radio Corporation of America, the National Broadcasting Company was particularly skilled in portraying itself as a news-gathering institution, the authoritative and essential aid to the listener eager to keep current on events. During World War II, the network added a fourth note to its musical signature to designate important war news reports, and in 1944 it published the promotional book *The Fourth Chime*, describing the NBC news operations at home and abroad and profiling members of the editorial and reporting staffs. One two-page spread, "The Door That Is Never Closed," places the news operation within a modern shrine of architectural grandeur and seems to equate its busy activities with those of an important federal agency, perhaps a quasi-secret one:

Dominating the prodigious gray limestone buildings that extend above Radio City's twelve teeming acres is the thin, slab-like pile of the RCA Building. On the fourth floor, opening off one of NBC's long corridors, is an ordinary door sandwiched between bustling offices. It bears the simple identification "404—News and Special Events."

This door is never locked, not even closed. Behind it is a small, unpretentious office whose lights are always on—Room 404, headquarters of NBC's efficient News and Special Events Department. Over this room . . . hangs a kind of restless but disciplined din; phone bells cut short with quick responses, the metallic tattoo of typewriters, the incessant chatter of teletype machines that hammer out an agitated world's hopes and fears. . . .

At sixty words a minute, 24 hours a day, this deluge of news reports [received by "trans-ocean phone, radiogram and telegram" from "seasoned NBC correspondents on duty at the world's strategic centers" and supplemented by three wire services] spills into Room 404—a harvest of words that must be sifted, separated and bound into five- and fifteen-minute bundles of radio news before it goes out over NBC microphones. This is done by a staff of writers and editors who have developed a style of writing that is inimitably "radio." . . .

Buttressed against a nearby wall are two glass-enclosed "speaker" studios. From here NBC home-front commentators broadcast the news "while it is happening"; from here trained technicians sitting at a monitoring board . . . push tiny buttons that bring to millions of Americans the voices of NBC correspondents scattered throughout the world.

From this "Room 404," the home of the Fourth Chime, NBC news broadcasts, accepted by millions as unbiased, unprejudiced and truthful, in themselves give purpose and substance to radio as a vigorous instrument of Democracy.[3]

Of course this hymnic publicity style seeks to lend the NBC news operation a unique identity while implicitly denying the existence of its competitors. *The Fourth Chime* also offers a map showing the locations of affiliates in a spread titled "NBC on the Home Front: 1942-1944."[4] The explanatory text again conveys the suggestion that the network holds a quasi-governmental authority by which its writers and newscasters, " . . . through their accurate, unbiased interpretation of the news at home and abroad, [have] told Americans how events were affecting their lives, shaping their destiny."[5]

"Destiny" had been an especially resonant word since Franklin Delano Roosevelt used it (in his second nomination acceptance speech in Philadelphia on June 17, 1936) to describe the mission of "this generation of Americans." That word reverberates through *The Fourth Chime*, and soon after FDR's death in 1945, NBC issued "for educational use" a two-volume set of twelve 78 r.p.m. disks containing excerpts from the late President's speeches, distributed under the title ". . . Rendezvous with Destiny." In the liner notes to the NBC Documentary Recording album, the anonymous copywriter proclaims,

It is doubtful whether "this generation of Americans" will experience events of greater stature than those encompassed in the period from 1933 to 1945.

For the first time radio was the chief medium by which a nation was kept abreast of the on-rushing events of one of the most significant periods in the world's history.

It is fitting, therefore, that radio should preserve for posterity this record of a memorable era . . . in the voice and words of one of its chief protagonists.

NBC presents this documentary recording of historic moments preceding and during the Second World War as reflected in the speeches of President Roosevelt— and broadcast over the nationwide facilities of the National Broadcasting Company.

Although the implication that one network held exclusive title to a four-term president's public utterances is patently incorrect, the representation of radio as "the chief medium" of news dissemination in the World War II era is a more viable claim. Microphones of CBS, MBS, ABC, and independent stations can be seen along with NBC's in photographs of President Roosevelt giving his Fireside Chats and speaking from Democratic convention and congressional rostrums. A respected organization with a fine eye for self-promoting devices, NBC was only one of the broadcast operations speaking with new confidence about their resources and their audiences.

Strongly loved by some and reviled by others, Franklin D. Roosevelt must be considered a radio personality as well as an object of others' reporting. In the period when radio was mastering its own resources, President Roosevelt honed a compelling style of platform and radio speaking. As with early-1930s "Amos 'n' Andy" episodes, so a few years later one could walk down many neighborhood sidewalks and follow Roosevelt's Fireside Chats as the sound of a radio in one house merged with the sound from the next one and the next. "I remember listening to President Roosevelt and thinking every time how beautifully he spoke. He made a very strong impression on me," says New York native Stella Saffan. During the war, Margaret Kirkpatrick affirms, "FDR's Fireside Chats were a must! When my husband was sent overseas in 1944, I returned home to live with my parents for the duration, as did many wives. My parents and I always gathered around for his broadcasts." In Bill Buri's view, "Roosevelt was magnetic . . . his voice, his diction. He was such a damned monarchist, but the people really loved him. Who else could say 'The only thing we have to fear is fear itself'? You have to be able to say that in a certain way, or you would get laughed out of the studio."

Roosevelt's radio personality strongly affected a guest of Jack Jennings's grandmother during the 1940 presidential campaign:

During the Depression "Mom" Jennings owned and operated a small country "Bon-Air" Hotel in the little cattle town of Kissimmee, Florida. One evening after supper the guests had gathered in the living room by the fireplace to listen to the new Philco console radio that had just been installed. "Gram" Wiggins was sitting in her rocking chair right next to it. The Franklin D. Roosevelt-Wendell Wilkie election was in full debate between the two presidential candidates. Wilkie made some disparaging remark about racing Roosevelt. Gram's temper flared as she took her walking stick and knocked the control knobs off of the new radio while exclaiming for all to hear, "Whoever heard of a Jackass outrunning a Thoroughbred!"

The remainder of the evening was spent listening to an old crystal set.

Near the end of the 1930s, radio mixed its usual entertainment and informational fare with reports of futuristic novelties, including demonstrations of television, at the New York World's Fair. However, other events were in the making, and they would push radio to new strategies for covering world events.

On August 30, 1939, N. D. Mallary, Jr., now head of a psychotherapy and family counseling clinic in Atlanta, was occupied in helping his girlfriend, Helen, and her recently widowed stepmother, Marty, settle into a newly rented apartment in Durham, North Carolina, where Helen was beginning her senior year at Duke University. Having known Helen since 1935 (when he was a high school lad of fourteen and a half and she was "a woman eighteen years old") and having "first kissed her at 9:30 p.m. on June 9, 1936," he had "won and lost her love" through a succession of Christmas, spring, and summer vacations. They had dated "constantly" in that last summer of the 1930s, and the relationship seemed to enter a new phase as he took charge of the move from Macon, Georgia:

We arrived on schedule, as did the moving van. We all set about getting the apartment in livable condition.

On September 3, 1939, after a good number of hours hanging curtain rods, curtains, towel rods, and can openers, while the women continued to unpack and put up, Helen and I were lying across her bed resting, and Marty was *in* her bed. We were listening to the radio when suddenly our program was interrupted—England and France had declared war against Germany. Hitler had invaded Poland on September 1st.

There is *no* good place to hear the news of the beginning of World War II, but certainly the least bad is in the arms of your girl. We did not fully comprehend it, but all of our respective lives would change drastically as a result of that announcement and subsequent events. For the moment, however, we continued with the necessary but mundane business of unpacking and getting an apartment livable.

Shifting the nation's focus from events in Europe, the Japanese attack on the United States military installation at Pearl Harbor on the early morning of December 7, 1941 was like the explosive burst from an old-fashioned photographer's flash pan, and moments in American lives were captured in memory.

Dr. Jeanne Kenmore recalls that day in Minneapolis: "On December 7, 1941 (I was eighteen), I was answering an ad in the Sunday paper. I was looking for a room to rent in someone's house. (There was no space in my family dwelling for me to live.) So, about 1 p.m. I rang someone's doorbell. A woman opened the door, looked at me, and asked, 'Have you heard what has happened? Japan has bombed some island that belongs to us.' She invited me in, I joined that family and listened for several hours, and— well, I did rent a bedroom where I could sleep. No eating in it, of course."

Wilton M. Browne had enrolled in the Civilian Conservation Corps in October 1936 and served in Pennsylvania and Oregon, at several South Carolina camps, and at District Headquarters in Fort McPherson, Georgia. In July 1941 he received an appointment as a CCC Subaltern (Administrative Assistant), and in December he was assigned to a camp on the Fort Jackson reservation. He remembers, "On Sunday, December 7 after midday dinner I was sitting in the barracks with nothing particular to do. I recalled that I had a small radio that had not worked for some time. At that time I had no knowledge of the workings of a radio, but to pass the time I decided to tinker with it. While I had it out of the small cabinet and was probing around, suddenly it came alive. The first and probably the only thing I heard was the news bulletin on the attack on Pearl Harbor."

Harry Boothby, now in his mid-seventies and residing in Shapleigh, Maine, was a young teacher at the Warren, Maine, High School when the news came: "In the early p.m. the radio stopped its program to announce the attack on Pearl Harbor. My friend and high school principal Wilbur Connon was making model airplanes from balsa wood, and I was correcting test papers. We knew our futures changed that day, and we spent the remainder of the afternoon talking about what we should do. Model airplanes and test papers could wait." (Soon Harry Boothby would volunteer his well-fleshed-out six-feet, six-inches frame for submarine duty in the Pacific—he often found himself stooping to survey the coast of Japan through a periscope—, and after the war he became simultaneously principal, teacher, and basketball coach at Warren High School until its closing when total enrollment reached thirty-three students.)

"Who could forget December 7, 1941, when the football broadcast was interrupted for the Pearl Harbor announcement?" Allen Hilborn asks. Musician John Butler remembers that the New York Philharmonic's concertmaster Mishel Piastro was playing the violin solos in Rimsky-Korsakov's *Capriccio Espagnol* when the symphony broadcast was interrupted. Elly Truebenbach says, "Like most people on that infamous December 7, the radio played a part in my memories. I was six years old, playing at the neighbors'. There was a broadcast of the Chicago Symphony playing when news of the Japanese attack came on. The most impressionable years of my life were influenced a great deal by the news reports we listened to about the wars across two oceans."

During that day, the news caught up with late sleepers and with young and old alike. Gloria Stallings remembers the confusion of "one dear old soul [who] happened to hear the announcement of the bombing of Pearl Harbor in Honolulu. She went from house to house and reported that the Japs had 'bummed hallelujah'." Margaret Kirkpatrick's college roommate awakened her from an afternoon nap to tell her the dreadful news: "My fiancé (now husband of fifty years) was a Naval Aviation Cadet stationed at Floyd Bennett Field in New York. We heard the commands for all military personnel to return to their bases immediately, and so began many years of worry and listening to all the news commentators, H. V. Kaltenborn among them." On December 7, Pat O'Shee and his parents were visiting Atlanta, and "when we came downstairs at the Hotel Henry Grady, everyone was gathered around the Atwater Kent console listening to the Pearl Harbor horror on WSB, 750. We still went to the Cyclorama at Grant Park and the Wren's Nest [home of "Uncle Remus" author Joel Chandler Harris] before returning to Birmingham and WWII." In Kentucky, John Simms had been to the movie matinee and, about 5:00, joined the usual Sunday family assembly of aunts, uncles, and their mates at his grandfather's house, where, in place of the usual lively bustle and conversation, he found everyone "seated around that Stromberg Carlson listening to the war news. Everybody was hushed—in absolute silence."

Thomas Fetters and his parents heard the news on one of those Sunday afternoon drives that would soon end for most citizens:

The most dramatic thing I ever witnessed was when I was just a month shy of four years old. We lived in Ohio and had gone for a ride on a December afternoon, and I recall crossing a big river valley on a spindly bridge (in the Akron area) and stopping about 3 p.m. for lunch. The radio was on, when everyone suddenly jumped to their feet and gathered around the floor model radio as the announcer told of the attack on Pearl Harbor. There were gasps and startled looks. My parents returned to the table obviously very upset, but the idea of war was still a bit vague for me. But not for long. In the months that followed I got my steel helmet and a plane silhouette guide and patrolled the sidewalk by my house, scanning the sky for Messerschmitts and Fokkers. Never saw one, but rest assured, my eyes were alert every day through 1942!

In Chicago, Glen Resch was initiated into a new stage of his young life when he heard an interruption of Jack Benny's 6:00 program:

It had to be something big—nothing had ever interrupted Jack Benny! The family wasn't in the living room that time, of course—the grownups had heard the news much earlier. We're eighteen hours behind 0755 Sunday in Hawaii, remember. My dad was an Army officer, and it meant more at our house. We soon moved to the first of several Army bases where we lived during the war years. Actually, I consider myself sort of a WWII vet, since I was closer to it than most ten year olds, my dad being an officer and all, the house full of stuff—maps, books, even (inactive) grenades and 105 mm shells! I stuck pins in the maps and read all the books (most of them "Restricted"). You could say I majored in World War II.

Monday, December 8, 1941, when President Roosevelt's address to the Congress was carried to the nervous nation, was another milestone radio day. Lessons were suspended in schools, and the students gathered wherever a radio was available. Ellen L. Edmonds, who calls that day her "most memorable occasion involving radio," explains, "Our seventh-grade teacher at Marshall School (on the island in Marshall, North Carolina) took the class of about thirty or thirty-five students outside to her car, and we stood and listened to President Franklin Roosevelt declare that we were at war! It was a cold, gray day, and for us life changed." Kathy Cunningham remembers "the smell of the wooden, oiled floors in the school in North Platte, Nebraska" that she attended. "We sat out in the massive entrance hall and listened to FDR declare war. I also remember my father's face the day before as we interrupted Sunday dinner to listen to the news accounts of Pearl Harbor."

Safe in family circles, children were told to expect significant consequences from those days. Pat Roach says, "I remember well being in the bed sick with the red measles at 15 McArthur Street, Brandon, the day Pearl Harbor was bombed. I can still see in my mind my parents and my aunt Emma Belle sitting close to the radio listening, and I remember my dad saying President Roosevelt had declared war. My daddy's brother,

Walter Percy, was over there in Pearl Harbor, and he was one of the lucky ones." John Idol offers another image of family listening:

When FDR addressed the nation following the attack on Pearl Harbor, my mother gathered all of her sons (five at the time) before the living room radio and asked us to listen quietly to President Roosevelt's words. I can't say that I remember his famous opening line. I do recall that I had never heard anything more solemn or so eloquently expressed. As a nine year old, I had sparse knowledge of the enemy my country was being called upon to fight, but I was moved to defend my own and to sacrifice for it.

Mother had a profounder feel for the sacrifices American families would be called upon to make. Her response was not to flag-waving but to loss of lives. Whereas her sons were behaving like little patriots, she began crying.

"Why are you crying?" we asked.

"I think that this thing will go on for so long that you all will be in it," she said.

Dottie Zungoli was working at the Penn Mutual Life Insurance Company offices in Philadelphia at the time of the "day of infamy" speech, and she recalls, "We all went up to the big dining room we had there. We all listened to one little radio—hundreds of people up there."

"I was in my teens throughout the war and very caught up in what was happening all around us," says George A. Walker, Jr., who explains, "I had twenty-three cousins in the Greater Boston area, and many of them were off to the war, and then in 1943 my sister joined the Marines (I followed her in '46). The radio and the newspapers were our only means of keeping track of all this. We hung on the evening news." The "baby brother" of Tom H. Newman's father "was a U.S. Marine in the Pacific as we listened to news of the war when I was five or six. Sadly, [my father] was called to the neighbor's phone one evening for the news of the tragic loss of his brother 'Buddy' on Iwo Jima." The earliest radio listening memories of Dorothy Stancliff, a native of Tidewater Virginia, "are of sitting around the kitchen table attuned to World War II news. My dad was in the Coast Guard."

Genella Olker particularly remembers, "The Battle of Britain and Bataan was followed closely by my father, who waited for each newscast. No one will ever forget Edward R. Murrow's 'This is London'." Meanwhile, Margaret Kirkpatrick, thinking of her fiancé in the service, stayed close to the dormitory radio: "While I was in college during the war (I graduated in 1942, and we were married the day I graduated; I had promised my mother I'd finish college before I was married!) we would huddle around the radio in one of our dorm rooms trying to hear all the news available while we knitted grey woolen scarves for the servicemen. They grew longer and

longer, with irregular margins and many holes, as we were not very efficient knitters, but we felt very patriotic."

Eager listeners sought war news at all hours. Margaret Kirkpatrick was
surprised late one night in the early months of the war: "I will never forget
shortly after December 7 listening to my little bedside radio and hearing an
interruption 'This is Manila; come in' in broken English and then no more.
I have always wondered how that got on the air in Ohio!" On the other
hand, many months later George Walker, Jr. had a special informant: "My
dad telephoned me about 4 a.m. on the 6th of June 1944 and told me that
the invasion had started and to put the radio on. It was all very real and
dynamic." Gus Wentz heard that news a few hours later: "The day the Allies landed in Europe started off much as usual, radio-wise, at our house—
the Griffin Shoe Polish program ('Everybody get ready, it's time to
shiiiiine!') at 8:00 (Charley Smithgall from WSB in Atlanta), but then was
interrupted by martial music (which really caught my attention because it
was so rare to hear my favorites) and the ongoing reports all day about the
D-Day invasions."

One aspect of radio's war coverage left Glen Resch puzzled: "A radio
journalist named Julian Bentley on WBBM, CBS in Chicago, kept me
abreast of events on Bataan, Guadalcanal, or the skies over London and
Midway. He used to sign off his fifteen-minute news with 'Seventy-three.
And good night.' Never did find out what 'Seventy-three' means."

"Radio was a companion to military personnel overseas during World
War II," "Ab" Snell remembers. "In England and France in 1945 I listened
to the radio in our hut or barracks and also in the Squadron dayroom on our
airbase. Some of the best music could be heard from a German station.
'Lord Haw Haw' and 'Axis Sally' would play modern American tunes interspersed with propaganda to try to demoralize the Allied military. Most
of my fellow pilots and airmen would listen to the music and pay little
attention to the propaganda. I will have to admit, they did know a lot about
what the Allies were doing or were planning to do."

James L. Sender's recollections of World War II further show that participants in great efforts also looked to radio for an accounting of those
efforts, as well as for relief from hours of homesickness or boredom:

In one way or another my fellow graduates of the [high school] class of '42 went
into the service, and by mid-'44 some of us were polishing our skills as infantry-
men (paratroop type) in California prior to service in the Pacific islands and even-
tually Japan.

The BMIB (Big Man in Barracks), as opposed to BMOC (Big Man on Campus), was usually the fellow who was lucky enough to own a small, honest-to-God

radio. They were about nine inches by four inches by five inches. And he decided what programs the troopers would enjoy. At 5 a.m. reveille the day began with "Reveille with Beverly." It usually started with a bugle call, then went into the Andrews Sisters' "Bugle Call Rag" and other such designed to get you awake and moving. Beverly also solicited postcard requests, birthday greetings, and so on. It was a good show and took our minds off those post-graduate courses we were taking in subjects such as "Introduction to Flame Throwers 101," "Do It Yourself Bangelore Torpedoes 130," and "The Romance of the Heavy Machine Gun."

And we closely monitored the news broadcasts . . . with a grain of salt, of course. When the news said they lost fifty planes and we lost five, that meant they lost forty and we lost twenty.

There were no restrictions on listening to radios in the barracks, other than [that] it better not be playing after "Lights out." Ha ha.

Living in Oak Ridge, Tennessee, in the latter stages of the war, Norma Brown Hanrahan especially recalls "the broadcast in 1945 after the Bomb was dropped on Hiroshima and the straining of mind to take in atomic matter and fission and destruction." Margaret Kirkpatrick remembers the report of Japan's surrender soon afterward: "The announcement that the war was over was joyously celebrated as we listened to the long-awaited news. My father opened a bottle of wine he had been saving from the year I was born, and I began counting the days until my husband and I would be together again." Larry Telles recollects the war's end from a younger perspective: "I remember one afternoon when I was eight; the year was 1945. My parents and I lived behind a soda fountain they owned on 38th Avenue in Oakland, California. I normally listened to the radio after school, before and after dinner. There was only one day that year I remember not listening to the radio. It was V-J Day. I celebrated with the people and kids dancing in the street and in our store."

Ellen L. Edmonds notes radio's part in welcoming a war hero home: "I recall vividly when Major Edward Rector of the Flying Tigers came home, and Marshall celebrated his homecoming with the first radio broadcast from our home town. Much ado to have him make a speech and broadcast live from Marshall, North Carolina. The whole county turned out—very patriotic event indeed!" She also sums up the medium's role in reporting the global conflict: "The radio kept us informed about the war, where our fighting men were—and the casualties. The bombings and the blackouts in London and Paris—and then the victories—the atom bomb—and our boys came marching home. Radio told us all these things, and how America rejoiced! We could hear the whistles and shouts in New York as they described these events on the radio."

If radio had signalled days of great national gladness in 1945, it also brought a solemn announcement from the Little White House in Warm Springs, Georgia, on April 12: President Roosevelt was dead. The degree of his physical weakness having been kept from the public for fear of encumbering the country's push toward victory, the news was all the more shocking for its suddenness. Dottie Zungoli and her friends heard the radio bulletin in Miami: "We just cried and cried and cried. We thought the world was going to end because we thought that he was the only one who could get us out of the war." Ellen Edmonds remembers that the President's "favorite song was 'Home on the Range.' It was played often that day." Gordon Kelley was "just an innocent eleven years of age" that day: "It was a young boy's disaster. I was not very worldly then and didn't realize the significance of the death of a U.S. president. All I knew was there was nothing but news on the radio. My favorite serials were not on the air. There was no Jack Armstrong, or Superman, or Captain Midnight. My heroes were silent for the first time in my memory, and it took a long time for me to realize what had happened. They returned the next day, but I spent a lonely Thursday without them."

John Idol describes the solemn funeral day which followed:

On the day FDR's body returned to Washington from Warm Springs, Mother turned on our Firestone console and asked us to have a seat. We listened as Arthur Godfrey and other correspondents narrated the event from their various observation posts. Born just days before FDR was elected, I had never known another President and was aware of how much he meant to my dad and his father, both Yellow Dog Democrats. I was sorry to be giving up so fine a man, my sorrow being no doubt heightened by the solemnity I heard in the familiar voice of Godfrey. But what I recall most vividly was the clomp, clomp, clomp of the horses as they drew the draped coffin down Pennsylvania Avenue. They were no sound effects for "Let's Pretend" or "The Lone Ranger" but, instead, undeniable tokens that FDR was taking his last ride.

For a time, postwar radio continued to lead as a broadcast news medium. "I listened to the Truman-Dewey radio coverage *all* night long," Mary Lee McCrackan says. "It was with a group of news-reporter friends, and about midnight the men left to go back to the office to rewrite their stories. I went to work with my civilian clothes on, and the election was still not decided for sure." Jim Fanning recalls "getting up on a Saturday morning in December 1946 and hearing about the Winecoff Hotel fire in downtown Atlanta. One couldn't believe it"; the images of people jumping to their deaths had to wait for the next day's newspapers. Nonetheless, radio commentators soon began to divide their time between that medium and television, where Douglas Edwards's "Camel News Caravan" was, at the beginning, little more than a quarter-hour's one- or two-camera view of an announcer reading the news and promoting the sponsor's cigarettes. As Chet Huntley was teamed with David Brinkley for television, the senior radio newscasters' quarter hours began to be shifted to other uses.

Some of those who were young in the 1930s and the 1940s prefer to recall the events and personalities of the era in a sweeping synthesis of radio voices. In Harriet Burt's view,

The most momentous events of the '30s and '40s played out before a national audience. Worried men with shaky jobs or no jobs at all heard FDR reassure a nation amidst the clang of bank doors. In the quiet of their safe living rooms, Americans listened to Edward R. Murrow describe the fires of London against a backdrop of ack-ack and bombs and sirens and the sound of Big Ben. They took heart when they heard Churchill's sonorous tones urge a people on to victory "on the beaches. . . ." Later, an entire nation listened prayerfully as correspondent Wright Bryan, native of a tiny Southern college town, described the uncertainty, hope, and triumph of D-Day. The death of a president, the downfall of a dictator, the enormity of an unbelievable weapon forged in unknown towns (one of which my father helped to build) were announced to "Mr. and Mrs. America and all the ships at sea" by Winchell, Heatter, Kaltenborn, and their fellows. War and peace, pageantry and pathos, funerals and even the wedding of a princess—all of these were experienced by those of us lucky enough to have known the Radio Age.

To have been alive in that age, and to have lived into the television age of Kennedy and King, men on the moon, bombs over Baghdad, and an unexpected outbreak of goodwill in Gaza, Moscow, and Berlin—I'd not trade those times for any others in history!

NOTES

1. Washington, D.C.: Smithsonian Institution Press, 1994; p. 120.
2. "Photography View: Setting the Standards for War Pictures," *New York Times*, 5 June 1994; 34H.
3. [N. p.]: National Broadcasting Company, 1944; pp. 12-13.
4. Ibid., 160-161.
5. Ibid.,160.

7

Sportscasts

An especially strong general sports avidity, coinciding with broadcasting's early years, prompted the buying or the building of many a radio apparatus. Set owners could expect to welcome (or to shun) visitors for championship prize fights, World Series baseball games, and New Year's Day football bowl games. Generally, sports events of national interest were not everyday occurrences in those days, and thus the "big fight" or the "big game" was all the more eagerly anticipated. When games could not be broadcast live from the field of play, they were often recreated from telegraphic reports by imaginative announcers. Although the first live broadcast of any baseball game took place during the 1921 regular season, for instance, the World Series for that year, pitting the New York Giants against the Yankees, was voiced in the studio by Thomas Cowan.[1]

In the 1920s and 1930s, the names of sports announcers such as Ted Husing, horse racing specialist Clem McCarthy, ringside reporter Don Dunphy, and baseball's "Red" Barber became as familiar as those of Knute Rockne, "Red" Grange, and Gene Tunney. In a long radio career Graham McNamee would serve as announcer for programs as diverse as "Cities Service Concerts" (beginning in 1927), "The Rudy Vallee Show" (1929), Ed Wynn's "The Fire Chief" (1932), and "Elsa Maxwell's Party Line" (1942), but he was best known as an NBC sportscaster who, among other accomplishments, brought Bill Stern to network radio. Although some listeners found Stern's play-by-play style to be over-excited, his "The Colgate Sports Newsreel" had a steady run from 1939 to 1951. Linking 1930s enthusiasms for aviation, baseball, and radio, Walter Lanier "Red" Barber interviewed Cincinnati Reds manager Bob O'Farrell in the air on June 9, 1934, during the first airplane flight ever taken by a baseball team.[2]

For every major city that boasted a winning or a characterful team, there was an announcer or a radio station known as "the Voice of" that team, and distant fans could follow their favorite teams or individual athletes on clear-channel or powerful regional stations. Guests, sometimes invited and some-times not, filled parlors, smoking rooms, lawns, sidewalks, parking lots, and town squares, anywhere a radio was provided, either with speakers or, in the earliest days, with someone who would repeat to the crowd what he heard over the headphones.

Championship prize fights brought out the radio crowds. Lois Garrison recalls that the first radio in Fitzgerald, Georgia, was set up at Halperin's Department Store for one of the Jack Dempsey-Gene Tunney fights of the mid-1920s, drawing "the whole town" to listen to speakers provided in surrounding blocks. Dottie Zungoli says that when Joe Louis was fighting his major bouts in the 1930s, her father "opened all the windows of our house—we had a lot of them—, and there must have been a hundred people standing outside listening to our radio." From a very young age (too young to recall which fight it was), Claire Caskey retains the memory of two uncles' driving forty miles over unpaved and heavily rutted roads to pick up his father and to drive another one hundred miles to try to hear the radio account of a championship contest. He does remember having cried when he was not allowed to go. Boxing was rough stuff meant only for grown-ups, he was told.

One fight brought special chagrin to many radio fans. John Butler re-calls the expectation:

For special broadcasts (prize fights, Fireside Chats, and so on) my father liked to position himself carefully in the dining/family room in our house in Minneapolis and make something of a ceremony of things—with snacks, water, etc., on hand. One particular occasion I remember was when he was gearing up to listen to a Joe Louis fight against Max Schmeling, and just as the first round started, Dad real-ized that the fudge he had planned to consume ceremoniously while listening was still in the kitchen. He went in to get it, and when he got back about a minute later, the fight was over!

Bill Buri anticipated hearing that fight on his attic radio in Pennsylvania, and he, too, was a listener who brought a sense of occasion to such events: "I can remember getting ready for things. I had a shoe box, and I would put two apples and a milk bottle of water and crackers in it. When the second Joe Louis-Max Schmeling bout came along, there I was sitting in front of the radio with the shoe box and the apples and the crackers. Just before it came on, I had to go to the bathroom, and when I got back, of course, Max Schmeling was out on the canvas."

While pioneer listeners, led by the ringside narrative, liked to visualize the dark drama of two sweating bodies sparring at and pounding upon each other, they preferred baseball among team sports. Maxine Trively pictures the group that gathered around her father's radio in Nebraska in the 1920s: "His friends, cigar smokers all, assembled to hear the World Series as Dad sat with his earphones on and relayed the plays, complete with his additional salty comments, sprinkled with cuss words. The air became blue with smoke and swearing when the baseball players scored or blew it!" The efforts of Owen Lyons, Jr.'s father to set up a radio to receive the St. Louis Cardinals games in a Missouri village in 1929 have already been detailed, but he adds, "In this same time period, my grandfather constructed his own crystal control radio and used it for many years with a set of headphones. He was semi-invalid and gained much of his pleasure from listening to the baseball games and other programs of the day." That family ardor for broadcast baseball brought Owen Lyons, Jr. a rare privilege in 1934:

My father gave me permission to skip school for a few days for a special reason. It had never happened before and never happened afterward. But this was the year that the St. Louis Cardinals played and defeated the Detroit Tigers in the World Series. It was almost like World War 1.5. In one game Cardinals outfielder Joe Medwick was thrown out of the game because the Tiger fans had become so outraged at his hits and scores that they pelted the outfield with vegetables, fruit, and other things and would not stop until he was out of the game. The Cardinals won anyway.

In the early 1930s, Percy M. Matthews anticipated listening to the World Series each fall during his school days in Camden, South Carolina: "One of the town's grocery stores had a radio up front close to the sidewalk. Our school was less than a mile away, so when school was let out, we boys would run to the store to listen, and always a crowd of men were there around the front and on the sidewalk. The great Mel Allen was the announcer—what a thrill to hear him describe the game." At about the same time in the town of Elloree, "Ab" Snell "would go to the drugstore or to a Gulf service station on the corner for the special broadcast of the baseball World Series. Dizzy Dean and his brother 'Daffy' (Paul) pitched for the St. Louis Cardinals. Boxing matches would also draw a crowd at the local service station."

Sports "philosophers" have long seen athletic events as ritualized realities, governed by necessary rule and quaint custom (the seventh-inning stretch, for instance). If so, then early sportscasting added its own layer of simulation. A telegraphed report of a baseball game in Boston, a football contest at Yale, or a boxing match in Philadelphia served as the announcer's script or, for the most imaginative recounters, as a cue sheet inviting elaboration through sound effects and the cunningly moderated urgency of the announcer's voice.

Many will remember that Ronald Reagan, later of Hollywood and Washington, gained his first more-than-local fame through studio re-creations of baseball games for WHO in Des Moines. James M. Roman of Montevallo, Alabama well recalls both the broadcast ritual and the pleasing microphone persona of a Birmingham announcer whose later prominence would involve decidedly unsportsmanlike conduct:

In the 1930s, radio station WBRC broadcast Birmingham Barons baseball games. When the Barons were playing on the road in such Southern League cities as Memphis, Nashville, and Atlanta, Western Union, using the American Morse Code ticker system, telegraphed play by play to WBRC. The game announcer, Eugene "Bull" Connor, called the game as if he were at the ball park itself. Of course, the radio audience had been advised earlier that the game was received by telegraph. But "Bull" had numerous sound effect gadgets, such as "canned crowd noise." One such gimmick was a gong for hitting when a player got a hit. One bong meant a single, two meant a double, three a triple, and four a home run.

The most unique sound of all was made when a player for either side made an out. "Bull" became famous for his saying "OW-oooot!" And even though the ticker tape may have sent only the word "out," "Bull" would ad lib by saying something like "There is a long fly-ball to deep right center, the centerfielder is chasing the ball, and . . . HE CAUGHT IT, a beautiful play . . . OW-oooot!"

About thirty years later, "Bull" Connor became nationally known in a much more negative way. In the 1960s, this same "Bull" Connor, as police commissioner of Birmingham, directed the use of dogs and fire hydrant water hoses to break up civil rights demonstrations. His tenacity in fighting integration no doubt gave Birmingham a negative reputation that still gets occasional mention in the media, even though it now is probably the most integrated city in the whole nation.

Yes, I prefer to remember the late "Bull" Connor for his unique style of calling baseball games on the radio.

In the mid-1930s, Claire Caskey spent his after-school hours as a Western Union messenger in Charlotte, and he recalls frequently walking past the large front window of Ivey's Department Store, where the WBT announcer passed the ticker tape across his fingertips and let it coil to the floor as he transported his listeners to Ebbets Field or Yankee Stadium. Thus in public view, and apparently without any sense that a minor fraud was being perpetrated, a game played in a major city became simultaneously an event shaped for the collective ear of Charlotte and, for the department store customers, a living tableau of up-to-date communications.

In Doris Swehla's Chicago family, "Radio was more than entertainment, of course. My father listened to the news each night and to every ball game ever announced. The sound of 'It's a *beautiful* day in Chicago,' as an opening to a game, was the most familiar Saturday sound" in the apartment. Reception conditions on an Illinois farm made Robert A. Waller "a lifelong Chicago White Sox fan (even though now living in Braves territory). Why? Because the Philco radio would not bring the Cubs games to a site 130 miles away. Later I had modest, but temporary, success in winning over some of my West Chicago relatives to support the South Siders rather than the North Siders in the days of GO GO Sox with Nellie Fox, Minnie Minoso, Billy Pierce, and others. Their allegiance has lapsed, I am sure, but mine persists due to that chance radio connection."

For Gray Whaley at age five or six, a special moment of 1930s baseball listening was captured in the announcer's "That's ball four!" when Lou Gehrig, already ill with the disease that now bears his name, was given a walk so that another RBI could be credited to his career record. More generally, Elly Truebenbach says, "Baseball distracted us for a few hours during those difficult times, and we were faithful fans of the original Milwaukee Brewers. As school children, my classmates and I didn't have the money to attend many games except for opening day. This was usually a chilly time in spring, but we bundled up and went to cheer for the cutest players. For some reason our teachers tolerated our playing hookey once a year. The rest of the time we contented ourselves listening to the games on the radio, dreaming of our heroes hitting home runs or making spectacular catches." Pat Roach, still a self-described "big baseball fan" at age fifty-eight, notes, "I remember well as a child how baseball was the thing in Carolina mill villages. I remember my daddy listening to the ball games— all of them on the radio."

The Atlanta Crackers of the Southern League, heard on a low-wattage local station in the 1940s, were a very different team from today's well-financed Atlanta Braves. Nonetheless, Bob Morgan developed a lifelong passion for baseball by listening to Crackers games on his hobbyist's crystal set in the late 1940s and trying to visualize the action called by Ernie Harwell, who later served as game announcer in Detroit: "I would put the crystal set on my bed and listen to it there. I became interested in baseball, but I knew very few of the rules at this time. As I listened to the games more and more, I learned just about all that I know about baseball, even up to now. The only thing that I got confused was this: I thought that the short-stop was between first base and second base. When I went to a game on Ponce de Leon Avenue, the home of the Crackers, I found out that the shortstop was between second base and third. There I learned by seeing."

After World War II, more teams playing greater varieties of sports were heard on more stations than ever before. Living in Cuba as a sales repre-sentative of a major U.S. drug manufacturer between 1951 and 1955, Bill Buri enjoyed hearing the local teams' games being broadcast in Spanish.

Football was a limited-season sport in the late 1930s and early 1940s, with national interest centering largely on a few college teams and on the bowl games. Many recall the dramatic circumstances in which the Rose Bowl contest was played in Durham, North Carolina, on January 1, 1942; the Japanese attack on Pearl Harbor less than a month earlier persuaded officials that Pasadena was a possible target, and Californians had to join the remainder of the country in hearing the radio account. "Ab" Snell counts a tense Pittsburgh-Duke gridiron battle among "a few special football games broadcast on radio. Duke's Eric Tipton kept Pittsburgh with their back against their own goal with his punting accuracy. Duke finally won by a touchdown." Marjorie Hunter terms it "a thrilling memory" when the first local station in Bloomington, Indiana, began transmitting in the 1940s: "What a thrill to hear the football game being broadcast across town."

Broadcasting of high school sports came with the increasing number of local stations. Holley Ulbrich remembers a time from 1949 or 1950:

I was about eight or nine, and my older sister had started high school, so she and my mother and I used to listen to the Torrington High School basketball games on WTOR in Torrington, Connecticut. Most of it I understood, but there were some repeated phrases like "top of the key" and "in the lane" that left me baffled— because I had never seen an actual basketball court or an actual basketball game. When I started high school in 1955 and began attending basketball games, the first game was a revelation to me, and for the first time all those radio broadcasts made sense! It would have been a lot easier to visualize the game from the radio report if I had ever seen a game played.

George A. Walker, Jr. offers a positive summation of the golden years of radio sportscasting. Thinking first of the championship bouts, he says, "The announcers for those matches were so colorful and got so excited themselves that they put you right there with them. It was the same with all the good radio sportscasters of that period, whether it was boxing, base-ball, football, or horse racing."

NOTES

1. For a succinct listing of other sportscasting "firsts," see Frank Buxton and Bill Owen, *The Big Broadcast, 1920-1950*, rev. ed. (New York: Viking, 1972); pp. 287-289.

2. Evan Wilson, "About the South," *Atlanta Journal-Constitution*, 5 June 1994; 2M.

8

Cultural, Educational, and Religious Programs

Lee De Forest (developer of the vacuum tube), Major Edwin Armstrong (FM experimenter), and other broadcasting pioneers expected that their new medium would become a great instrument of education and high culture. "Uplift" was a frequently invoked aspiration in the Washington Radio Conferences taking place at about the time of NBC's founding in 1926 and CBS's debut in 1927. Although radio became a largely commercial medium, those early hopes were encoded in the "public service" programming requirements of the Federal Communications Commission, successor to the Federal Radio Commission. To earn its license renewal, each station had to show that it regularly devoted a portion of its airtime to programs "in the public interest," and many stations went far beyond the minimum requirements, which were, at any rate, rather broadly defined.

Still, some listeners hoped for better fare (and more of it), while others sulked in disappointment. A letters-to-the-editor skirmish early in 1937 typifies these views of radio's role. On successive Sundays in January 1937, *The Washington Post* published letters from two gentlewomen, both politely suggesting that radio mind its manners. Clara Louise John's plea for more cultural programs was seconded by Mary L. Boyce's letter, printed on the January 15 editorial page[1], which found that radio offered too much "horseplay," too many high-tension salesmen, and too many "funnies." Trustingly, she asserted that she would prefer to hear more piano music. In response to these genteel pleas came a wrathful lecture on popular taste, signed only "J.W.W., Bethesda, Md." and printed in the January 31 "Excerpts from Our Letters" column:

The recent comment in these columns on radio programs merits attention. . . .

[One] writer is disappointed at the increasing trend to cry up the wares and to horseplay down to a vastly inferior audience. Frankly, I'm alarmed at these and other indications of dry rot, callow under-development, childlike immaturity that simply won't grow up, or whatever it is that ails us! For such things are "morons" made. . . . Can anyone listen to radio thrillers, educational programs eased in with frills and mental anesthetics, the blues, bossy bellowing softly to her mate, and tell me America has come of age? Why clutter up with clatter an already short life?[2]

These letters were published about eleven years after the founding of the first network, and 1937 would prove to be approximately the midpoint between the debut of programmed radio and its metamorphosis in the 1950s in response to the growth of television. Was radio already beyond redemption in 1937, as J.W.W. implied?

A sampling of *The Washington Post*'s January 31, 1937 radio columns, programming notes, and advertisements might initially seem to justify J.W.W.'s sweeping condemnation. RCA Victor was hawking its new line of "Magic Eye—Magic Brain—Magic Voice—Metal Tubes" radios, offering in those phrases three lures for consumer-fantasists, one for the practical buyer. In apparent defiance of common sense, ventriloquist Edgar Bergen and his wooden friends were becoming increasingly frequent guests on Rudy Vallee's variety program (and soon would have their own show). Fred Astaire was breathlessly reported to have chosen "dilapidated clothing" rather than his trademark top hat and tails for a dancing appearance— on the radio! KNX, the Columbia network's new Los Angeles station, received a package in response to Eddie Cantor's publicity-stunting national search for a "missing trained flea"; inside the box was a three-month-old terrier guaranteed to be hosting "a flea answering to the name of Oscar." Thus far, the evidence offers no eloquent brief for radio.

At the same time, however, Louisville's WAVE and WHAS, network affiliates with already distinguished records of public service, struggled valiantly against the Ohio River floods, borrowing transmitter time from Nashville, Memphis, Chicago, and Cincinnati stations to keep an anxious listenership informed and, where possible, entertained.[3] The summer of 1937 would see the beginning of a new radio "culture war": the NBC Blue network aired the first of its "Streamlined Shakespeare" programs in June, and CBS countered with its own Shakespeare adaptations. In the same period, radio versions of plays by Eugene O'Neill were given, despite the widespread notion that his works were strongly "modern" and thus hopelessly "difficult" to comprehend. In short, while radio offered plenty of entertainment fodder in 1937 (and in all the other years of its early decades), it also provided much information and public service as well as some programming for a high culture audience. It was, for the most part, a commercial medium, but those who knew when and where to listen found satisfaction in the Monday evening "light classics," band concerts, and operetta programs, in the Saturday afternoon Metropolitan Opera broadcasts (still one of radio's longest traditions), and especially in the diversity of Sunday presentations.

"Mostly," says Dr. Jeanne Kenmore, "I was a musical snob. I preferred the symphony hours, the Saturday performances from the Metropolitan Opera House in New York, 'The Telephone Hour' with its famous singers, and so on." Owens Pomeroy, co-founder of the Golden Radio Buffs of Maryland and editor of its newsletter, remembers the variety of Sunday programs:

Sunday was a great day for radio listening, although it did not include the traditional soap operas and children's adventure stories. A typical day in 1942 would start with organ recitals by E. Power Biggs. Commando Mary spoke to the home front at 9:15, while those in search of inspiration could turn to "The Radio Pulpit," "The CBS Church of the Air," "Wings Over Jordan," or the Salt Lake City Tabernacle Choir. Egon Petri gave a twenty-five minute piano recital at 11:00 a.m., and then it was time for "Invitation to Learning."

Sunday afternoon offered a wide choice of programming. For news analysis you could choose from Morgan Beatty, Quincy Howe, William L. Shirer, Edward R. Murrow, Drew Pearson, Gabriel Heatter, Eric Sevareid, and Walter Winchell. If we could only get that kind of variety in news opinions today. Those who preferred cultural programs could listen to baritone John Charles Thomas, the New York Philharmonic Orchestra, the NBC Symphony, the Metropolitan Opera Auditions, or "The American Album of Familiar Music," starring Frank Munn, "the golden voice of radio," and Vivian Della Chiesa.

Glen Resch also remembers that Sunday radio had a distinctive pace and content: "Sundays? A different venue altogether. Most of the family's in the living room. Only in later years did I discover what would come to be called the Intellectual Ghetto—the Longines Symphonette, 'CBS Is There,' and the NBC Symphony, Arturo—for God's sake—Toscanini conducting! Ten-year-old kid. Wish I could get *those* tapes."

"Classical music was (in retrospective consideration) surprisingly available on the radio," says John Butler, who found many means of expanding his musical knowledge and discrimination:

Major symphony orchestras broadcast regularly; works were commissioned for radio performance from major composers; CBS maintained an excellent radio symphony, and NBC founded its own symphony orchestra especially for Arturo Toscanini—unquestionably the preeminent conductor of his day.

I remember well a sort of "club" I belonged to as a teenager in Chicago. One of our major radio stations (I *think* WGN) had its primary classical-music "disc-jockey" (not a term then in use, if memory serves) meet once or twice a month in a studio at the Merchandise Mart (a building roughly the size of Rhode Island) and play privately for those assembled some of the newer and rarer recordings, all on clumsy, scratchy 78 r.p.m. discs, of course. In addition to playing the music, discussions of the composers and the works at hand were a part of the program. I made my first acquaintance with the works of Carl Nielsen and Gustav Mahler at these meetings, for example.

A surprising amount of music literature came to me by way of radio programs' theme songs and background music—much of it ingrained in my "mind's ear" for years before I discovered the names of the works. Sibelius's *Second Symphony* (played *passionately* on one of those ubiquitous "studio organs") and Debussy's *Clair de lune* I remember from a couple of different afternoon soap opera themes. Respighi's *Fountains of Rome* still evokes "Grand Central Station" for me ("crossroads of a million private lives—gigantic stage on which are played a thousand dramas daily," according to the opening announcement).

I also confess to a real fondness for some pretty trivial pieces I learned through this medium. (Poldini's *Poupee valsante* is a pretty good example, courtesy of "The Stillicious Story Hour.") My mother always listened to the Mormon Tabernacle Choir on Sunday mornings, but I found that pretty dull. There were also the unbearable Hartz Mountain Canaries, tweeting their fool heads off to another "studio organ." Everyone was so amazed at how those damned birds "sang with the music." Nuts—they simply chirped maddeningly away at any sound. Probably a pneumatic drill would have served just as well.

Actually, the quality of some of the classical music programs was not so terrific, as I recall. I always felt that "The Hour of Charm," with Phil Spitalny's All-Girl Orchestra, and featuring Evelyn and her Magic Violin, was pretty bad. The Longines Symphonette was another one that didn't do much for me. Even back then I knew (as a teenager) what horrible editing liberties were being taken by Paul Lavalle for his Cities Service Band of America broadcasts. (You want the *1812 Overture* to last three minutes?—no problem for Paul!)

"It was on our Zenith radio that I heard my first symphony orchestra," says Malcolm Usrey of his Texas Panhandle upbringing:

Early one evening, when one of my older brothers was fiddling with the dials, he pulled in one of the most heavenly sounds I had ever heard. At the time, I had no idea that I was hearing classical music played by a symphony orchestra; it was magnificent, and I was hooked. What my brother and I listened to was totally unlike any music I had experienced. Even at the time, I realized what we were hearing was not D. W. "Pappy" O'Daniel's band that helped O'Daniel become a Texas governor. It was not the Dallas-based Stamps-Baxter Quartet. It was not the nasal-toned singers and finger-plucked guitar and banjo and rosin-stroked fiddle strings of "The Grand Ole Opry." It was only later that I realized what I was hearing. That evening when I first heard a symphony orchestra stands vividly in my memory, and symphonies playing classical music remain my favorite whether at a live concert, from the radio, or from tapes and CDs.

As the years passed, my family and I enjoyed musical programs played by symphony orchestras—the NBC Symphony; Phil Spitalny's All-Girl Orchestra, which featured Evelyn and her Magic Violin; the Longines-Wittenauer Orchestra; and others whose names I can no longer recall.

"Monday night's 'The Bell Telephone Hour' and 'The Voice of Firestone' provided me with my first acquaintance with opera, which I now dearly love," Gus Wentz declares as he recalls those programs' signature pieces, "The Bell Telephone Waltz" and "If I Could Tell You," the latter written by the sponsor's wife, Mrs. Harvey Firestone.

Margaret Kirkpatrick found an agreeable variety of music on the radio:

I grew up with Saturday afternoon opera broadcasts—every Saturday. (No wonder I became an opera buff.) My favorite memories of my father are seeing him sitting in his easy chair with his feet on the hassock, helping conduct the orchestra.

Sunday mornings I was awakened by the Mormon Tabernacle Choir. I miss it. It started Sundays out in such a beautiful way.

My children grew up on Long Island, New York, listening to the classical music station in New York City, WQXR. I'm so pleased that they still like that kind of music and are bringing up their children to appreciate fine music.

Bill Buri discovered a pleasing variety of ethnic music in a Sunday program called "Music from the Bush Veldt." Pat O'Shee did not like the musical horseplay of that Sunday violinist, Jack Benny, preferring his non-musical sketches instead.

Growing up in Macon, Georgia, in the 1930s, N. D. Mallary, Jr. carried away from Frances Holt's seventh grade schoolroom a deep appreciation of recited poetry. That skilful teacher would read and *mis*read poems, would rush them and read them flatly, then would read them again "like a pro." In that way she persuaded her students that poetry had expressive value, and she had prepared Nelson Mallary to be a ready listener when he discovered one of the best known of all non-network programs, "Moon River," broadcast each evening at midnight by Cincinnati's WLW. "It was a program of poetry read to organ music," he recalls:

Ed Fick and I would often slip away from a dance (Armory or Shrine Mosque) and go down to the NU-WAY Wiener Stand on Cotton Avenue, where they had a radio, and catch the program. If nothing more, we'd always try to catch the theme poem . . . the opening one, or the signature, which spoke of the river as an "enchanting white ribbon / Twined in the hair of night" and yet flowing "down the valley of a thousand yesterdays."

Whispering these words in some fair damsel's ear, at a later date, always seemed to have a salutary effect.

In time I began to haunt our local radio station, WMAZ, whenever Marion Bragg was broadcasting his "Words and Melody, with Marion Bragg." I studied his techniques, much like Frank Sinatra watched Tommy Dorsey breathe as he played the trombone.

"Radio knew how to celebrate a holiday," says Mike O'Donnell, thinking of family Christmas seasons that began with the purchase of a tree on December 13, then the family's decorating ritual, and then each evening his lying "on the floor with my head just under the tree amidst gaily wrapped packages. The room was left dark at night, lit only by the multi-colored tree, and the radio was always tuned to Jack Benny, Amos 'n' Andy, Lionel Barrymore as Scrooge, and Bing Crosby singing 'White Christmas.' Holiday shows would not come on until two weeks before Christmas Day, but then every show you ordinarily listened to would have a Yuletide theme. These were then and are [on tape] today some of the best episodes of these shows."

Others valued the educational and informational programs that radio provided. John Nesbitt's "The Passing Parade" told the stories of those who had left, in the poetic phrase quoted in the program's standard opening, "footprints on the sands of time." Aside from his "most favorite" programs starring Jack Benny and Eddie Cantor, "Ab" Snell lists two other programs he considered worth tolerating static to hear: "We, the People" and Robert Ripley's "Believe It or Not." "The strange happenings told on these programs stimulated my curiosity," he says. On Sunday mornings in Milwaukee, Elly Truebenbach's family listened to a radio sermon (to be described below). Then, "After scouring and shining my soul, I tuned to a Chicago station to sharpen my mind. Carson Pirie Scott, a department store, sponsored a series of lectures mostly for adults, but I loved to listen to the ones about history or natural science and occasionally sent for a copy of the lecture."

Created by George V. Denny, Jr. for NBC in 1935 and moving to ABC in 1943, "America's Town Meeting of the Air" set the pattern for programs involving the audience in discussion of the issues of the day, and it remained on the air on Thursday or Tuesday evenings and finally on Sundays over a three-decade span. The Reverend Philip Humason Steinmetz knew the program in its vintage years: "In about 1938, when I was serving a church in New Milford, Pennsylvania, we had a group of men who gathered in the local barbershop each week to listen to the 'Town Meeting,' which always ended with a question for listeners to discuss. We stayed late some nights talking about the topic of the week."

From her 1930s schooldays in Chicago, Doris Swehla remembers radio's lending its resources during medical and weather emergencies: "Before Salk and Sabin, polio epidemics were a tragic reality, and children died. During one especially severe epidemic, schools were closed, and assignments were given over the radio so we could keep up on our studies. We didn't have a desk, so we improvised. A leaf from the kitchen table was laid across the arms of the dark maroon overstuffed chair in the living room, and I listened to the radio teacher and did the work on the makeshift desk. This education arrangement was also used once when the temperature stayed below zero for a week."

Doris Swehla's mother, Lois Robinson, adds an anecdote illustrating her own experience with Chicago radio's professionalism: "In the 1950s a radio station in downtown Chicago had a segment which highlighted interesting features of the area, and individuals were invited to make a short— maybe even just one-minute—presentation. Somehow I was chosen to represent the Bellwood, Illinois, Garden Club. I was nervous before my turn, and they told me we'd 'just go over' my talk first, before we went on the air. So I 'rehearsed' with no stress at all and was very relaxed. They had tricked me, though, and that had been the actual performance."

During World War II, radio was used to promote international understanding, especially among allies. In 1942, J. B. Priestley was heard on "Britain Speaks" each Tuesday. In the summer of the same year NBC carried "Britain to America" each Sunday at 5:30. Jeanne Kenmore recalls,

In the 1940s there was a radio program whose purpose was to "connect" England and the U.S.A., to help people in each country feel some common bond with people in the other. I listened each Sunday morning. Half an hour. Each week one occupation would be selected. Then an American in England would interview someone who worked in that occupation—perhaps a bank clerk, a shoe repairman, a musician in an orchestra, a fireman, and so on—for fifteen minutes from England. Then an English voice would interview an American counterpart here—someone with the same occupation. I loved the show.

Part of my pleasure in the program was the fact that I had had a pen pal in England from 1941 onward. During the war I sent packages of food—tins, boxes, and so on. I never could understand why her family had problems trying to figure out what to do with certain packages. *Royal* puddings, for example. Obvious, right? No, they had to ask me in the next letter how one used the item!

Religious programming ran the full range from evangelical fervor to theological discussion, and early Sunday afternoon network programs offered dramatizations and talks for those of one major faith or another. Aimee Semple McPherson owned one of the first radio stations assigned to a religious organization (KFSG, "Kall Foursquare Gospel"), and Billy Sunday and Father Coughlin would, in their respective controversial ways, garner millions of listeners. Barbara Lyon Franklin says, "At family reunions, we still talk about the late night advertisements for "Last Supper tablecloths"— a promotion that struck her and her sister, listening in bed in the 1940s, as an odd bit of commercialization.

For Ellen Edmonds and her family, religious broadcasting was more than a Sunday matter: "Daytime radio included the early morning broadcast of Ralph Sexton, evangelist, on 'Send the Light,' now a very popular TV program—fifty or more years of broadcasting the Gospel. We could get some station from Johnson City, Tennessee, broadcasting John A. Leland's 'Evangelistic Hour.' Gospel music was sponsored by products like Rumford Baking Powder or White Lily Flour. Sunday programs were mostly religious, like 'The Old Fashioned Revival Hour' from Long Beach, California. (We listened faithfully.)"

Gus Wentz says, "Sunday at our house was mostly given over to church activities, but . . . I can vaguely remember hearing some religious program which began with a woman screeching some song and my dad rushing to the radio to snap her off." Roger Rollin adds, "I still vividly remember our preacher one Sunday morning inveighing against those who stayed away from Sunday evening services because they were listening to a wooden dummy [Charlie McCarthy] rather than to the Word of the Lord. That preacher had me again, but I figured that since my parents were listening to that same wooden dummy, I'd probably be spared damnation."

George A. Walker, Jr. came from a different background:

My dad was a newspaper reporter, editor, and later publisher. He was quite liberal, about twenty or thirty years ahead of the time, and as a result we never listened to any religious broadcasts on the radio. There was no rule. It just did not come up. My sister and I were raised Catholic, and there was no problem about that.

He and my mum did like to listen to Father Coughlin on Sunday afternoons. He was an outspoken Catholic priest who at first supported FDR and then turned vehemently on him and the New Deal. [Father Coughlin] was quite a convincing speaker and may have been a grand uncle of Rush Limbaugh. He ended up verbally assaulting communism, Wall Street, and Jews. He was literally turned off by the Church in 1942 and was directed to discontinue broadcasting.

James Sender adds that for a time "Father Coughlin apparently had a larger audience than the Pope. Each week when he was speaking, any child had better not be. People loved him or hated him, but they all listened to him—people of all faiths."

According to Elly Truebenbach, "The Sunday afternoon sermon broadcast from St. Louis was a must for our family. This rousing lesson was delivered by a Dr. Walter Mayer, whose voice seemed to stay at maximum volume for an hour. I didn't need television to help me see this fervent son of Lutheranism: his face was deep red, his collar was tight, and his wavy white mane shuddered with every word."

Born in 1945 in Sumter, South Carolina, a city with a very large black population, Lemie Lentz grew up listening in the 1950s to live weekly broadcasts from the black churches, sponsored by funeral homes, before going to Sunday school at her own white church. When she later went to live in the Philippines, her father sent her tapes of those broadcasts, and they made her very homesick: "I cried," she says.

NOTES

1. "Letters," 8.
2. Ibid., p. 9B.
3. *Washington Post*, 31 January 1937; features section, 4-5.

9

Morning to Mid-Afternoon Programs

For weekdays, radio quickly learned to keep its daytime programs light (except during the serial dramas), varied, and carefully paced. Especially in mid-morning and after lunch, the progression of fifteen- and thirty-minute shows mirrored the home listener's movement through a succession of cleaning and cooking tasks. The longer breakfast-hour programs were divided into short segments, many featuring the antics and patter of genial cast members, so that the radio became a pleasant but undemanding accompaniment to the departures of household members to work or to school, with wifely or motherly admonitions and reminders fresh in their ears. Even the more "serious" radio "talks" tended to draw from the well of popular sentiment; no pause longer than the frequently suggested second cup of coffee was required for absorbing radio's advice or advocacies. In some homes, on the other hand, one or two favorite romantic serials received absolute attention. Grandmothers were especially liable to letting the door knocker knock and the telephone ringer ring during the select quarter of an hour occupied by "Our Gal Sunday" or "Young Widder Brown."

Local stations often began their broadcast days with pre-dawn "rise and shine" programs, supplying weather information, news, and music to set a cheerful pace for scrambling eggs and frying bacon in the farm kitchen. From her childhood in the late 1940s and early 1950s, Lemie Lentz remembers the familiar greeting at 5:30 or 6:00 each morning from WIS in Columbia, South Carolina: "This is Bob Bailey, your home farm county agent, reminding you that 'He who plants a seed beneath the sod . . . and waits for the seed to raise a clod . . . , he trusts in God." The earlier the hour, it seems, the more welcome were the conventional pieties.

Belonging to an earlier generation of listeners, Marshall Ramsey, Jr. sampled a variety of radio day-starters:

A program I particularly recall was one which came on every morning during the early 1940s, and I associate it mostly with my old friend Bunky Bruce, whose mom always had the radio turned on (and up) early in the morning. She liked WREC in Memphis, Tennessee. Louis Fosse was the d.j., and the sponsor was Griffin Dynashine, with the theme song "Shine your shoes and wear a smile, / Shine your shoes and be in style. / When you hear that familiar chime—ding, dong, ding, dong— / It's time to shine— / Everybody get ready— / It's time to shine." After that, Texas Jim Robinson would come on "riding down the airways with my saddle bag of songs, out from the plains of the West . . . [to] sing my favorite songs to you. . . ." (I can sing this just as naturally today as then!) At the end of the program, he'd close with the same song in the past tense.

In the late 1930s and early 1940s, when we would be visiting my mother's family in North Carolina, it would be a special thing to get up before daybreak when everyone was milking, feeding, and so on, and my great aunt Priscilla was in the kitchen frying bacon and fixing biscuits. She always listened to Arthur Godfrey. We never heard that one at home, as no one was up that early there.

(Before becoming a CBS network morning presence for many years, Arthur Godfrey was heard in early morning slots from New York and Washington, D.C., stations.)

In the Minneapolis-St. Paul market, the preferred early morning fare maintained a distinctly urban tone, according to Corinne Sawyer, who would later become the hostess of a television homemakers' show:

Everybody in the Twin Cities listened to "The Dayton Reporter" every morning, Monday through Friday, starting at 7:00 on WCCO, the CBS outlet.

Every morning the program was identical to all previous programs. The announcer spun a record—usually easy listening material, occasionally a novelty number, once in a while a show tune or light classics, often a vocal by a popular singer, but never ever anything loud or jazzy. (This was the Big Band era, so there was a lot of Glenn Miller and the Dorseys, some Sinatra, Patti Page . . . but Benny Goodman and Gene Krupa? Never that I can remember). Then the announcer gave the time, a weather report, and the weather prediction for the day. On the hour and half hour, the announcer gave a brief résumé of the news. And between records and weather reports, a woman (she was "The Dayton Reporter") gave a brief announcement of some item or other that could be found that day at Dayton's department store in downtown Minneapolis. The items could be one-day sale items or regular features, high-end designer merchandise or everyday items like a vacuum cleaner or a set of dishtowels . . . or even just the records that were played on the air, which were always available in Dayton's music department.

Sound boring? Maybe so, but it played behind my family's conversations as we had breakfast every morning through the '30s, and we relied on it utterly to know what to wear as we walked to school. And we weren't unique. You couldn't talk to anyone who hadn't heard "The Dayton Reporter". . . and if the weather report was faulty and it turned wet instead of fair, there were dozens of kids at school besides me without their galoshes and raincoats. We took that program as gospel.

I also know that the program continued into the '40s because in 1943, when "The Dayton Reporter" had to go to the hospital for an appendectomy and WCCO hastily held a series of auditions, I won the job as substitute, a job that continued for three months because the patient developed complications and had to have further bed rest. I thought that I had arrived; to me, "The Dayton Reporter" was as much of a celebrity as any we had in the Twin Cities.

When I left the Twin Cities for good in 1947, the program was still on the air.

Among early morning network programs, Don McNeill's "The Breakfast Club" was a longtime favorite, starting life as a sustaining program in the early 1930s, gradually building a loyal audience and attracting sponsors, and later being challenged in popularity only by Arthur Godfrey. Children who were home from school because of real illnesses or "radio flu" loved to listen with their mothers. Roger Rollin details the McNeill program's appeal:

Bedfast-type illnesses (which, for my cautious mother, most of my sniffles and sneezes were) meant an unaccustomed luxury—weekday morning and afternoon radio. I always started off the day with Don McNeill and "The Breakfast Club," a variety show broadcast out of Chicago. McNeill was a jovial teller of jokes and inspirational stories (an early Arthur Godfrey, who had a very similar show). There were also boy and girl singers, and my favorite feature, "The March Around the Breakfast Table," when the studio band would play a lively Sousa tune and Don would exhort us all to get up and march around.

Elly Truebenbach listened to "The Breakfast Club" on Milwaukee's WTMJ when she was a kindergartener: "It was mostly a program to waken sleepy adults, but there was a part of the program that I looked forward to—the 'March Around the Breakfast Table.' I guess this was supposed to get one's blood circulating for the day ahead, and for me, it sure was fun. Our kitchen table was pushed up against the wall on one end, making it difficult to march around, but our dining room table was perfect. I can still see the sun shining on the lace tablecloth and the cut glass bowl in the center of the table. I marched until I was dizzy." From his South Dakota childhood, Ken Weigel sees "The Breakfast Club" as "the one morning show that could be called a ritual at our house," and he too felt obligated to join in the exercise routine: "Mom and I 'marched around the breakfast table' so many times we wore a rut in the floor." Jim Fanning, listening in Atlanta, regarded the McNeill march as a familiar feature of sick days at home, but he also remembers "Aunt Jenny's True-Life Stories" and "The Kate Smith Show" as programs having recuperative value. Aunt Jenny's stories were dramatizations of problems from the lives of studio "guests," but these romantic tales were offered in single outings, not serialized. Kate Smith, bold of voice, held exclusive performance rights to Irving Berlin's "God Bless America" for several years, and her frequent performances of it brought a comfortingly familiar patriotic note to daytime radio during World War II.

For Bill Buri, daytime radio meant the conversation programs presided over by Ed and Pegeen Fitzgerald and later by John Gambling. Lacking the staff musicians, cast members, and studio audiences of the McNeill and Godfrey programs, the Fitzgeralds opened the microphones to their lives as a couple, domestic spats and all, and from their 1927 beginnings they welcomed generations of listeners on a succession of New York area stations: WOR, WJZ, and WNYC. "They were beautiful people" is Bill Buri's assessment of their long-time broadcast presence. In later years these domestic visits were broadcast from their Manhattan apartment, and Pegeen Fitzgerald (and her many cats) continued the program from her husband's death in 1982 until the medical leave-of-absence from which she proved unable to return in 1988.

With the shift from a wartime to a peacetime economy, early afternoon quiz and contest shows became a daytime staple, especially on the Mutual network. Five days a week the names of sponsors and prize-giving companies were reeled off in a litany of product worship. Offering modest prizes for answers to easy questions, Tom Moore presided genially over "Ladies Fair" from Florida, while Jack Bailey, at once loud and avuncular, shouted to his Hollywood studio audience each afternoon, "Would *you* like to be Queen for a Day?" and invariably received a resounding "Yes-s-s!" in reply. In each program, three ladies from the audience were invited to reveal the personal needs or wishes that would come true for the day's winner (along with lunch at a restaurant frequented by movie types, a limousine tour, and the piling up of prizes from brand-name contributors). Listeners noticed that contestants requesting Bibles usually registered higher on the applause meter than their rivals on a given day, and participants pleading for assistance for ailing family members (especially children) also weighed heavily in the audience's choice. Lemie Lentz says that her father found "Queen for a Day" particularly distasteful; he objected to the public parading of private griefs and longings, especially when some contestants broke into tears and sobs in the process of telling their "stories." "My daddy would always say, 'Don't put your business on the street,'" Lemie Lentz recalls, and she reports that father and daughter alike judged "Queen for a Day" to be "pitiful and embarrassing," adding that they "felt sorry for the people" thus exploited.

At a young age, Ken Weigel experienced the reach of genial Jack Bailey's program:

One day in 1946 an aunt of mine in Los Angeles attended a broadcast of a new (1945) program called "Queen for a Day." The show had a gimmick whereby a large roulette wheel, marked with the names of the forty-eight states, was given a spin. The pointer stopped on a "State of the Day," and a person from that state was picked from the audience. On this particular day, the pointer fell on South Dakota, and my aunt, a native South Dakotan, was picked from the audience to name an out-of-town Queen for a Day from her home town. Before the whole world she named my mother. Back home in Aberdeen, radio station KSDN hauled its mothballed red carpet out of storage and gave Mom a royal on-the-air reception and showered her with gifts, à la Jack Bailey. It was quite a big deal for a beaming kid of five. Since that is my earliest recollection of radio, I suspect my lifelong partiality for the medium dates from that broadcast.

Also imprinted on youthful memories in that period was the absorption of mothers, aunts, grandmothers, and neighbors in romantic serials, beginning about lunch time and running until mid-afternoon. Older women called them "pieces," as if they were the radio drama equivalents of the melodic *morceaux* heard in salon recitals. "We didn't really say 'soap opera' in the 1930s and 1940s, although the daytime serials of the day *were* sponsored by soap companies," Doris Swehla remarks: "We just said, 'my program' or called it by name: 'Lorenzo Jones,' the inventor and his long-suffering wife Belle; 'Just Plain Bill' Davidson, Barber of Hartville; 'Our Gal Sunday,' from a little mining town in the West, who found happiness as the wife of England's richest, most handsome lord, Henry Brinthrop; 'The Romance of Helen Trent,' who, 'when life dashes her against the rocks of despair, fights back bravely to prove what so many women long to prove in their own lives—that romance can *begin* at thirty-five, and even beyond!'"

"My mother's favorite soaps," Ken Weigel recalls from the 1940s, "were 'Ma Perkins,' 'Young Dr. Malone,' 'Life Can Be Beautiful,' 'The Story of

Mary Marlin,' 'When a Girl Marries,' and 'Lorenzo Jones.' Since coming to the Old Time Radio hobby, I've identified them by their theme songs. Today, whenever I hear 'Funiculi, Funicula' ('Lorenzo Jones') or 'Clair de lune' ('Mary Marlin'), I'm reminded of lazy afternoons spent playing with toys on a warm linoleum floor." Susan Taylor counts "Big Sister," "Our Gal Sunday," and especially "Vic and Sade" as her favorites, confessing, "I used to try to 'play sick' to stay home from school, and I reveled in summertime when I could hear them every day. At night my family would gather for 'One Man's Family,' which we couldn't miss!"

"Radio was a medium for voices and the spoken word," declares Owens Pomeroy, and he finds that true in recollections of daytime serials:

If we listen hard, we can still hear the worried voice of the announcer as he leads us into another episode of "Just Plain Bill"—"Danger threatens Bill Davidson and Nancy, his beloved daughter, and Kelly Donovan, her husband, because of the mysterious, sinister actions of Ira Brewster, who beat Kelly for district attorney by lying about Nancy's supposed parentage"—or "the real life drama of Helen Trent, who, when life mocks at her, breaks her hopes, dashes her against the rocks of despair, fights back bravely, successfully. . . ."

Doom hung over the heads of so many soap opera heroines, the afternoons seemed awash with tears. Ma Perkins, suffering with the tribulations of her two daughters, Fay and Evey, went through 7,065 broadcasts in twenty-seven years. Other long-running shows included "One Man's Family" with 3,256 episodes and "Just Plain Bill" with 3,062 episodes. We worried over "When a Girl Marries," "Our Gal Sunday," "Stella Dallas," "Young Widder Brown," "The Right to Happiness," "Aunt Jenny," "Pepper Young's Family," "Portia Faces Life," "Those We Love," "Light of the World," "Big Sister," "Young Dr. Malone," "Mary Noble, Backstage Wife," "The Brighter Day," "David Harum," "Lorenzo Jones," "Life Can Be Beautiful," and so many other weepers, it's surprising the housework ever got done.

Although his monitoring of them was necessarily intermittent, Roger Rollin knew the serials and the family sagas:

What I really looked forward to in home-from-school days was, of course, the soap operas—"One Man's Family," "The Goldbergs," "Stella Dallas," "Mary Noble, Backstage Wife," to name a few. It was always hard to pick which show to listen to because the major networks ran competing fifteen-minute soaps for two to three hours weekday afternoons. On the other hand, it didn't make a lot of difference, either, because since I heard the soaps so infrequently, I had no idea what their complicated story lines entailed. If you were able to listen to the same soap for two or three days, you could get some sense of what was going on, but that was about all. Didn't matter. It was radio drama, and I loved it. My impression is that my mother, unlike some housewives, didn't listen much and had no show she always listened to. Too busy keeping the house for Dad and me, I guess.

On the other hand, Fulton C. Hines notes that during his own grammar school days, his father "would come home daily for lunch, and 'Helen Trent,' 'Our Gal Sunday,' and 'Young Widder Brown' were more important than what he had to eat."

Young listeners measured their own family lives against those portrayed in the continuing stories. Constance S. Lackey, recalling "radio's glorious days," confesses, "I was a pre-teen then and spent too much time imagining how life was lived in each radio household. Coming from an extremely dysfunctional family, it provided me with a much-appreciated escape." Malcolm Usrey's family in "the low, wind-raked hills of the Texas Panhandle," was simply large, but he found "Stella Dallas," "Ma Perkins," "Portia Faces Life," "Just Plain Bill," and especially "One Man's Family" to be transporting. Heard in a half-hour weekly format in its early years, Carlton E. Morse's family drama did assume serial form in the 1940s, counting up books and chapters in the Barbour family chronicles. Although this was an early evening feature, it is almost always remembered in relation to the daytime serials, as Malcolm Usrey does here. Calling it "the best of the soap operas," he says that the story of the Barbours, "who lived in an exotic place called San Francisco, [represented] a kind of life that sent my imagination soaring. The members of the Barbour family became as real to me and my family as if we lived next door to them. My sister sent away for a booklet about the Barbours with photographs and biographical sketches of the clan." These promotional booklets, called "Memory Books," were offered annually for several years, and they clinched the sense that the program was populated by a real and ever-changing family.

Radio serial time passed differently for young listeners and for their elders. Elly Truebenbach found that an annual sampling was enough: "About once every winter I managed to get sick enough to stay at home in bed. Mom would bring a small portable radio to my bedside to entertain me. I would get my yearly dose of 'Stella Dallas' and somebody's 'Backstage Wife.' Old Ma Perkins suffered under the sponsorship of Oxydol for many years. There weren't many listening options on WTMJ, so I had to be satisfied with the soaps. Fortunately, the plots moved very slowly so that from year to year I could keep up with the story line nicely." For Margaret Kirkpatrick, the soap operas brought adult voices into a home centered around the needs of children: "When I was a young wife with small children in the late '40s, I loved to listen to some 'soaps'—'Mary Noble, Backstage Wife' (and later Bob and Ray's parody 'Mary Backstage, Noble Wife'), and 'One Man's Family,' which was on for years and years. The soaps made the time pass faster when you were home with two small children. You could listen while cooking or baking, or mopping runny noses, or changing diapers." Maxine Trively confirms that the serials "made ironing and sewing and mending much more tolerable." Robert Cox adds, "I got quite a few spankings at age two or three when I'd climb on a chair and cut off the radio that Mom had on a shelf. She listened to soap operas as she went about her housework. Well, maybe I didn't like 'When a Girl Marries' or 'Portia Faces Life.' It took Mom a while to figure out the name of [the latter] one. She couldn't understand what the announcer was saying. She thought it was 'Wash Your Face with Light.' "

In retrospect, Constance Lackey finds humor, intended and unintended, in the episodic programs: "'The Romance of Helen Trent': God bless her, the dear lady never aged beyond thirty-five. Her ever-faithful boyfriend Gil was an inspiration to all." Of "Our Gal Sunday," the story of the mining town girl "who married an honest to God English lord named Henry Brinthrop, mercifully I don't remember if she flunked handling the fish knife" at the aristocratic table. For Constance Lackey, however, her "loves" among afternoon radio characters were the family described in the announcer's opening as the inhabitants of "the small house halfway up in the next block, radio's home folks, 'Vic and Sade,' written by Paul Rhymer." This soap opera parody was so popular that at one time the cast did separate readings of the script each day for NBC, CBS, and Mutual. As Constance Lackey recalls, "Sade's favorite supper was 'beef punkles.' Do not forget their male friend with the marvelous name of Rishingan Fishigan who happened to live in Sishigan, Michigan."

In some homes, special circumstances governed romantic serial listening. Dorothy Stancliff says, "Our laundress listened to soap operas. I used to hide under the tablecloth while she ironed so I could listen, since Mother frowned upon it." For Rose Marcaccio's immigrant mother, however, daytime programs were very useful: "My mother learned to speak English by listening to the radio. She would always listen to Kate Smith. At noon we would be home for lunch. If Kate would say a word she didn't know, she would ask us and then repeat it for a while. She would always listen to 'Helen Trent,' then tell us about it, and we would correct her."

The soap opera habit could become behavior altering. Ruby Fisher remembers wryly, "My daddy finally bought a radio. We were so glad. Being country girls, my sisters and I had to work in the fields, but we would get awfully thirsty about soap opera time, so we would go to the house for water—and listen to 'Portia Faces Life' and 'When a Girl Marries' and 'Stella Dallas.' We didn't care if the grass was growing. We had to keep up with the soaps." Kathy Chastine confesses that in the 1940s, "I managed to get myself and my mother 'hooked' on 'Young Widder Brown,' among others of the soaps. We really enjoyed them. I no longer care for what they call the soap operas today, but twenty or so years after we had stopped listening to the soaps, I dreamed I was in a plane crash. I bailed out along with my companion, just as we were approaching the beautiful mountains of South America. I looked over, and to my surprise my companion was Young Widow Brown! Don't ask me why she stuck in my mind."

In the Nebraska home of her youth, Maxine Trively recalls, "There were times in the day when we staked out a close-by chair to listen to 'Myrt and Marge' coming on with their theme song, 'Poor Butterfly.' " Constance Lackey sums up that pioneering serial as "a mother-daughter soap about the perils of show business," adding, "I'll never forget my shock at seeing a photo of the duo in a magazine. Yipe! In retrospect, I now realize that Ma looked like a retired madam." For Dottie Zingoli, the shock came with the program's sudden end: "The last time that they were on the radio, they stopped in the middle, and one of them said, 'I can't go on anymore'—they were real mother and daughter—and that was the end of 'Myrt and Marge.' "

Favorite soap operas wove themselves into real-life family histories. In Max Salathiel's Oklahoma family, he reports, "One of my great grand-mothers listened to the daytime soaps every day. One of her favorite shows was 'One Man's Family.' She would allow nothing to keep her from listen-ing to it. When the soaps moved to television in later years, she would schedule her dinner early to not interfere with her shows. One evening she left the table at her usual time, went to her room, turned on 'One Man's Family,' sat in her rocking chair, and died at the age of ninety-two. When my grandmother went to check on her, she was sitting in her chair with 'One Man's Family' on the television." From an earlier day Doris Swehla remembers a similarly poignant involvement:

After my little crippled, almost-blind grandmother moved from Greenville, Mis-sissippi, to live with us in Al Capone's and John Dillinger's Chicago, the charac-ters in these daytime programs became her friends. She didn't know the neighbors, but she spent time with her radio friends every day. Dearest to her heart was "Oxydol's Own Ma Perkins." In 1943, Grandma fell and broke her hip and even-tually died from the shock. She was delirious and not coherent most of the time.

But toward the end she laughed and pointed and said, "Oh, look! There's Ma Perkins." Then [referring to the title character's lumberyard assistant and confidant] she chuckled and said, "And there goes Shuffle," as if she had just seen a close, dear friend. The programs weren't her entertainment; they were her life.

Social and economic changes after World War II—and, most of all, the development of network television—began to reduce the audience numbers for radio serials, and CBS gave pink slips to the last remaining soap operas in 1959 and 1960. By happenstance, John Butler remembers the end of a radio genre:

The hard-core soap operas—"Ma Perkins," "Stella Dallas" ("Lolly, honey . . ."), "Mary Noble," "The Romance of Helen Trent," "Our Gal Sunday," and so on *ad nauseum*—weren't for me, of course, but I inevitably had to hear the occasional episode here and there, since I was a real *artist* at playing sick and staying home from school. (My house specialty was the mysterious stomach cramp.) I recall that many years after I had hung around the house, having to remember to *look sick*, I had occasion to hear how old Helen Trent finally wrapped things up. I was in graduate school in 1959 and was teaching part time in a small town about fifty miles from the campus at the University of Georgia. It had probably been ten or fifteen years since I had last heard an episode of "The Romance of Helen Trent" on the radio, but as I frantically tried, day after day, to find something of interest to listen to on the radio during my hours of daily commuting, I discovered that Helen Trent was still having a romance, and nothing much seemed to have changed (translation: she still hadn't married old Gil Whatsisname). About half way through the school year they announced that after something like twenty-five years, the serial was going off the radio, and in the short time remaining, they managed to tidily wrap up all the loose ends that had been hanging for twenty-five years. As I recall, she married Gil, thus proving that "just because a woman is past forty, romance in life need not be over."

The mismatching of program and listener is a frequent theme of 1920s radio cartoons. The grandfatherly listener is confused by the "story time" host's signoff: "And now, little kiddies, 'Sweet dreams.' Run off to your trundle beds and sleep tight." Anonymous illustration for Maxson Foxhall Judell's "The Fun Shop" column, The *Atlanta Constitution*, June 6, 1924, 17. Reprinted with permission from The *Atlanta Journal* and The *Atlanta Constitution*.

While most early radio cartoons ridiculed the medium and its fans, The *Chicago Tribune*'s editorial cartoonist John T. McCutcheon saw radio's capability of bringing the wide world into the modest 1924 home. John T. McCutcheon, "The Radio," The *Chicago Tribune*, November 19, 1924, 1. © Copyrighted Chicago Tribune Company. All rights reserved. Used with permission.

Fun indoors –
with a Radiola

Good music, a glowing fire . . . *comfort!* Jokes, speeches, songs, dancing . . . *fun!* The best times of the winter, right at home, with a Radiola.

Everywhere—city, suburb, and far-away farm —Radiola III-a will bring in music and laughter—news and exciting new interests. It is low in cost—but big in performance, and with its four tubes it gets distance *on dry batteries.* It brings in programs from the country over, brings them in always clear—always *real!*

Radiola III-a. With four Radiotrons WD-11, headphones, and Radiola Loudspeaker.

Radiola III. With two Radiotrons WD-11 and headphones.

You can always add Radiola Balanced (push-pull) Amplifier, with two Radiotrons WD-11, to make a four tube set out of Radiola III.

RADIO CORPORATION
OF AMERICA
Sales Offices:
233 Broadway, New York
10 So. La Salle St., Chicago, Ill.
28 Geary St., San Francisco, Cal.

This symbol of quality is your protection

"There's a Radiola for every purse"

Radiola
REG. U.S. PAT. OFF.

Countering the widely held impression that radio sets were unsightly and temperamental, manufacturers associated their products with the joys and routines of family life, as this 1925 RCA Radiola advertisement shows. Radiola advertisement, *National Geographic*, 47 (March 1925), n.p. Reprinted with permission of General Electric Company.

GASOLINE ALLEY
—WHY HANG AROUND AND DO NOTHING?

Frank King's popular comic strip "Gasoline Alley" chronicled its age's preoccupation with new-fangled devices. On January 30, 1925, Avery discovered the perils of maintaining the radio aerial. Reprinted by permission: Tribune Media Services.

The wake-up exercise program was a frequent feature of early radio, as Gaar Williams's 1934 panel shows. Reprinted by permission: Tribune Media Services.

By 1935 the young hitchhiker had become choosy about his transportation, as another Gaar Williams panel illustrates. Reprinted by permission: Tribune Media Services.

SPARKS FROM THE CAT'S WHISKER

Little Raymond has scampered downstairs ahead of everybody, clamped the headset over his ears, and tickled the cat's whisker. Tinny carols are coming in from Pittsburgh.

This was in 1921. There were only a few thousand radio receivers in the entire country then.

Today, you sit in an armchair . . . touch a button . . . and hear, just as if it were in the room with you, a program of Christmas music, drama, comedy, and news from virtually everywhere in the world.

There are about 27,500,000 homes equipped with radio sets in the United States today. Plus 6 million sets in motor cars.

And from an average of $60 in 1923, the average price of radios came down last year to $30 a set.

How has it been done?

Modern methods of mass production to supply national markets created by advertising.

N.W. AYER & SON, INC.

Time, December 25, 1939

Appearing in a weekly newsmagazine on the last Christmas Day of the 1930s, this house promotion for the Ayer advertising agency portrays radio as a matured medium, worthy of audiences' attention and prospective advertisers' consideration. For the 1939 listener, little Raymond's cat's whisker set, a prized gift eighteen Christmases ago, represents the long-gone "primitive" days of radiophonic communication. N. W. Ayer & Son, Inc. advertisement, *Time*, 34 (December 25, 1939), 41. Courtesy of N. W. Ayer & Partners. © N. W. Ayer & Son, Inc., 1939.

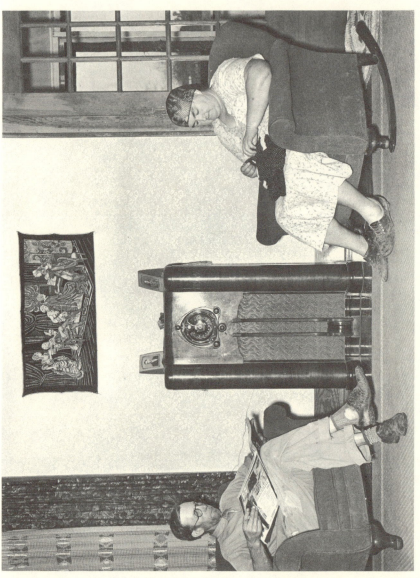

Documenting the success of a New Deal effort, Farm Security Administration photographer Russell Lee recorded this 1939 image of a Hidalgo County, Texas, couple and the newly acquired Zenith console. Russell Lee, "FSA clients at home; Hidalgo County, Texas, 1939." Photoduplication Service, The Library of Congress.

LITTLE JOHNNY CODY AND THE THREE MILE LONG CORD.

EVEN ON A HIKE OUT IN THE WOODS JOHNNY WOULD'NT MISS JACK ARMSTRONG and LITTLE ORPHAN ANNIE FOR THE WORLD!

School-age children often had to choose between outdoor activities and the afternoon adventure serial broadcasts. Here John V. Cody retrospectively solves the dilemma of his youth. Original drawing. "Courtesy John V. Cody."

"Don't Cry Mother.. It's <u>Only</u> A Program!"

OF COURSE daughter is wrong. It's not just a program—it's real and the people in it live! Mother's tears and smiles are the natural reaction of one good neighbor to another neighbor's everyday problems.

She shares the heartbreak of a girl who is hundreds of miles away—yes, farther than distance itself, for she lives in the land of make-believe. But it isn't make-believe to this lady because, thanks to the golden tone of her General Electric Radio, every program is close, intimate and personal—an actual visit from the interesting neighbors on the other side of the dial.

What a wonderful thing this radio is! Its magic conjures people, nations, castles and kings right out of the air! It carries you on thrilling journeys to exciting places—brings colorful people to call who become closer friends than the folks next door. Summons interesting guests whose songs and smiles crowd with pleasure hours that once were empty and lonely for so many of us—brings countless bits of radiant color to weave into the pattern of gray days.

The golden tone of the General Electric Radio affords such realistic reproduction that every word and sound sweeps in with full depth and color. It's almost like another dimension in radio. And, listening to G-E, all barriers of time and space seem to fall away. The unseen curtain of distance is lifted.

Great improvements are constantly being made in G-E Radios. G-E engineers have perfected a new Beam-a-scope (eliminating aerial and ground wires), a new Dynapower speaker, a new super-powered chassis, a new tone monitor circuit, and other great contributions to finer radio reproduction. These developments mean reception of greater depth and brilliancy of tone—*realism!* All this adds up to greater radio enjoyment—a better seat at the greatest show in the world.

Radio plays such an important part in your daily life that you should enjoy it at its best. You can, for G-E golden-tone radios are priced to fit all purses.

And remember—it ceases to be "*only a program*" when it comes to you via the rich, golden tone of the new General Electric Radio.

GENERAL  ELECTRIC RADIO

LISTEN TO THE GOLDEN ♪ TONE OF GENERAL ELECTRIC

This 1940 General Electric Radio advertisement proclaims in sympathy with the soap opera listener, "She shares the heartbreak of a girl who is hundreds of miles away." Papa is puzzled, and "of course daughter is wrong" to dismiss the serial as "*only a program*." General Electric Radio advertisement, *Life,* 8, 8 (February 19, 1940), cover 2. Reprinted with permission of General Electric Company.

Babysitting his younger brother for a long afternoon, John V. Cody has lost track of the time and suddenly realizes, when he hears the 7 p.m. "Amos 'n' Andy" program from nearby houses, that he is two hours late for supper. (His account appears on page 138). Original drawing. "Courtesy John V. Cody."

10

Children's Adventure Programs

In the 1930s and 1940s, the after-school hours of elementary grade children fell into conventional patterns. Some had afternoon newspaper routes to run or chores to perform. Others were committed to Scout meetings or to swimming lessons at the "Y" or to that often unpleasant interlude known as the "music lesson." For still others the journey from the schoolhouse door to the home front porch or kitchen door could be a labyrinthine trek involving treehouses, basement workshops, park or schoolyard slides or jungle gyms, soda fountains, and other fascinating and pleasurable places. Changing seasons led to piles of autumn leaves to kick up or to tumble in, winter-white hills for sledding, and spring baseball diamonds to trace. Whatever options they pursued in the hour or two after the last school bell of the day, most children began to feel a homeward pull about 4:30 or 5:00 Eastern Standard Time (or the equivalent hour in other time zones or under War Time). That homing tendency might have been encouraged by parental precept ("No allowance next week if you're not home on time") or by the ominous lengthening and massing of shadows, but the imminence of the radio "children's hour" was a strong inducement for the "red-blooded American boys and girls" who saw themselves reflected in the hearty enthusiasms of the breakfast drink or cereal commercials as well as in the easily visualized exploits of the heroes and heroines of fifteen-minute serial episodes and half-hour adventure stories.

During that transitional time from daylight into evening, the seemingly benevolent networks, collaborating with the promotional and program production agents of breakfast food manufacturers, spread out an aural comics page where Buck Rogers, young Jimmie Allen, Hop Harrigan, Jack Armstrong, Superman, Captain Midnight, and Sky King flew into the skies (never colliding with each other, by a miracle of scheduling); Mark Trail took to the forest, Sergeant Preston of the Yukon to the snowfields; Chandu the Magician vexed his opponents; Terry Lee and Pat Ryan fought pirates of many kinds; Tom Mix, Bobby Benson and the B-Bar-B Riders, and Straight Arrow left hoofprints on the plains; Don Winslow sailed for the U.S. Navy; and Little Orphan Annie, alternately known as Radio Orphan Annie, bravely shook her auburn locks as she and her dog Sandy pursued the path of the picturesquely homeless. Depending on the local affiliate's indulgence in these matters, there might be three to five quarter-hour serial episodes capped by the half-hour grandeur of "The Lone Ranger," a general favorite whose superior production values and firmly moral tone impressed even its youngest listeners.

City and rural youngsters alike had to fit their chores and other family obligations to the program starting times—or pay the consequences. John Butler says of his Minneapolis boyhood, "The late afternoon 'cereal operas' were of course my favorites: 'Tom Mix,' 'I Love a Mystery,' 'Orphan Annie,' 'Captain Midnight,' etc., etc. I always had to finish my 'chores' before being allowed to flop down on the floor in front of the radio to tune in. I remember being out in the garage shoveling coal any number of times while Jack, Doc, and Reggie were in there 'loving' a mystery without me because I'd been dilatory." Time-discipline was equally strict in the central Illinois farm house where Robert A. Waller listened: "Farm rituals were tied to mealtime in my upbringing. Thus, supper ('dinner' to city folks) was always at 6 p.m., at which time a series of four fifteen-minute adventure stories was our constant listening fare. After all chores were completed in the evening, my high school homework was done at the dining room table listening to the radio. To this day I have vivid recollections of working over the algebra and geometry problems while listening to 'The Lone Ranger.' Being able to give reasonable concentration to two areas at once is a skill that has served me in good stead even to this day" in university teaching and administrative positions.

As a rural North Carolina youngster, John L. Idol, Jr. was determined to be within earshot of the family radio at the crucial times:

I grew up in a large family, the second of eight children. To lighten their duties around the house and to teach us how to handle responsibility, Mom and Dad made up a duty roster, assigning us chores ranging from milking cows and slopping pigs to mopping floors and washing dishes. Those outside chores took me away from some of my favorite shows—"The Lone Ranger," "Jack Armstrong,"

"Hop Harrigan," and "Let's Pretend." Since my sister had the good sense to be born near the end of the lineup of kids, the outside chores had to be endured by my brothers and me. But, out of my love of my radio heroes and the longing to share the marvelous adventures of characters on "Let's Pretend," I brushed aside all snide remarks about being a sissy and volunteered to do only household chores. That nurturing of my imagination has served me well as a student and teacher of literature.

For others, tuning in was simply a matter of choosing to halt outdoor activity for the day. Roger Rollin remembers of his youth in the late 1930s and early 1940s in Pittsburgh: "After school was always a dilemma. Should I stay in and listen to the kids' shows that started at 4:00 or go out and play? It was always a relief when really wretched weather made the decision for me." Elly Truebenbach, having spent the first twenty-one years of her life in the "formidable winters" of Milwaukee, recalls, "After an hour or two playing in the snow between the time school let out and suppertime, I would come in with tingling fingers and toes and listen to 'The Green Hornet,' 'The Lone Ranger,' or 'Tom Mix.' (The Ralston-Purina Company sponsored 'Tom Mix,' and Hot Ralston, which I prepared myself, was my Saturday breakfast. Not that it was especially tasty, but, gosh, Tom Mix ate it.)" Carol Norrgard of St. Louis Park, Minnesota, followed a similar pattern: "After school on winter days in the late '30s I often went sliding or skating. When I came home, I'd heat up leftover breakfast cocoa and take it into the living room to enjoy while listening to one of the radio serials. I'd open the cabinet doors on our Stromberg Carlson console, curl up in a chair beside it, and listen to the latest exciting episode. I liked 'Orphan Annie' and 'Renfrew of the Mounties,' but my favorite was 'Jack Armstrong.' I'd sing along with the 'Won't you try Wheaties' commercial—I still remember it. The show was a fifteen-minute journey into adventure." Further south, Percy M. Matthews remembers his first listening experiences in about 1933, when one of his playmates' family "got a radio with a large oval speaker on top and with about six knobs to turn to bring in the station, WBT in Charlotte. Each afternoon at 5:00 we boys made a beeline to his house to listen to 'The Adventures of Buck Rogers in the Twenty-Fifth Century.' What a program to stir the imaginations of a group of young boys! This program was a great topic of conversation among us."

When afternoon serials were introduced in the early 1930s, children soon discovered that the fading light from living room, kitchen, or parlor windows provided an appropriate atmosphere for staring toward the console or the tabletop cathedral radio and letting imagination reshape the surrounding space. Margaret Kirkpatrick remembers such a setting in her grandparents' house in Minnesota during her early elementary school days: "There was a big rectangular black box about two and a half feet long and one and a half feet high sitting on a table in the dining room. I would rush home after school and seat myself on a large upholstered stool in front of the set. How I loved my grandfather with his storybook white hair and mustache. He would enthusiastically listen to my shows with me, he in his Morris chair and I on my stool. He would 'tune' the set for me. If I remember correctly, there were three big dials, each of which had to be set to a specific number for a certain station" for such program choices as "Lone Wolf Tribe," "Sergeant Preston," and "Jack Armstrong."

A decade later, the World War II-era boyhood of Jack French (who would become a career FBI agent and is now the editor of the periodical *Radio Recall*) sounds like a model of enlightened child rearing, with allowance being made for the younger family members' own interests:

I grew up in Kaukauna, Wisconsin, when radio was an integral part of my family's life and lifestyle. We did not have a strong antenna, so all of the radios we had (one in the playroom, one in the living room, and one in the family car) usually could pull in only the Mutual network from Chicago.

For me and my little friends, the most important radio time was from 5 to 6 p.m., Monday through Friday, and Saturday mornings. Our parents had designated those times for our use . . . an exclusive use, I might add, in households of friends who only had one radio. My father had installed a golden pine picnic table in the playroom, and our small radio perched on one end. The evening pre-supper programs varied over the years, but for most of the childhood in Kaukauna, the most remembered were "The Adventures of Superman," "Captain Midnight," and "The Tom Mix Ralston Straight-Shooters."

At the end of World War II the French clan moved to Rhinelander, Wisconsin, where other networks could be received. Jack French notes, "Our smaller home (or larger family) did not permit the use of a playroom, so the picnic table went into a corner of the living room, and that's where we listened to the new half-hour kids' adventure shows: 'Sky King,' 'Straight Arrow,' and 'Tennessee Jed.'"

In typical households during the 1930s and 1940s there might be a solitary listener to the afternoon adventures or half a dozen, sprawled in a fan-shaped pattern and facing radio-ward, "with our elbows on the floor and our chins cupped in our hands," as Walter M. Keepers, Jr. describes the scene from his Philadelphia childhood. Jim Fanning, growing up during World War II as the only child in his Atlanta family of "radio junkies," sensed that his mother yielded the listening area to his choices—"Jack

Armstrong," "Don Winslow of the Navy," "Little Orphan Annie," "Dick Tracy," and, at 6:30, "The Lone Ranger"—as she prepared the 7:00 meal. Yet "she, I am sure, listened to my programs as well," being a companion presence but not an intrusive one. Jim Harmon, author of several books on radio and Western film heroes, recalls the domestic scene in Mt. Carmel, Illinois, after his family got its first radio, a Crosley, in 1936: "My father would sometimes listen 'with one ear' during 'the children's hour.' He several times questioned the propriety of a young lady like [Jack Armstrong's cousin] Betty being dragged to dangerous parts of the globe. My mother would listen too, as she prepared dinner just beyond the doorway. She did not like the paramilitarism of 'Captain Midnight,' but not enough to forbid me to listen."

Wherever they listened, enthusiasts learned that promptness in reaching the radio and warming up its tubes (if it were not already playing for another listener to another kind of program) was rewarded with the familiar sounds of the favored program's standard opening. Rushing wind and excited voices—"Look! Up in the sky . . . It's a bird . . . . It's a plane. . . . It's SUPERMAN" (with a booming, faintly Brooklynese accent on the SOOP-syllable)—announced another episode in the adventures of the character who was "faster than a speeding bullet" (gun effect), "more powerful than a locomotive" (train effect), "able to leap tall buildings at a single bound" (a renewed rush of air, yielding to Jackson Beck's avuncular promotion of Kellogg's Pep cereal). "Hop Harrigan" began with a simulation of plane-to-control-tower radio communications, "Dick Tracy" entered with a fleet of squad cars sounding their sirens and pacing through their gears ("Let's go, men!"), and "Terry and the Pirates" opened with the confused cries and other noises of an oriental harbor. The tolling of a huge clock and the swooping of an airplane blended to herald the arrival of Captain Midnight and his Secret Squadron associates.

The musical openings of "Little Orphan Annie," "Jack Armstrong," and "Tom Mix" invited singing along, and such participation etched the lyrics in the memories of thousands. "It's amazing how the theme songs of the programs we listened to every evening between 4:30 and 6:00 imprinted themselves on our consciousness," says mystery writer Corinne Holt Sawyer as she breaks into a mini-recital: "Who's that little chatter-box . . . / Who can it be, / It's Little Orphan Annie" and Jack Armstrong's "Raise the flag for Hudson High, boys, / Show them how we stand."

The "Jack Armstrong" opening was shrewdly divided between character evocation (the rah-rahing for the high school that Jack Armstrong ironically seldom seemed to have time to attend) and commercial appeal, as the vocal quartet's medley shifted into a closely harmonized stanza:

Won't you TRY Wheaties,
The cereal with all of the bran.
Won't you TRY Wheaties,
The best food in all of the land.

For masterful blending of the listener's entertainment and the sponsor's promotional interests, one can look to "The Tom Mix Ralston Straight-Shooters" (in which the leading role was never played by the film star for whom the series was named). James L. Sender remembers the opening shout, "Here come the Tom Mix Ralston Straight-Shooters," followed by "lots of hoofbeats and cowboy yells." Originally broadcast three times a week on NBC and later five times per week on Mutual, each episode began and ended in seasonally adjusted lyric praise of a Ralston product. "Start th' mornin' with Hot Ralston" was the opening plea in winter months; "Shredded Ralston for your breakfast" highlighted the product of choice for the remainder of the year. In these variant opening lines (sung to the same melody), a "Westernized" effect was immediately established through a sliding of pitch on the first note—a deep-in-the-heart-of-Texas "lonesome cowboy" equivalent of the New Orleans blue note. At the close of the program the sung message took on a greater urgency: "Take a tip from Tom [pronounced TAWM]; go and tell your mom, 'Hot Ralston can't [pronounced CAIN'T] be beat.' " In the program's early days on NBC, the "Tom Mix" music further verified its Western identity through its guitar accompaniment and the plaintive appeal of its "Git along, little dogies" singing style. When the program entered the Mutual afternoon lineup in the mid-1940s, the ubiquitous studio organ provided the instrumental support to the singing of Curley Bradley, well seasoned in the title role by then, while rhythmic slapping was added to simulate the prancing of Mix's noted Italo-American horse, Tony. In these ways the opening and closing themes were cunningly shaped so that character, regional identification, sponsor's name, and musical appeal were quickly and inextricably fused in the ears of those who aspired to be counted among the "Straight-Shooters."

The opening music for "The Lone Ranger" did cause some confusions of cultural identity. Elton Dorval remembers a crisis from his grammar school days:

President Roosevelt created the WPA back in the 1930s to put people to work during the Depression. The WPA orchestra toured the country and gave concerts at the public schools. Around 1937, when I was seven years old, the WPA orchestra visited my grade school here in Racine, Wisconsin. The entire school population assembled in the gym, and we students made ourselves comfortable on the floor. I made sure I sat near my true love, Marguerite. She always resented my attentions, and I was continually trying to impress her.

The WPA orchestra opened their concert with a stirring rendition of my favorite song. When they finished, the leader asked if anyone could name that music. I jumped up and shouted, "That's the Lone Ranger song!!"

"Wrong," answered the leader. "It was the *William Tell* Overture."

So much for impressing Marguerite. I wished I could have crawled down a crack in the floor.

The afternoon adventure programs, then, boasted ear-catching openings and closings variously keyed to character, setting, action-charged atmosphere, and sponsor identification. Equally familiar was the rich voice that unified each of these quarter- or half-hour exercises in commercial (or public service) announcements, sound effects, excited dialog, and music. The announcer-host-narrators were "stars" in their own way: they projected equal enthusiasm for the sponsor's product, for the evolving story line, and for the premiums that often made a cunning link between product and story. Who could doubt Pierre André's assurance that a Little Orphan Annie Shake-Up Mug was a snack time and mealtime necessity or that a Secret Squadron membership and a decoder badge (both obtainable for an Ovaltine seal and a "thin dime") were essential for full participation in the exploits of Captain Midnight and his companions? Offering the homey credibility of a Western sage, the Old Wrangler (played by Percy Hemus until his death in 1942) stepped out of the "Tom Mix" story line to perform a large share of the narration and commercial duties, dropping word endings and otherwise seizing every opportunity to simulate tumbleweed country dialect.

Most announcer-hosts, communicating in regionally neutral standard English, used the full range of tones from friendly confiding to compelling urgency. Their persuasive articulation gave rise to the widespread belief by schoolchildren that an announcer could be fired if he ever mispronounced a single word. Fred Foy and his predecessors (one of whom, Brace Beemer, had graduated to the title role) brought The Lone Ranger and Tonto onto the western scene with rich-toned authority: "Return with us now to those thrilling days of yesteryear. From out of the pass come the thundering hoofbeats . . . "—what veteran listener could not join in reciting that earnest-sounding invitation? Evoking a more modern West where Silver and Scout would be replaced by the *Songbird*, Mike Wallace was as effective in selling "Sky King" and Peter Pan Peanut Butter on ABC and then on Mutual radio in the mid-1940s as he would later be a cunning interrogator of "60 Minutes" interviewees. Although the writer or the producer might be credited above closing music in a very few adventure series, the announcer's name was usually the sole non-character identification used in a typical episode. Sounding like a favorite uncle or a genial neighbor, the announcer embodied the sponsor and his product, and even his closing tag "This program came to you FROM . . . CHICAGO" carried a tremendous ring of authority. Thus assured, none would dare believe that it came from Cleveland.

For many who grew up in the heyday of the afternoon radio adventures, memories of eagerly awaited sponsors' premiums are as vivid as recollections of the programs themselves. Owens Pomeroy says of his collecting habit, "I glance in my closet at the Little Orphan Annie Shake-Up Mug, the Dick Tracy badge that I had to take Syrup of Figs to get, the Green Hornet Ring, and the Tom Mix Straight-Shooter medal . . . and memories come flooding back." James L. Sender remembers of the "Tom Mix" program, "For a boxtop you could get a genuine horseshoe nail from the great horse Tony, and it could be made into a ring." "I found myself ordering every radio premium announced, sending in my ten cents along with a box top or inner seal and waiting expectantly for the secret decoder badge, ring, or whatever to arrive," adds Chuck Juzek concerning his radio days in the late 1930s and early 1940s. Joan Waller recalls from her listening in a Chicago suburb, "Missing a commercial proved almost as much a disappointment as missing a moment of the action itself. I enjoyed sending for the advertised products, especially those, like the decoder ring, which became part of the story." On an Illinois tenant farm in the same late-Depression years, Joan Waller's future husband Robert saw the premium offers from a different perspective: "Being too poor to send off for the decoder ring, I frequently copied the clues about the next program in hopes of breaking the code. I do not recall any successes, but it was fun trying."

Analyzing the premium phenomenon from the perspective of one who knew it first-hand, Roger Rollin observes:

Afternoon kid shows must have been in intense competition for their youthful audiences because they were always offering inducements. "For ten cents and a Wheaties boxtop" or their equivalent one could join a show's fan club, receiving an official membership card and perhaps a Secret Decoder Ring with which one could decipher the Secret Messages delivered at the end of each program. Or there were premiums like the Don Winslow stamp and pad I obtained with an anchor in the middle of the rubber stamp and my initials on either side. I held on to that self-contained stamp and pad for years. Such items seldom cost more than twenty-five cents, and they were not always shoddy, so they must have been loss leaders for the shows' sponsors. The main trouble with them was the wait: after one had been able to persuade one's parents to part with a very scarce dime or quarter and had devoured enough cereal to get the required number of box tops, and after one had sent the requisites off to the address given over the air, the wait—what seemed like months, but which more than likely was only weeks—was agonizing. "Any mail for me?" was the first thing said to one's mother upon getting home after school, and since one never got any mail that one hadn't initiated, the day when the answer was "Yes" was a day of bliss.

General Mills's Wheaties ("Jack Armstrong"), Kellogg's Pep ("Superman") and other cereals ("Mark Trail"), Nabisco ("Straight Arrow"), Quaker Oats ("Dick Tracy" and "Terry and the Pirates"), Ralston ("Tom Mix"), Derby Brands' Peter Pan Peanut Butter ("Sky King"), and other sponsors sent out premiums by the many thousands, but Ovaltine, in its sponsorship of "Little Orphan Annie" and later "Captain Midnight," doubtless achieved the pinnacle in the number and variety of premiums offered. Radio club memberships were geared to annual renewals, and Orphan Annie Shake-Up Mugs were promoted each year in must-have "new colors." Doris Swehla has especially fond memories of an early mug that "had a picture of Orphan Annie holding a mug with a picture of Orphan Annie holding a mug . . ." ad infinitum. In Talking Rock, Georgia, Evelyn B. Thomason recalls the operation of another frequently updated premium: "'Little Orphan Annie' offered a ring with a dial on it which had letters under numbers, and periodically the announcer would present a message in number code which I could decipher by turning the numbers on the dial and revealing the letters beneath. The message was a clue regarding whatever peril was in progress at the time." Bill Buri adds, "I was a military cryptanalyst in World War II, and I often thought, 'Boy, if I had that Orphan Annie decoder ring, I could really make out!' "

"Be the first in your block to receive" the current premium, the persuasive Pierre André often urged in his extended Ovaltine commercials framing the story portion of each "Orphan Annie" episode. In Lynnfield, Massachusetts, illustrator John V. Cody experienced both triumph and disappointment in the ownership of his 1930s Little Orphan Annie "decoder pin [by which] you were enabled to solve the code given at the end of each broadcast and thereby know, *in advance*, what was going to happen in the next day's broadcast. When I received my pin, all the gang would be over at my house to learn what was coming up with our little heroine. I was a real big shot and would make a big show of decoding the 'exceedingly difficult' code. Suffice to say, others later received the pin, and my big shot status soon evaporated."

Indeed, in the 1930s and 1940s many a child became acquainted with the premium caveat that expectation must finally be measured against reality. The Captain Midnight periscope proved to be two very small shafts of decidedly non-strategic metal, the smaller cylinder limply hanging from one end of the larger one. In Oakland, Larry Telles discovered another problem:

In 1949 I received my Captain Midnight Key-O-Matic Code-A-Graph by sending the label from Ovaltine and ten cents in coin (I think) to an address given to me by Pierre André. After using the Code-A-Graph for about a week, I ran into trouble. I lost the little odd-shaped key that changed the codes. Over the next three weeks I copied down the secret code messages, hoping that a miracle would happen and I would find my key. One afternoon about a month after my losing the key, my mother gave me my blue jeans from the clothesline. When I threw them on the bed, I noticed that something small and shiny fell out of the cuff of the pants. It was the missing key, and I was back in the secret code business again.

Even premiums from the vaunted "The Lone Ranger" program sometimes failed to meet expectations, as Roger Koonce remembers: "I once sent off for a Silver Bullet Ring. It had been described in glorious terms, and I could hardly wait. When it finally arrived, I was greatly disappointed. The radium glow, found when you removed the bottom of the bullet, was fainter than the dial on my watch." On the other hand, the regional sponsor of "The Lone Ranger" pleased Pat O'Shee when it extended an offer of Southern hospitality over Birmingham's Blue network affiliate, WSGN: "Merita Bread offered us a tour of the bakery. I went."

The disappointments of some premium collectors did not deter others. Some premium seekers, in fact, resorted to various stratagems to satisfy their longings. "I sent for many radio premiums," Elton Dorval says, "and for some reason never saved any. I sure saved everything else. I remember decoder badges, a ring that glowed in the dark, a periscope so one could look around corners, and so on. 'Little Orphan Annie' had great premiums, but my mother would never buy Ovaltine, saying it was too expensive. Then I discovered that Mary, one of my grade school classmates, drank Ovaltine every morning and didn't listen to 'Little Orphan Annie.' I talked her into saving the foil seal from her next jar of Ovaltine and was able to get an Annie premium. What a thrill to be able to decode the next secret message." Larry Telles was a loyal, yet conflicted, young fan: "I ate Langendorf Bread since it sponsored 'Red Ryder,' and I wanted my parents to alternate between Langendorf and Kilpatrick's Bread, which sponsored 'The Cisco Kid.' They didn't think too much of that idea. When The Lone Ranger endorsed Cheerios, I ate them. When he switched to Wheaties, so did I. But none of my best pals would touch Straight Arrow's cereal, Nabisco Shredded Wheat. I still eat that cereal to this day at least once a week. My parents didn't like to buy Sergeant Preston's cereal—Quaker Puffed Rice and Quaker Puffed Wheat—because they said it tasted like air. But I sure was an advertiser's dream."

Future engineer Thomas Fetters seemed much more interested in the premiums than in particular heroes. Growing up in Iowa with a local Mutual station and nearby NBC, CBS, and Blue network affiliates to choose from, he remembers:

I never really got in the regular habit of listening to one of the kids' shows in the afternoon, but would dial around until I found a good one. More often than not, I would hear Tom Mix get into big trouble and never learn how he got out. I did write away for the premiums with the box tops. We had a lot of cereal without tops, and Mom would complain that I wouldn't eat it. Cheerios, Kix, and Kellogg's Corn Flakes were good, but there were several brands that I just couldn't take. I got the Lone Ranger silver bullet with the spilling atoms inside, and decoders with whistles, and an atomic bomb ring, and some other stuff. Somehow it all disappeared when we moved, and I never saw it again.

Theme music, character names, announcers' and actors' voices, sponsor and product identifications, and places of broadcast origination became increasingly familiar to two-, three-, and five-day-a-week listeners, but what of the exciting stories, the ostensible central interest in all of that packaging? Today listeners recall pieces of story line—Superman is occupied elsewhere, and Lois Lane is tied up in a shack full of dynamite as the fire set by her captors circles closer and closer (for three or four episodes, it seems); Tom Mix is battling a giant enemy balloon hovering over the plains (for weeks)—, but few could trace a full plot without the prompting of taped copies of the broadcasts. Here Ken Weigel offers a valuable caution:

I'm aware of all the popular shows that my parents listened to in my polliwog days, but my recall for specifics has been dimmed by the rude intrusion of thirty-five years. I'm amazed by some radio fans who claim to remember the secret messages they decoded from "Captain Midnight" or specific episodes, like the time Hop Harrigan brought Nimitz down on the Japs in the China Sea by tapping out an SOS on his molar, or some such stuff. What recall! Me, I can't remember what I had for lunch yesterday without first consulting my vest. I suspect these people have memories like Fibber's, of which Molly said, "Himself here has such a good memory, he remembers things that didn't happen."

On the other hand, Ron Sayles of Milwaukee has good reason to remember "one moment in Old Time Radio that stands out in my ever-fading memory." He observes that the radio adaptation of the "Buck Rogers in the Twenty-Fifth Century" comic strip "wasn't a great show as shows go, but because of it I have a lifelong love of science fiction." Moreover, a rather minor plot detail became a family joke:

This show, to the best of my knowledge, was on every day at about 4:00. I do remember that the first thing I did when I came home from school was to tune this program in to see what kind of problems Buck had to face.

The story that comes to mind had some robots burrowing to the center of the earth. If a robot got out of line, the supervisor would tell the robot to shape up or it would be taken to the disassembly plant. That in itself is not memorable. What is memorable is that my eighty-five-year-old mother, who is now in a nursing home, still throws that line at me when I go to see her. She will tell me to do this or that, and if I don't, she will send me to the disassembly plant.

After fifty years, it stuck.

Corinne Holt Sawyer never forgot the lesson that she and her younger sister Madeline learned through another pioneering radio serial during the early 1930s:

They started a new series during "The Children's Hour" one year . . . "Chandu the Magician." I don't remember all the details except that a killer had decided to knock off five famous men and (for reasons that were probably clarified at the time, but which I can't remember now) he killed each one in some way associated with one of the five senses. I can remember that one man had his tongue torn out (and presumably bled to death) amid horrible and vivid screams and gurgles. . . .

The villain had dispatched three of the victims in three separate episodes. My sister and I—perhaps nine and eleven at the time—were glued to the set for the fourth episode, when a man was killed "through the ear" (stabbed with a long hatpin through the ear canal!), again accompanied by ghastly screams. This time, my mother—who at that hour was usually occupied in the kitchen making dinner—somehow overheard the program, or at least the part where the murder victim was screeching his last. In she charged and flipped off the set! She decreed we would listen to no more Chandu . . . not the rest of that week, not ever! It was too gruesome for two grade-school girls, she said. We were obedient children, so we never did find out how the fifth victim died.

Introduced as a quarter-hour serial on CBS in July 1933, "Jack Armstrong" underwent several changes of time and episode frequency, but it proved to be one of the most durable afternoon adventure programs. In 1934 it was trimmed from six to five days a week, in 1936 it moved to NBC, in 1941 it shifted to Mutual, and in 1942 it came to the Blue network (later ABC), where, under the title "Armstrong of the SBI," it underwent a final transformation into the newly prevailing half-hour alternating-days format in its final year, 1950 and 1951. Wheaties remained the loyal sponsor, but several actors essayed the title role initiated, as Corinne Sawyer remembers, "by Don Ameche's kid brother, Jim, who had a highly identifiable voice, very much like Don's in timbre and accents."

Glen Resch speaks for many when he says, "The don't-miss biggie of early evening radio for me was 'Jack Armstrong, the All-American Boy' from WMAQ, NBC in Chicago. Weekdays at 5:30 found me, with a couple of toy cars, probably, in front of our Sparton (that's Sparks-Withington Radio Corp.) floor console in the living room, never missing this one." For Jane A. Kobler the program title "Jack Armstrong" recalls many afternoons of play with her siblings:

It is 5:00 p.m. My two brothers and I are sitting on the floor in the living room. We will soon be called to dinner; the aroma of Mom's cooking is coming from the kitchen. Our favorite program at this hour is just beginning: "Jack Armstrong, the All-American Boy." I still remember the lyrics of the theme, "Wave the flag for Hudson High, boys. . . . " We are playing cards. This was the beauty of radio, that there could be interaction with each other while listening. We sometimes would be building different structures with my brother's Erector Set, Tinker Toys, or Mechano Bricks, at the same time enjoying the adventures of this high school hero, Jack Armstrong.

For Fulton C. Hines in Florence, South Carolina, that program was simply "a must," while Hal Higdon, a Chicago native, calls it his "favorite," although he adds succinctly, "Don't remember much about the program, just the theme song."

Although Glen Resch was aware that "Little Orphan Annie" was to be heard "someplace on the dial" at 6:00 Chicago time, he "was forced to eschew [her radio company] because she was a GIRL (ugh)" and because she appeared opposite Goodman and Jane Ace in "Easy Aces"—"not exactly kid's fare—maybe I was precocious—but one of the funniest things I ever heard on radio." Despite having carried all or most of the "Orphan Annie" theme lyrics in her prodigious memory for decades, Corinne Sawyer observes, "My sister and I didn't much like Annie; we got a negative feeling because of the comic strip (in which she was a tiresome, blank-eyed girl, and still is, I hear!) She was much more like Nancy Drew, on the air, but we still preferred Jack Armstrong." Roger Rollin confirms both of those opinions: "Little Orphan Annie was something of a pain, primarily, of course, because she was a *girl*. A lot better was Don Winslow of the Navy, whom one could look up to. How could you look up to a little red-headed girl with no retinas?"

A short-lived (1932-1933) but effective radio serial was "Lone Wolf Tribe" (often recalled under the title "Wolf Paw"), with Chief Whirling Thunder. For Doris Swehla it was one of the earliest programs she could remember: "Wolf Paw was an Indian chief, and the stories were reminiscent of 'Hiawatha.' The sponsor was Juicy Fruit gum. If you sent in five Juicy Fruit wrappers, Wolf Paw sent you a genuine Indian arrowhead." Margaret Kirkpatrick numbered "Wolf Paw" among her childhood favorites too. "I sent for the ring," she says, "and still remember his trademark words 'Oh wa ho se walk ee.' (I wonder what they were supposed to mean.)"

The exotic serial "The Devil Bird" ran on CBS only from 1932 to 1933, but James L. Sender recalls its vivid opening as well as its story premise and premium offer: "Tropical jungle sounds, drums, and the eerie cry of the Amazonian 'devil bird.' Commander Davis and his three Eagle Scout assistants—Red, Dana, and Skeebo—have various adventures with primitive tribes in South America. They sent a stylized face of the 'devil bird' on a piece of old copper. It looked like something from the Maya period."

In the early 1940s, afternoon radio offered Roger Rollin a plethora of choices:

I could tune in to some of my favorites—Westerns like "Tom Mix," "Renfrew of the Mounted," or "Sky King," which improbably combined my personal favorite thing, aviation, with cowboy-type stuff. Or there were adventure shows like "Jack Armstrong," though "the All-American Boy" could be a bit much to take when one was a pale, skinny twelve, with few opportunities for rescuing girls or defeating spies, and for whom the command "Wave the flag for Hudson High, boys, / Show them how she stands" spoke of an impossibly remote world of serious education and football heroics. I suppose my favorite was Captain Midnight, whose thing, like mine, was airplanes and flying. Trouble is, as I recall, the Captain seemed to spend more time on the ground than in the air, and on the ground he was just like any other hero. Far beyond his show was another, which I heard only a few times, when atmospheric conditions allowed me to pick up a station in Cleveland, Ohio. What made the show so special was that it supposedly featured my all-time personal hero, "Colonel" Roscoe Turner, the epitome of glamorous real-life aviation supermen, only three-time winner of the Thompson Trophy Race, the world's greatest aviation competition, and holder of many flying records. As I recall, despite my efforts to catch "his" program through the static and its fading in and out, it was a standard aviation-adventure show. But because it carried my hero's name, it was nonpareil.

On the air from 1937 to 1939 and again from 1943 to 1948, the "Terry and the Pirates" radio serial invited comparison with the comic strip on which it was based. "Compared to Jack Armstrong, I didn't care that much for [the radio] Terry," says feature writer and original comic art collector Hal Higdon, explaining, "Maybe it was because the fantasy world I encountered on the radio paled beside Milton Caniff's classic strip." On the other hand, Elton Dorval finds that the radio adaptation led to a special fame and perhaps ultimately to his career choice:

That early interest in "Terry" the radio program made me a diehard fan of "Terry" the comic strip. I sought out and began collecting "Terry" comic books. About that time I decided that I wanted to become a comic strip artist and began corresponding with Milton Caniff. We exchanged letters for the next forty-three years. I finally met him when he invited me to the dedication of the Milton Caniff Library at Ohio State University, his alma mater. Later I was privileged to have my likeness used for a major character [Val Elton] in a "Steve Canyon" story. Talk about the "thrill that comes once in a lifetime." I did become a commercial artist, so possibly a radio program was responsible.

Elton Dorval remains an avid collector of children's adventure serial episodes on tape, and he is a contributor of text and artwork to the Southeastern Wisconsin Comics Club.

Latecomers in the post-World War II years found their afternoon adventure listening choices altered and diminished. Pressure against comic book violence began to have a spillover influence on children's radio programming, and the national Parent-Teacher Association, through its official journal, insisted that children ought to remain outside at play, rather than filling their heads each weekday afternoon with the nightmare-inducing crises of radio cliffhanger endings. The producers of these programs attempted to blunt such criticism by reshaping the children's hour into blocks of alternating half-hour self-contained stories featuring some familiar (Jack Armstrong and Sky King) and some new-to-radio (Clyde Beatty and Straight Arrow) characters. As Jack French aptly observes, this change was less than satisfying to seasoned listeners: "While it was convenient for us kids to listen to a thirty-minute show of Bobby Benson and the B-Bar-B Riders, it was just as easy to miss one show or another, since each program was complete in itself. So listener loyalty among the small-fry diminished, as indeed it did with me." In some mid-century years the program alternation patterns became annoyingly troublesome to keep up with: "Jack Armstrong" took the Monday-Wednesday-Friday pattern and "Sky King" the Tuesday-Thursday slots at the same time during one week, and in the following week these programs traded their on-air days. Soon the available audience found its time better spent in squinting at a black and white picture on a small television screen, attempting to catch glimpses of Pinky Lee and Captain Video through the electronic snow.

One character who made the transition from radio to television is The Lone Ranger. Known from the Fran Striker Grosset and Dunlap books and from later Whitman Big Little Books, the character was also adapted to movie serials, a comic strip, and Dell comic books, but by almost unanimous consent his exploits are best remembered through the grandest of the radio adventure series. Sad indeed was the child who was denied this three-times-a-week experience. Gray Whaley, now an industrial machinery manufacturer in Florida, remembers being reared by a "very German" (i.e., strict) grandmother in East Orange, New Jersey, in the late 1930s and, at the age of six, being "whisked away" to bed every evening at 7:28, just two seemingly eternal minutes before the scheduled starting time of the program that all the other kids talked about at school. Sometimes he twirled the dial frantically, hoping to catch an early start of this program before the immutable bedtime moment, but, alas, "It was two years later before I heard it on radio." Roger Koonce faced a similar prohibition: "My parents refused to leave the radio on during supper (my mother claimed that the pace of the *William Tell* Overture was bad for her digestion), and therefore I missed many of the episodes. My greatest thrill was to find out that supper would be delayed and that I could tune in." For Frank Raines, the listening dilemma was deciding whether half a program was better than none at all: "H. V. Kaltenborn was the commentator that I most easily remember because his program aired at 6:45 p.m. [on NBC affiliate WSB at 750 on the dial], half-way through "The Lone Ranger" [played by transcription at 6:30 Central War Time on WGST, 920 on the AM band], and since my father felt that keeping up with world events during World War II had a higher priority than The Lone Ranger's pursuit of truth and justice in the early American West, I felt like I was the only person in the Atlanta market who didn't know the result of The Lone Ranger's latest scrape with the diabolical outlaw Butch Cavendish" and his gang.

The desire to hear "The Lone Ranger" developed early negotiating skills in Brenda Seabrooke, who faced a time conflict at 6 p.m. three days a week: "This was about the time my mother made me practice the piano every day," she explains. "I convinced her that I had to listen to it before I went up to the cold front room where the piano lived. She believed me because I was crazy about horses and, of course, there were horse sounds on the show, hoofbeats and neighs. For a wonderful half hour I could listen to The Lone Ranger and Tonto outsmarting the bad guys while I drew pictures and put off the inevitable—one, two, three, four, practicing is such a bore."

Bill MacDonald of Blaine, Minnesota, recalls the airtime of "The Lone Ranger" as a moment of group crisis, resolved through neighborly generosity:

My favorite radio program, during my youth, was "The Lone Ranger." I particularly remember the years 1948 and 1949 when I was an eleven-years-old baseball player for the Morgan Park GFC Midgets. We practiced in the early evening hours, generally around 6 p.m. Our coach, Don Derbeshire, was a stickler on hard practices and complete commitment from the players. But he and the team members had one particular weakness, "The Lone Ranger." The George W. Trendle classic came on at 6:30 p.m., thirty minutes after we began ball practice. Our mission was to listen to that program.

With no reasonably priced portable radio on the market and no electricity close to the practice field, we had to rely on the good graces of the nearby homeowners to provide the means to hear that great Western. They were the "Joneses," the "Smiths," and the "Browns"; their names have long since escaped me. They provided radio access to our team over those two years. And gracious they were. We would gather on their front porch where they would bring a radio along with a pitcher of Kool-Aid and a plate of fresh cookies for our enjoyment. Although I continue to hear the voices of the radio actors in my mind, I have long since forgotten the story lines. But they were our heroes, the good guys, the guys we tried to emulate. Somehow they made our lives a little more complete and well rounded.

Times like that don't exist anymore. Who of the younger generation today would sit on someone's porch, sip a small glass of Kool-Aid, and listen to some radio program?

Most are gone now. Don has passed on, as have several members of the ball club. The other players and the ballpark homeowners have also gone their way. As for The Lone Ranger and Tonto, they're still alive, and will be long after I'm gone.

Owens L. Pomeroy, author of three books on radio, supplies earlier memories of this durable program:

Giants ruled the airwaves in those golden days. I first heard "The Lone Ranger" in the mid-1930s, and the actor playing the part at that time was Earle W. Graser. John Todd, a former Shakespearean actor, was the faithful Indian companion Tonto, who nursed the Texas Ranger back to health after an ambush. Remember when Tonto made a black mask out of the Ranger's vest and dubbed him the *Lone* Ranger? Remember when Tonto would refer to The Lone Ranger as "Kemo Sabe"? According to the story the words meant "Faithful Friend." Something else you might not have known about The Lone Ranger: he was a blood relative of The Green Hornet's father!

That program, like many of the other great shows, was broadcast live for more than twenty years. The pounding of horses' hooves was created with coconut shells hitting different surfaces, and the gunshots were rat traps hitting an empty tin drum. But they were far more real to us than the blood-spattered shootouts of "The Godfather" or "Bonnie and Clyde."

"One 'The Lone Ranger' show was so sad it made me cry," says another veteran listener, Robert Cox, who also enjoyed "Smilin' Ed's Buster Brown Gang," "Tom Mix," and "The Cisco Kid" during the 1940s:

I don't quite recall what kind of fix The Lone Ranger was in, but I think he was lost on the desert or something, and he was sure that he and Silver would die. He was down to his last two silver bullets. He was saving them to shoot himself and Silver with. "And this one is for you, big fellow," he said.

I sat there like a little idiot with tears streaming down my cheeks.

"What's the matter?" Dad asked repeatedly. "Do you have a stomach ache? Are you sick?"

Each time I'd shake my head, "No."

"Is it that story?"

It was the story, but I shook my head, "No." I was embarrassed to be crying over a radio show and was mad at myself and mad at the [program] for putting such a sad show on in the first place.

Even in its thirtieth year "The Lone Ranger" was "must" listening, while other children's radio adventures were rapidly disappearing. In an account that tells much about listener loyalty in the early 1950s days of radio drama's waning, Darrell E. Boomgaarden retraces a family trip from Chula Vista, California (where his father was stationed as a U.S. Navy chief) to grandparents' homes in Minnesota and Texas. The 1948 Hudson carried the Lone Ranger fan, his little sister, his parents, and "a considerable collection of traveling stuff." Since the car had a radio but no air conditioning, the father, "a pretty careful planner," scheduled the departure and paced the journey so that the desert crossings would occur in the cooler night hours:

I remember it was night, the moon was full, and you could see pretty well. We were traveling along at a decent clip with not another car in sight on the old main two-lane highways of the day. My sister was asleep, and Mom was dozing. Dad had the window down, with his arm resting on the door like he always did, smoking cigarettes, kind of communing with himself.

Well, there weren't any Game Boys or portable TVs back in those days for six-year-old boys to while away the time during these long trips, so I was a little restless. I remember standing up in the back and hanging over the front bench seat between my dad and my mom, watching the desert go by. After a while, I worked up enough courage to break in on my dad's reverie to ask him to turn on the radio and see if we could get a show. It was pretty risky, breaking in on him like that, 'cause you'd never know just how he'd react. But this time he must have been ready to move on to something else 'cause he said that that sounded like a good idea, and he reached over and turned the radio on.

I thought I'd died and gone to heaven because luck was with me that time. After just a little fumbling around to get a station, what came out loud and clear was nothing less than "The Lone Ranger"! And believe it or not, I'd hit it just right, and it was the very beginning of the show!

I can't tell you what the show was about anymore; it was a lot of years ago. All I remember was it was "The Lone Ranger" and the adventure was all around me. I was a living part of it . . . it was a warm, luscious feeling. After all, wasn't I in the middle of a big desert, and all around me was sagebrush and cactus? I was there! Riding along with the Masked Man and Indian, sharing in the chase and the shooting! It was all as plain as day in front of me; the imagination was extra-energized; I was part of the Lone Ranger adventure sure enough! My body might have been riding along in a car along a darkened desert highway hunched over a bench seat, hanging on every word that came from the radio, but my mind was seventy years in the past in the middle of a shoot-out with the bad guys. I was in heaven. . . .

Then we started to go behind a mountain . . . and the reception began to fade. Other stations began to interfere, and I'd hear strains of "Blueberry Hill" instead of Tonto. A couple of times the show would come back just as strong as ever, but it was just a tease. "The Lone Ranger" was fading out, growing weaker and weaker by the second . . . and the show wasn't over! There was a lot of the show left, hours and hours in the mind of six-year-old. I was beside myself.

I tried everything. I got Dad to move the dial to keep the reception as clear as possible. (I wasn't allowed to touch the radio at that time.) It helped some, but I could tell that it was just a matter of time. I asked Dad to slow down, even to turn around and go back so that we could at least hear the end of the show. You can imagine the response I got to that suggestion.

And then . . . it was gone. With a click, Dad turned the radio off and returned to whatever thoughts I'd interrupted before. There was silence now, just the steady hum of the car moving along a desert highway on a moonlit night. I never found out how The Lone Ranger got the best of the bad guys that time. I consoled myself with the sure faith that he'd come out the winner no matter what the odds. But the feeling was strong within me that I'd somehow let The Lone Ranger down, not being there with him at the showdown. It was a hard burden to bear when you were only six years old.

As radio stations increasingly streamlined their formats in the 1950s, even "The Lone Ranger" faded from network schedules, and fewer and fewer smaller stations received shipments of sixteen-inch transcriptions for playing in local markets. "Kemo Sabe" jokes proliferated as Cold War cynicism filtered down to the schoolyard. In a small South Georgia town the third grade teacher (equally adept at wielding the multiplication tables and a ruler) startled every young sensibility within earshot when she recited, in a very rare offhand moment at morning recess one day, the very mildly racy rhyme about Tonto's having lost his underwear and his existential assessment of the crisis: "Me no care. Lone Ranger buy me 'nother pair." Her young charges had never supposed that the aging teacher knew many subjects beyond the multiplication tables—*certainly not* The Lone Ranger's "faithful Indian companion Tonto"—and *especially not* Tonto's underwear. After that revisionist treatment, the hero's moral authority was permanently diminished, at least for one group gathered that day around the elementary school steps.

Yet it is that moral authority that most listeners remember. Gordon Kelley, author of a Scarecrow Press book on the radio, television, and film adaptations of the Sherlock Holmes character, retains the impressions formed in his boyhood during the late 1930s and early 1940s as he heard his favorite program on WIBC, the Mutual affiliate in Indianapolis: "I eagerly listened to each episode as Tonto and The Ranger successfully fought and subdued various outlaws, all the while teaching us morals and ideals that being good, honest and law abiding was the only way to go. I would get as close to the old cathedral [radio] as I could and be transported to the Western lands where the stories took place. It was heaven for a small boy."

11

Other Children's Programs

If the hour before or during supper was the best time for catching the attention of schoolchildren on weekdays, then Saturday mornings and Sundays offered still further opportunities for drawing young listeners to the radio. While afternoon adventure programs dramatizing a hero's or a heroine's exploits seemed most appealing to children in the middle elementary grades, other afternoon and many weekend offerings captured the imaginations of moppets in the pre-kindergarten to early elementary school years. These programs centered around a "kindly" host or hostess who offered the home listeners (and sometimes a studio group) a variety of storytelling, singing, game playing, and learning experiences.

Usually inexpensive to produce, young children's programs were a part of commercial radio's pioneering days, and early programs in this genre set the pattern of offering memberships and prizes or tokens, as one listener remembers: "When I was about eight years old, in 1922, my father had a crystal set complete with earphones. I became a member of the Bob Emery Big Brother Club, sponsored by General Electric in the Boston area, where I grew up. Membership pins were a small replica of a light bulb!"

In Marion Holtzclaw's young experience, one program heard on the single available receiver was a draw for an entire neighborhood:

About seventy-three years ago I lived in a town in New Jersey called Nutley. It was a nice town, and still is, except it has grown considerably.

The street on which I lived was called Wharton Avenue. There were many small one-family houses on the street, and they were quite close together. The houses were occupied by young people, and there were many children all about the same age, and they all played together.

There was one house about five doors down the street from ours that was different. It was occupied by an older couple who had no children and were very friendly to us. We thought they were very special, particularly because they had a "crystal radio" with earphones—two sets. No one else on the street had a radio.

At that time there was a program called "Uncle Wiggily," a very popular children's program, that came on for one-half an hour at 5:00 each afternoon five days a week. The man of the house used to invite two or three different children to come in and listen to this program, sharing the earphones.

Nurse Jane Fuzzy Wuzzy, a large gray mouse, was our favorite character on this program (next to Uncle Wiggily, of course). She was his housekeeper, I believe. The programs depicted some event in the lives of these two characters and their friends, and they all ended in the same or a similar way: "If the tea kettle doesn't boil over and scald the baby rabbit's ears, we'll be back tomorrow with another event in the life of Uncle Wiggily."

Uncle Wiggily was, of course, drawn from widely read children's books. Within a few years, children could find radio represented in the popular series books that they paged through while they listened. Issued in 1927, *Billy Whiskers and the Radio* was the twenty-ninth in a series, with an anonymous text illustrated by Frances Brundage.[1] Here an animal crew from Mr. Watson's farm near Mapledale, Wisconsin, first hears the local furniture company's station JZY and then invades the studio to "perform," to the engineer's chagrin. *Miss Minerva Broadcasts Billy* is one of Emma Speed Sampson's contributions to the series about the comic results of the natural confusion arising when adults reared in the nineteenth century must deal with the human, mechanical, and electrical progeny of the twentieth.[2]

Between the late 1920s and the early 1940s, the growing size and popularity of the Sunday comics sections in metropolitan newspapers paralleled the increasing listenership and programming variety of radio. While some newspapers regarded radio stations as "enemy" competitors for advertising dollars, other newspapers owned and enthusiastically promoted broadcast outlets. These interests met in early Sunday morning "read the comics to the kiddies" programs. Having established a presence on New York's WOR for five (sometimes six) afternoons a week in the mid-1920s, "Uncle Don" Carney also undertook a fifteen-minute reading of the Hearst comics at 8:45 on Sunday mornings. Fulton Hines, grateful for this comics recitation, especially remembers "Uncle Don's" claim to have an "autogyro—a car that operated as a helicopter."

Similar comics-reading programs were heard in other markets. Born in Los Angeles in 1934 and reared in the suburb of Lynwood, Barbara

Abercrombie "never missed" the comics-man program "early Sunday morning before time to eat breakfast and get ready for Sunday school." As she further recalls, "In the Los Angeles area children would get up early and bring the paper in, open it to the 'funnies,' and someone would read the funnies to us, every word, panel by panel, telling us where to look, when to turn the page, and explaining some things too. This program was so very enjoyable and now with hindsight very helpful to our parents too. All this had to have been in the early '40s." Reform Mayor Fiorello H. LaGuardia, who was to be the subject of the 1959 Jerry Bock-Sheldon Harnick musical comedy *Fiorello!*, earned the gratitude of his younger constituents when he read the comic pages over municipal station WNYC during the 1945 New York City newspaper strike.

Aside from its entertainment value, radio could be a special boon to weather-watchful New Englanders, even young ones. In the late 1930s on school mornings in East Parsonsfield, Maine, Frank Day would not step out of his family's house without first tuning to Portland's WCSH, where Arlyn E. Barnard detailed the weather and road conditions that a student would face on his way to the schoolhouse. Known as "the 3-A Safety Man," Mr. Barnard invariably closed his early morning report with the double admonition: "Be careful; walk safely." Since then Professor Day has followed many paths in teaching, academic administration, journalism and literary criticism, and volunteer police work, and he has ventured into Rumania (several years before the 1993 Soviet thaw) and Bangladesh on Fulbright Fellowships, but in all those succeeding years he has carried in his head that solicitous voice, warning, "Put on your slickers and your rubbers before starting out this morning, boys and girls. Be careful; walk safely."

Anticipating public television's "Mister Rogers' Neighborhood," early radio programs for young children were often hosted by a genial "uncle." For every veteran listener who insists that he or she heard Uncle Don Carney make the notorious dismissive remark, there is another listener who insists that it never happened. The Reverend Philip Humason Steinmetz offers an alternate attribution of the legendary 1920s open-microphone disaster: "There was a children's program called 'Uncle WIP' on WIP, the station of Gimbel's department store in Philadelphia. One night Uncle WIP, having finished and thinking the mike was dead (it wasn't), sighed and said, 'That should take care of the little bastards for another day.' He lost the job."

Many local stations offered early bedtime readings by a "story lady," often a staff member of the local library, but none was more beloved than Nila Mack, who brought "Let's Pretend" to CBS in 1934 as a Saturday evening program, carried it to a twice-weekly late afternoon time in 1938, and presided over it in a twenty-five minute Saturday morning slot until her death early in 1953. (The program survived her for almost two years, leaving the air in October 1954.) "The world of imagination opened for me when I was a very young child," says Ann C. Bowers. "The path into this world was a radio program entitled 'Let's Pretend.' The theme song of 'Let's Pretend' was similar to an appetizer; I remember smiling in anticipation each time I heard it. That warmth deep within returns even today, fifty years later, when I recall that tune." She further explains,

I usually chose a special place in which to listen, a place where I would not be interrupted. Often that place was under the dining room table. Sometimes my mother would cover it with a blanket, making a wonderfully private setting for me. With a pillow or two and perhaps some dolls for company, that spot was transported into the story being told that morning. I sometimes drew things on the bottom of the table as I listened. The last time I saw its underside, chalk marks were still visible.

The stories were told in a manner which encouraged me to join the characters in my mind, to feel their joys and sorrows, to see the scenes they saw. I truly think it inspired an active use of my imagination—and left me with a skill which still enriches my life.

Norma Brown Hanrahan still associates "Let's Pretend" with the ritual of "sweeping the front porch on Saturday mornings . . . with [her] mind in the make-believe of the program," and in continuing gratitude to its long-time cereal sponsor, James C. Fanning, now a chemistry professor in his sixties, "still eat[s] Cream of Wheat because of that show." Doris Swehla declares, "More than fifty years later I still know the jingle: 'Cream of Wheat is so good to eat, / Yes, we have it every day . . . .'"

For Dr. Jeanne Kenmore, the memory of hearing Nila Mack and her "Pretenders" while growing up in Minneapolis was deeply engrained. "Even as an adult I would listen in my car to [that] particular show," she says. "A child would send in the names of three objects. Any three. Perhaps 'dog, buffalo, cowboy.' And a half-hour show would be built around the three words. Good stories, too." Harry Durham declares, "My favorite children's program was Saturday morning's 'Let's Pretend.' Whenever the harp run sounded that signified the troupe was moving to the location of today's story, I was pulled right along with them. Those shows were pure magic for me."

Another highly popular young children's program, beginning on the Blue network in 1932 after a few months as a local presentation of WGN in Chicago, was officially titled "The Singing Story Lady," but most remember hostess Ireene Wicker as simply "The Singing Lady." (According to a widely circulated account, she added an *e* to the spelling of her first name for astrological "good fortune" purposes.) Long running as a quarter-hour afternoon feature four or five times per week, it was heard in a half-hour Sunday morning format for one season on NBC, and in 1975 it ended as it had started, as a local program in New York. Roger Rollin recalls the program in its late 1930s glory: "When I was small, I loved The Singing Lady, who told children's stories and sang in a most gentle and lilting voice. She was, of course, The Perfect Mother no one has."

Birthday greetings were included in some children's programs. "Dressing for kindergarten in front of the Warm Morning stove" in Knoxville, Tennessee, in the mid-1930s, Harriet Burt recalls, "I heard 'Popeye the Sailor' and listened for the birthday list." Chicago's WLS offered the early morning program "Jolly Joe," hosted by Joe Kelly, who would later serve as host and questioner on the popular 1940s Sunday afternoon network program "The Quiz Kids." As Elton Dorval remembers, "Listeners would send in their birth dates, and every day Jolly Joe would acknowledge who was celebrating a birthday that day by singing his birthday song, 'Birthdays come but once a year, / So we send this message clear, / Happy Birthday, Elton, dear, / Happy Birthday 'til next year.' Years later, when I became a father, the Jolly Joe birthday song became a part of each child's birthday celebration. Now they have children of their own, and the Jolly Joe birthday song continues to be part of the event. The power of old time radio, yes?"

Doris Swehla and Elton Dorval remember another regular segment of "Jolly Joe" in interestingly comparable ways. Having come to Chicago from a small Mississippi town, Doris Swehla was impressed by the efficiency of the program's "'big old dressing race.' From his place in the studio, Jolly Joe could see all the kids in 'Chicagoland,' and one morning the girls won the race, and the next day the boys won. Once in a while the boys would win two days in a row, which, of course, resulted in my getting dressed the next day with the speed of light." By Elton Dorval's account, "Every morning Jolly Joe had a 'who gets dressed fastest' contest, pitting boys against the girls. I never got dressed until the contest started so that I could do my bit to help the boys win. Winners were decided when Jolly Joe looked through his magic telescope wherein he could see into every home and thereby determine who got dressed the fastest. (What a dirty old man, watching all the little girls get dressed.)"

In the 1940s, Saturday mornings increasingly became a time when networks and local stations threw together an assortment of music, comedy, adventure, and other programs. From his postwar Saturdays in Wisconsin,

Jack French remembers the mixing of " 'Archie Andrews,' 'The Billie Burke Show' (not a kids' show, but we listened to it anyway), 'Let's Pretend,' and 'The House of Mystery.' The latter, [reshaped from a weekday afternoon fifteen-minute serial format into a half-hour program and] sponsored by Post Corn Toasties, was a deliciously spooky show for kids that always ended each mystery with a scientific, 'aw-shucks' explanation so no youngsters had nightmares later. Of course, it was also made less scary by the fact that we were listening to it in the morning sunshine, not the after-dark hours."

Ken Weigel recalls his listening choices from the 1940s in South Dakota:

My favorite shows came on Saturday morning—Big Jon and Sparkie's "No School Today" and "Archie Andrews." [Based on the Bob Montana comic book characters,] "Archie" was formula gee-whiz stuff, but it was like eavesdropping on the neighbors. Every week you knew Jughead would do or say something completely harebrained, and Veronica would charm Archie into a helpless puddle of giggles. In the last scene the writers invariably steered everyone into one room, with everyone talking at the same time. Into the center of this noisy confusion stepped Mr. Andrews, who dispelled the chaos this way: "Quiet, everyone . . . [bedlam increases] . . . quiet! . . . [bedlam grows louder; exasperated:] . . . QUI-ET! [silence]. This has gone far enough! Too far, in fact!"

"No School Today" played to the younger set. Every Saturday morning Sparkie came back from the movies and told Big Jon about the perilous serial adventures of "Mayor Plumbfront" and "Captain Jupiter," a thrilling outer space saga that went on for several hundred pulse-pounding chapters. It was pretty heady stuff for a nine year old like myself. Even today, whenever I hear "The Teddy Bears' Picnic"—the "No School Today" theme—I think of that serial, and I get a great rush of apprehension; my skin gets clammy, my mouth gets dry, my veins flatten out, my tonsils wobble, my liver turns to goulash, my heart goes bowling, and I feel nine again. When I was nine, I was a very sick child.

Amazingly, this effect was created by one man, Jon Arthur, playing all the dramatic roles, with the musical assistance of William J. Mahoney, Jr. as Gil Hooley, the director of the Leprechaun Marching Band.

Although he protests that weekend mornings were for outdoor play, and Saturdays meant preparing for the delights of the local movie theater ("twelve cents for a ticket and five cents for a Clark Bar"), Roger Rollin mentions some radio oddities that he caught during inclement weather or in periods of illness:

There were two strange shows sponsored by pet products companies. One was "The Hartz Mountain Canary Hour" [alternately titled "American Radio Warblers," "Radio Canaries," and "Canary Pet Show" in its Mutual run from the late 1930s to the early 1950s], which featured popular tunes twittered, through some recording sleight of hand, by songbirds. Why I listened to this I have no earthly idea. The other was a show sponsored by Thrivo Dog Food. It featured supposed kid sisters who sang old favorites. I can't remember their names, but I can remember—what a weird and wondrous thing memory is!—their theme song:

> We feed our doggie Thrivo,
> He's very much alive-o,
> He's full of pep and vim.
> If you want a healthy pup,
> You'd better hurry up,
> Buy Thrivo for him!

Our dogs ate table scraps—and thrived.

Another Saturday morning show I heard occasionally was a drama series called "The Lincoln Highway." The premise was that along this first coast-to-coast highway there were a million stories, and today you'd hear one of them. The main thing that attracted me to this program was that I kept hoping one of their shows would be set in my area—the Lincoln Highway ran only about ten miles from where we lived, and I had been on it a number of times. But glamorous McKeesport, Pennsylvania, was never the locale for one of these radio dramas.

Today serving as host of "Heritage Radio Theatre" on the Yesterday-USA Satellite Superstation, Tom Heathwood entered the radio profession at the age of twelve or thirteen as a "Junior Announcer" on Boston ABC affiliate WCOP, where his childhood listening quickly blended into the beginnings of his adult interests. He remembers the hectic time of live children's shows: "Life on a Saturday was fast-paced at the studio. There were two 'local' kids' shows, playbacks after the broadcasts, discussions about 'next week' and time with the host of 'The Children's Song Bag,' Voltarine Block. Live audiences disappeared after 12 noon, and the station was quieter in the afternoon," when airtime was taken over by disc jockeys and their patter.

NOTES

1. Akron and New York: Saalfield, 1927.
2 .Chicago: Reilly and Lee, 1925.

12

Comedy Programs

"Make me laugh and I'll keep your tubes glowing," early listeners seemed to say to the radios that brought them the friendly patter and brief sketches of music-and-talk zanies such as Billy Jones and Ernie Hare and Stoopnagle and Budd (Chase Taylor and Budd Hulick). Freeman Gosden and Charles Correll, traveling directors on the amateur theatricals circuit, shaped their blackface routines into radio's "Sam and Henry" and later "Amos 'n' Andy." Weary of touring, Jim and Marian Jordan entered the Chicago broadcasting scene in the early 1930s and, through months of experimenting, created the Wistful Vista townscape of "Fibber McGee and Molly."

Layered like geologic strata, styles and sources of radio comedy accumulated in the 1930s. As vaudeville collapsed under the competition of Hollywood, its stage stars found their way to radio studios, and by mid-decade Eddie Cantor, Ed Wynn, and Jack Benny could be heard in weekly comedy-variety shows. After a period of straight-arming radio as a rival medium, the movie studios began to appreciate the publicity benefits of having their contract performers appear as hosts or featured guests on evening network programs. From the late 1930s forward, headliner variety shows shared schedule space with increasing numbers of situation or "place" comedies that explored the laugh potential of family life ("The Aldrich Family," "Vic and Sade," "The Life of Riley"), workplace "families" ("Duffy's Tavern"), immigrant enclaves ("The Goldbergs," "Life with Luigi"), and such institutions as the high school and the boarding house ("Our Miss Brooks") and the quiet college campus ("The Halls of Ivy"). Fred Allen toured Allen's Alley in a patentedly acerbic way, while Fanny

Brice (as Baby Snooks) turned brattiness and Dennis Day (as the light-brained radio tenor) turned dumbness into comedic art. The Bickersons bickered, initially in a recurring spot on "The Charlie McCarthy Show" and then on their own program. George Burns and Gracie Allen and Jane and Goodman Ace played sharps and flats on domestic themes.

During the Depression and World War II eras, the presence of one or two "never-miss" comedy favorites was reason enough to carve the purchase price of a radio from all but the slimmest of family budgets. "In those dark days," experienced listeners insist, "we needed to laugh," and the radio was a renewable source of laughter close at hand—the table radio next to the armchair, the console a few steps across the room. In the post-World War II world, radio's familiar comic ensemble families, risibly dysfunctional as they might have seemed then, ironically lent a comforting sense of normalcy to a time of great social and economic change.

In Ken Weigel's useful word, listeners knew and imitated the "speechways" of their favorites. Doris Swehla describes such radio anticipations: "Our family used quotes from the 'running gags'—a gag line sure to be repeated in every show: 'That's a good i-dee, Lum' from 'Lum 'n' Abner'; 'If I dood it, I get a whippin' . . . I dood it' from Red Skelton's 'mean widdle kid' character Junior; 'Buzz me, Miss Blue' [in the Kingfish's executive-parody tone] from 'Amos 'n' Andy'; 'Where does an alien go to register?' from Bob Hope; 'I betcha' [from the pesky neighborhood girl Teeny] in 'Fibber McGee and Molly.' The line itself wasn't really funny, but if a show didn't manage to fit it in, we felt like something was missing."

Even intonations of voice and sound effects were eagerly listened for. The "Blondie" show opened with the announcer's warning "Don't touch that dial" and then Dagwood's man-boy cry "Blonn-dieee," to which Arthur Lake always seemed to add a syllable or two, as he would also do many times in the film series based on Chic Young's comic strip. Fibber McGee often drove the stiff Mayor La Trivia into a whirlwind of spoonerisms, followed by a pause and then the mayor's officiously threatening "McGeeeee. . . ." Of course the weekly avalanche from the McGees' hall closet is many times familiar, and the various alarms and sonorous traps in Jack Benny's vault delighted listeners, as did the screeching arrival of Mr. Dithers's limousine at the curb in "Blondie" and the bumpy bassoon bridge and the yucking laugh that announced Mortimer Snerd's entrance on Edgar Bergen's program. Through changes of sponsors, Jones and Hare were "The Happiness [Candy] Boys," "The Interwoven [Sox] Pair," and "The Tastyeast Bakers," but they carried their cheerful greeting "How do you doodle-

doodle-doodle-doodle-do?" from one shift of program title to another. Martha Caskey recalls their parting words with fondness: "Now we're sorry we must leave you, / But we have to say 'Adieu,' / In each town and village small / Hope that we have pleased you all. / We're the Interwoven Pair."

Rudy Vallee hosted one of the biggest variety programs of the 1930s, but his guests were better comedians than he. Corinne Sawyer remembers:

"I used to be a Westerner till Fleischmann's brought me yeast . . .": That's just one of the wretched jokes that Rudy Vallee had on his variety show ["The Fleischmann Hour"], and one my sister and I simply adored. (Why do kids like rotten and obvious plays on words so much?)

I remember when Vallee introduced Edgar Bergen and Charlie McCarthy, who became so popular they eventually got their own programs. [Vallee] never had quite the same success with any other of the comic acts he featured (Vera Vague was one I recall). McCarthy started trading insults with Vallee and moved on to take W. C. Fields as a favorite target on his own show. The main thing about which McCarthy (and other comics) made fun of Vallee was his wealth. Supposedly he had saved his money from when he was a popular crooner and romantic actor, had invested brilliantly, and now was too wealthy to have to work if he didn't want to. There was a running gag about Vallee buying a new car every week on the flimsiest of excuses: "I had to. The old one was facing the wrong way!" "I had to. The ashtrays in the old car were all full!" Again, weak gags, but we kids loved them!

"Speaking of weak gags," Corinne Sawyer continues, " I cannot imagine what I ever thought was funny about Joe Penner—kind of the 'Pee Wee' [Herman] of his day, with a funny hat and rolled up trouser cuffs. I don't remember any of Penner's gags, but I certainly remember one of his lines that, whenever repeated, was sure to bring laughter and applause: 'Wanna buy a duck?' It was repeated at least once on every show, sometimes in highly inappropriate circumstances. It was like 'Laugh In's' 'Here come da judge' or 'Sock it to me!' . . . lines that took on a life of their own. Penner died in the early 1940s at the height of his limited popularity." Death came to him at age forty-four, while he was attempting to redirect his career to the stage.

For N. D. Mallary, Jr., the Sunday evening of radio comedy included the Jack Benny and Fred Allen programs, but it was "capped" by Eddie Cantor on "The Chase and Sanborn Hour" from 1931 to 1934:

Eddie Cantor came to radio from the Broadway stage, where he starred in the *Ziegfield Follies* and such hit musicals as *Kid Boots* and *Whoopee*. He had been a singing waiter in a Coney Island saloon (where he claimed to have developed his singing style of dancing all around to escape, he said, food being thrown at him) and then in burlesque and vaudeville. Throughout the 1930s he was one of the top attractions in radio and in many of these years was *the* top attraction. Many top stars were his protégés, including Bobby Breen, Deanna Durbin, and Dinah Shore. He also introduced George Burns and Gracie Allen to radio.

Cantor earned his place at the top as a comedian but I enjoyed him most for the songs he sang: "If You Knew Susie," "Makin' Whoopee," "When I'm in Washington," "Now's th' Time to Fall in Love," and his closing signature "I love to spend this Sunday with you, / As friend to friend, I'm sorry it's through; / Let's make a date, for next Sunday night, / I'm here to stay, 'twill be my delight, / To bring again, to sing again the things you want me to, / I love to spend each Sunday with you."

Although "The Amos 'n' Andy Show" became a part of CBS's formidable Sunday evening comedy lineup in the late 1940s, it began its network existence on NBC in 1929 as a late evening quarter-hour daily program, then became an early evening fixture during five or, for a time, six days a week. At the 7:00 to 7:15 time, the program became a national institution, and, as Owens L. Pomeroy puts it, there were "few people in the United States who didn't stop everything to hear the 'Amos and Andy' show." Young and old knew its starting time, as an anecdote from L. William Ice demonstrates: "My kindergarten teacher was teaching the class to tell time by setting a 'clock' at various times and asking the class to tell her what time the clock indicated. She set the clock at 7:00 and asked what time it was, to which I promptly replied, 'Amos and Andy time.' It *was*, at our house and many others." So it was in John V. Cody's experience:

It was a beautiful, warm summer day. I was ten years old, and I had the lovely duty of minding my kid brother Jerry, age five. We had had several small adventures during the afternoon, and I remember strolling down Tower Hill Avenue, the two of us without a care in the world. All of the windows along the street were open to the balmy breezes.

Suddenly, it seems, my peace was shattered!! I heard the theme song (or words) of "Amos and Andy"! How could this be? They were on at 7 p.m., and I was supposed to be home for supper at 5 p.m.!!

Whooeee!! My father wanted everyone at the table at 5, without fail. I dragged Jerry home at the gallop. Happy to say, my parents were so relieved to see us that I got off with just a stiff talking to.

Radio really indicated what we *should* be doing at certain times of the day, especially in the evening.

Many listeners still quote favorite "Amos 'n' Andy" lines. Owens Pomeroy, for instance, remembers when Andy had bought a house and asked the Kingfish what he thought of the deal. " 'Andy,' he said, 'that is a stucco house, . . . and you is the stuckee.' " Mary Lee McCrackan recalls how a name mentioned on the program in the 1930s caused a sensation in Richmond, Virginia, where Freeman Gosden, who played Amos, had been born:

The "Amos and Andy Show" had a significant impact in goings-on at the Second Baptist Church of Richmond, which we attended. "Amos" [Gosden] had grown up attending our church, and during one broadcast he made reference to Henry Hotchkiss of our Second Baptist Church who had unfortunately married an Episcopalian and seldom came back to our church. The Sunday after Amos mentioned us, no one talked of anything else. We were famous, or so it seemed to us. The Baptist old ladies' home moved their supper hour back because so many little ole ladies were skipping dessert to run and hear every word of "Amos and Andy."

"Of course we listened to 'Amos and Andy' every evening," says the Reverend Philip Humason Steinmetz, but he also remembers the team of Eddie East and Ralph Dumke, who brightened the Depression decade with "Sisters of the Skillet," a parody of household hints programs, and its successor "The Quality Twins." "I wish they were on today," he says of both comedy duos; "Lake Wobegone has to fill the gap."

"Everybody listened to Jack Benny," Corinne Sawyer declares. "Our family dinner hour was inflexible, but even we listened. That was the one show we had playing while we sat at the dinner table. Once a week the music ran the scale upward—sol, sol-sharp, la, ti, do—and our whole family sang with the commercial, 'J-E-L-L-O.' We could also recite the flavors right with Don Wilson, the announcer: 'Strawberry, raspberry, cherry, orange, lemon, and lime.' The order of that recital never varied, any more than our listening habits."

In contrast to "Amos 'n' Andy," where two men played most of the roles for many years, "The Jack Benny Show" had a large cast, the members of which are variously remembered today. Marshall Ramsey, Jr. was especially struck by the routines in which Mel Blanc, who also played the "role" of Benny's temperamental Maxwell car, was featured as a Mexican who responded to a series of questions with either the name "Sy" or the affirmative "Si!," and he remembers Sheldon Leonard in a number of con-man roles. Corinne Sawyer recalls "when Kenny Baker (the tenor who did one musical number and played a feckless juvenile of incredible naiveté) left the program and was replaced by Dennis Day (also a tenor who did one musical number and played an unworldly and boyish innocent)." Eddie Anderson, playing Benny's driver Rochester with a rough-throated agreeableness, was a favorite of many. N. D. Mallary, Jr. recalls "the great efforts of Rochester to get Jack's vintage Maxwell started, with Mel Blanc doing the sound effects." Mel Blanc is also fondly remembered for his occasional appearances as the railway station public address announcer who invariably called, "Train now loading on track three. All aboard for Anaheim, Azusa, and *Cuc*-a-monga," with a rhythmic snap and a strategic pause on the name of the latter destination.

Jack Benny's radio character was the essence of penny-pinching. As Jeanne Kenmore puts it, he was "very tight. About once a month the script would call for him to descend to his cellar (lots of clanging chains and squeaking doors) to get two dollars to pay someone on his staff." N. D. Mallary, Jr. remembers it a little differently: "The many trips Jack made with Rochester to his subterranean vault down long, echoing corridors and past many steel doors locked with many chains . . . to get a nickel." He also heard an unforgettable illustration of Benny's supposed stinginess: "One of the classic skits of all time involved a holdup man who demanded of Jack, 'Your money or your life.' We of the radio audience were treated to one of the longest planned silences ever aired. Finally, the holdup man yelled, 'Well?,' and Benny petulantly replied, 'I'm thinking it over.' The second longest silence involved his telephone conversation with Jack Warner, head of Warner Brothers Studios, demanding to play the lead in a new movie. After his demand Jack started listening and occasionally muttering 'but . . . but . . . but . . . but'." Hal Higdon remembers how the studio audience's tittering during Benny's pauses enhanced the effect of the famous street robbery sketch. "It was a popular bit. Jack reprised it for months after," he says.

Listeners seemed especially eager to visualize the faces of Benny's players. Jack Benny's own face and distinctive walk were well known from his films, but, as Roger Rollin says, "One's image of the supporting players was more dim. I had a vague sense that Don Wilson, Benny's jovial announcer, was chubby and that his resident tenor, Dennis Day, looked as boyish as he sounded, but Mary Livingston, Benny's wife, and Phil Harris, Benny's comic bandleader, presented no clear image for me." Pat O'Shee notes, "We could not, of course, see Jack Benny's face on radio, when he was upstaged by Mary Livingston, Rochester, or even Don Wilson and Phil Harris, but the imagination filled in the blanks to make his nonplussed, silent exasperation equally as funny as if we had seen him. As a matter of fact, I did not enjoy him on TV as I did for a decade on radio; for me, TV was anticlimactic." Roger Koonce also found the Benny supporting players to be less than expected in the TV version: "Of that group, only Jack

Benny looked like I imagined he would. The others were great disappointments when they were recreated on the tiny black and white screen of our Zenith. The screen in my head was as big as I needed, and everything was in color."

In many listeners' recollections, Jack Benny's name is inextricably linked with Fred Allen's because of one of the most cleverly executed publicity ploys in broadcast history. "Benny had a manufactured 'feud' going with Fred Allen," Corinne Sawyer says, adding, "My family was not very sophisticated, and Allen's satire was a bit over our heads, but Mom and Dad listened to the Allen show all the same—mainly, I think, to get the latest in the Allen-Benny feud." Once again, N. D. Mallary, Jr. provides useful details:

Immediately following Jack Benny's Sunday evening half hour was Fred Allen's "Town Hall Tonight" and his wife, Portland Hoffa. It was somewhat later on the "Texaco Star Theater," however, that Fred first strolled down Allen's Alley and met Senator Claghorn (Kenny Delmar), Titus Moody (Parker Fennelly), Mrs. Nussbaum (Minerva Pious), and Ajax Cassidy (Peter Donald).

The "feud" between good friends Jack Benny and Fred Allen aroused such listener interest in the 1930s that when the two met on Benny's show on March 14, 1937, purportedly to do physical battle with each other, radio survey figures showed that only one of Franklin D. Roosevelt's Fireside Chats had ever drawn a larger audience. There was such a demand for tickets to the broadcast that it had to be held in the ballroom of the Hotel Pierre in New York.

"It seems like I could listen to Fred Allen's voice and envision his horribly baggy eyes," says Pat O'Shee, who continues, "The Trip Down Allen's Alley was my favorite part of the program. There was Mrs. Nussbaum, who would answer Allen's knock on the door with an ascending 'Noooooooo?'" Owens Pomeroy wistfully declares, "If we could only walk down Allen's Alley again and hear Senator Claghorn, Titus Moody, Mrs. Nussbaum and 'mine husband Pierre,' I'd gladly trade all the so-called situation comedies on TV for the privilege." Bill Buri calls Allen's program "one of the most intelligent comedy shows," and Harriet Burt takes special pleasure in a coincidence: "Sunday, October 23, 1932, has been called 'a truly historical date in radio'—the broadcast debut of Fred Allen and, incidentally, the day I was born. Arriving thus just in time for the 'golden age of the airwaves,' I became well acquainted with radio's varied offerings."

Another Sunday evening comedy powerhouse was Edgar Bergen, with his alter egos Charlie McCarthy, Mortimer Snerd, and Effie Klinker, supported by Ray Noble as the affable bandleader and a parade of guests including Dorothy Lamour, W. C. Fields, Mae West, and Marilyn Monroe. Jim Fanning says, "My mother was particularly fond of 'Edgar Bergen and Charlie McCarthy.' She and the lady next door used to rehash the program the next day, laughing again at the jokes." In Pat O'Shee's view, "Edgar Bergen's genius was that he could be the most devastated butt of the jokes he put into Charlie McCarthy's mouth. Then he would put Mortimer Snerd on his lap and be very indulgent and understanding of the stupidities he put into wonderfully lovable Mortimer Snerd's mouth. (I was fascinated by the very authentic-looking Charlie McCarthy and Mortimer Snerd dummies on the ninth—TOY—floor of Famous-Barr department store, 7th at Olive, St. Louis, during WWII.)" Jeanne Kenmore remembers Charlie McCarthy as one of the raciest things in radio: "Jokes never carried innuendoes that were sexual—except what Charlie hinted at to stars like Marilyn Monroe, Jeanette MacDonald, Myrna Loy, and others. During the half hour Charlie would flirt scandalously with any woman guest and compete in some verbal way with the male guest. Gales of laughter."

If, for many years, Sundays meant Jack Benny, Fred Allen, Edgar Bergen, and Blondie (with the belated addition of "Amos 'n' Andy"), Tuesday evening also became a reliable time for laughter, especially in the 1940s. H. K. Hinkley declares, "My favorite night for listening was Tuesday; that was when Bob Hope, Red Skelton, and Fibber McGee and Molly were on. These shows particularly appealed to that young boy." Marshall Ramsey, Jr. remembers Tuesdays as active radio evenings in his home too: "We station-switched, and while Dad usually handled the dial work, we pretty much liked the same programs."

Born with the radio debut of Fred Allen, Harriet Burt also knew the peril of listening to Bob Hope's "Pepsodent Show" during a civilian defense drill in Knoxville, Tennessee:

It was "Pepsodent night" in wartime America and, like literally thousands of others across the nation, my big sister and I were settled close to our small radio. Outside, a peculiar wailing rose and fell: *why* did they have to go and interrupt Bob Hope? Douse the lights! Draw the curtains! Close the blinds before the air-raid warden comes by!

The radio—could that tiny little glow from the dial really be seen for miles? Often enough I had heard the broadcasters warn that enemy bombers could home in on the light of a single candle. The dilemma was real in my mind: miss Bob, or risk the safety of Knoxville. Quick as thought, I grabbed the radio, slid it under one of the twin beds, and plopped myself sideways across a mattress. Its telltale light safely hidden beneath me, the radio played on through the blackout, right through to "Thanks for the memories."

In the recollections of World War II listeners, Bob Hope is forever linked with the defense effort. Like Jack Benny, he often broadcast from military camps and hospitals. In Pat O'Shee's estimate, "Bob Hope, of course, became a national hero in WWII because of his USO shows. Frances Langford, who went with Bob on his 'I Never Left Home' USO tours, was a fine songstress whom Bob made to 'appear' to the imagination as a luscious female. Les Brown and his Band of Renown supplied the excellent instrumentals. Bob had his monologue, as he still does." Roger Rollin looked forward to "the occasional swapping of guest appearances on each other's shows by Bing Crosby [host of the 'Kraft Music Hall'] and Bob Hope," who were sure to engage in "laugh-a-second banter" and to join voices in one of their musical duets.

Like Edgar Bergen on Sundays, Tuesday evenings' Red Skelton had a variety of recurrent characters personified by various intonations. Tom Fetters, as a potential Red Skelton listener, was scared off for a time by a misunderstood announcement:

In 1947, I went to bed about 8:30 or 9:00, as I was nine. But I did have a radio, and although I was supposed to go to sleep, I sometimes turned it on low and listened to far-away stations with some of the great evening shows. One night I turned the dial just at the hour and heard the announcer introduce "The Red Skeleton Show!" I only paused a moment and shut the set off. I knew that show would be far too scary and my mom wouldn't want me listening to anything so gruesome. It was a few years later that I heard "The Red Skelton Show" and enjoyed the adventures of the Mean Widdle Kid! I still have sharp memories of just how scary that "Red Skeleton" show would have been, though.

Tuesday nights at 9:30 meant one thing for a majority of listeners: "Fibber McGee and Molly," more formally known in its heyday as "The Johnson's Wax Program." Harlow Wilcox was one of the most genial announcers in radio, and Wistful Vista's tireless telephone operator Myrt was one of the most memorable nonspeaking roles ever created for the medium. Each week McGee involved a sizable portion of his town's populace in one or another of his schemes, which were usually Rube Goldbergian contrivances for avoiding the obvious means to an end. The McGee house was open to drop-in visitors such as little Teeny (played in a pouty-whiny voice by Marian Jordan), who got under McGee's skin as he got under others', and the crochety Old Timer, ever ready to follow one of McGee's shaggy dog stories with "but that ain't the way I heared it!" The Old Timer was a favorite of Pat O'Shee, who says, "His subjects always interested little me."

"Fibber told whoppers, of course," says Roger Rollin, "but what drew the biggest laugh was something we *expected* to happen now and then. He would go to the hall closet to get something, and when he opened the door, incredible stuff fell out with a lot of interesting noises." Every listener to Jim and Marian Jordan's program remembers Molly's weekly warning, "Oh, no, McGee, don't open that . . . ," followed by a crash and, after the briefest of pauses, the tinkle of a bell rolling on the floor near the notorious hall closet. Pat O'Shee's impression was that "when the door opened, tons of junk tumbled onto Fibber and the floor. I had a closet like that in Chattanooga." Constance S. Lackey says of Fibber, "Each house I have lived in has had one closet named for him. The McGees were such a joy." Likewise Trina Nochisaki says: "I still call my junk drawers and closets 'Fibber McGee's Closet'." "You could just see it happen," comments Martha Caskey about that sound effect which Trina Nochisaki describes as "all the assorted paraphernalia and junk tumbling out and making a great racket." George Robinson did see it happen because a high school friend (whose father was an NBC executive) often provided passes for witnessing a variety of Chicago broadcasts, including "Fibber McGee and Molly." He was impressed by the sound effects man, whose "gadgets . . . were truly a Fibber McGee's closet."

In Roger Rollin's recollection, one typical "Fibber and Molly" script illustrated changing times: "The McGees were driving to the airport to meet someone, when Molly remembered that she had left the roast in the oven. Fibber tried to get off the highway, but couldn't. In the '30s such highways were new to the U.S.A." In that simpler time, McGee enjoyed his fishing and camping trips and his lodge buddies, and Molly enjoyed her husband's company on leisurely shopping trips to the downtown Bon Ton department store, where they encountered many of their friends, including Water Commissioner Throckmorton P. Gildersleeve.

"The Great Gildersleeve" is one of radio's most significant spinoffs. Harold Peary had developed the character on "Fibber McGee and Molly" in the late 1930s, but in 1941 Peary's waxy-voiced public servant moved away from Wistful Vista and into a Sunday early evening half hour on NBC, where the expansive comic egotist resettled in Summerfield and became president of the Gildersleeve Girdle Company. The program later moved to Wednesdays, and Willard Waterman, whose intonation most listeners found to be an almost perfect match of Peary's, assumed the title role from 1950 to 1957. A bachelor whose life was complicated by his responsibility for his niece and nephew, Gildersleeve hopelessly pursued some ladies while others hopelessly pursued him.

Like "Fibber McGee and Molly," "The Great Gildersleeve" evoked small-city life through the weekly appearances of such characters as the barber, the eagerly available widow, and Mr. Peavey, the pinched-voiced druggist. The latter character has encouraged an avocation of Dr. Mickey Smith, F.A.P. Barnard Professor of Pharmacy Administration at the University of Mississippi and author of the book *Pharmacy and Medicine on the Air*. A self-described "'born again' radio buff," he was nudged into collecting broadcast tapes by an early 1970s *Time* article on vintage programs.[1] "I started looking for pharmacy in the programs," he says, and "It was my good friend, Richard Q. Peavey, R.Ph., who ultimately convinced me that the history of radio included a sequence on the history of pharmacy. Mr. Peavey receives and deserves much attention" in Mickey Smith's booklet *Reflections of Pharmacy in Old-Time Radio*, published by the American Institute of the History of Pharmacy in 1986.

Heritage Radio Theatre host Tom Heathwood characterizes "The Great Gildersleeve" as "one of the happiest shows ever broadcast," and he describes the program, its characters, and its casts in avid detail:

Gildy became guardian of niece Marjorie, played by Lurene Tuttle, Louise Erickson, and Marylee Robb, and nephew Leroy, played by Walter Tetley, who had a marvelously convincing teen-ager's voice. Marjorie's boyfriend, Bronco, was played by a young Dick Crenna. Rounding out the new family was Birdie Lee Coglin, the Gildersleeve maid as played by Lillian Randolph.

Important, too, in the development of each week's plot were Richard LeGrand, who played Mr. Peavey, who was frequently heard to say "Well, now, I wouldn't say that" in mild refutation of what Gildy might be expounding on at any particular moment, and Earl Ross, originally Gildy's nemesis as Judge Horace Hooker, who became one of his best friends as time passed on the show, though he retained the personality of "that old goat." Judge Hooker, Mr. Peavey, Chief Gates (Ken Christy), and Gildy made up "The Jolly Boys," a local fraternal club specializing in barbershop harmony. The loves in the great man's life were Shirley Mitchell, who played a scheming Southern belle widow; Leila Ransom, her cousin; Adeline Fairchild, played by Una Merkel; nurse Kathryn Milford, played by Cathy Lewis and Eve Goodwin; and the school principal, played by Bea Benaderet.

The show adapted to the times. Many of the shows helped to build good morale during WWII and encouraged all kinds of patriotic behavior by the listeners. It was shows like this that kept us able to keep our country going in its most crucial time. The show taught good morals and respect for fellow man. I only shudder to think what Gildy would think of the "new generation."

During his childhood in the mid-1940s, Roger Koonce was especially fond of the family and small town comedies. He says of Harold Peary's Gildersleeve, "He had an engaging laugh which I tried to imitate." He also has very distinct recollections of hearing another general favorite: "After our baths and before we went to sleep, my older sister and I were allowed to listen to a couple of programs from our beds. The old Philco was located in my parents' room, and it was turned up loud enough for us to hear such programs as 'The Aldrich Family.' The program began with Mrs. Aldrich's voice calling 'Hennnnnnry, Hennnry Aldrich!' Then an obviously adolescent voice [Ezra Stone's during most of the show's run] would respond, 'Coming, Mother.' I identified with the Aldrich family and was distressed when they left the airways." As for riveter Chester A. Riley and his family, Roger Koonce says, "'The Life of Riley' was never quite as good when it moved to TV. Digger O'Dell, 'the friendly undertaker' ('You're looking fine, verrrry natural') and the Riley family looked better in my head than as a result of some casting director's decision."

If "Fibber McGee and Molly" and "The Great Gildersleeve" represent "town populace" comedy, then "Easy Aces" and "Burns and Allen" typify the comedy of domestic differences. Owens L. Pomeroy fondly recalls how Goodman Ace was the foil to his wife Jane's insistent malapropisms: "Remember when she wanted to go into acting: 'I get the smell of the old goosegrease; I want to get behind the footnotes; I want to see my name up in tights.'" Ironically, the dialogue's dependence on verbal slips gave "Easy Aces" a literate, sophisticated overall tone. Vaudeville veterans Burns and Allen used a somewhat broader delivery for similar material. On radio, Pat O'Shee declares, "George Burns was funnier then than he is now, mainly because he could be the butt of Gracie Allen's humor. The outstanding example of this was Gracie's saying, 'George, turn the radio dial. I love to see your muscles BULGE.'"

Glen Resch grew skeptical of the popular taste in large-cast comedy shows played before studio audiences, and he casts his vote elsewhere: "I guess we laughed, all right, at Jack Benny. You know how a studio audience evokes the radio audience's response. There was a New York elevator operators' strike in the late '40s. Programs aired without studio audiences for a few weeks. I remember that the only thing we really laughed at then was Henry Morgan—funniest guy ever to collide with a radio beam, I still think—and that all the other programs really needed a live audience environment or it just didn't carry on radio." Morgan's listeners also delighted in his habit of alienating his own sponsors by questioning the worth or quality of their products. This was a costly habit to Morgan, but his devotees found it a refreshing change from comedy and variety programs that carried their sponsors' names in their titles, in the names of their singing groups, and in broad and often heavy-handed transitions into commercials.

Stanley C. Morrison remembers a fresh wind that blew from Boston's WHDH from 1946 to 1950—Bob Elliott and Ray Goulding, who would appear in a variety of network venues beginning in the 1950s: "Their characters were always funny. The females they impersonated were incredibly dumb. The male relatives were usually con men with wild ideas about getting rich. One program offered a do-it-yourself brain surgery kit for 'only 25¢.' They reported that a number of listeners ordered them! I listened alone at home and laughed a lot. (I never got my quarter back!) They were absolutely hilarious!" Working various shifts for Mutual and NBC, Bob and Ray perfected their parody soap operas ("The Life and Loves of Linda Lovely"), adventure serials ("Nat Neffer, Boy Spot Welding King of the World"), man-in-the-street interviews (Wally Ballou, who forever jumped his cue and, in consequence, clipped his name in coming on the air), and detective programs ("Mr. Trace, Keener Than Most Persons").

Postwar radio brought other fresh voices and perspectives, even in the soon-to-disappear genre of radio situation comedy. Marlin Hurt, a white male, lifted his black maid character from "Fibber McGee and Molly" and created his own "Marlin Hurt and Beulah Show" in 1945. Barbara Franklin remembers that after she and her siblings finished their chores on the family's Virginia farm, "the reward we looked forward to was being able to listen to a comedy show that starred 'Beulah'." Other listeners of the late 1940s and early 1950s found new comedies featuring high schoolers, their bewildered parents, and their teachers. The female ingenue and the cracked-voiced adolescent male were the comedy voices of the moment in "A Date with Judy," "Meet Millie," and "Meet Corliss Archer," and Eve Arden as "Our Miss Brooks" was surrounded by naifs—not only her high school English students but also her landlady and the eligible but unromantic biology teacher, Mr. Boynton.

Returning from military service in Europe and moving his family to New Haven to begin graduate study in 1955, Roger Rollin was comforted to find "one of my longtime favorites, Eve Arden," still on the air. Prevented from owning a television set by the graduate scholar's financial pinch, the Rollin family was contented well enough with radio during four years at Yale, "and if radio (old style) were dying, one hardly knew." The inevitable transition to television was eased by the nostalgic radio voice of Jean Shepherd, of whom Roger Rollin says,

Nothing had been heard like him before, with his reminiscences of growing up in industrial Ohio (which sounded very much like my growing up in industrial western Pennsylvania), his comic meditations on life, love, and the human condition (I can still remember his ironic account of reading, on the fender of a car rusting in a junk yard, "Rocket 88!"), and his wacky schemes (a man in touch with him by a car phone—very rare then—agreeing to tell the Lincoln Tunnel toll taker he had no money and seeing what would happen). I thought he was a genius. Still do. An urban predecessor of Garrison Keillor.

Jean Shepherd and Garrison Keillor have been fully aware of their debts to earlier radio comedy and of the possibilities of recycling its distinctive humor. Shepherd has contributed a fond foreword to a published collection of Paul Rhymer's "Vic and Sade" scripts.[2] Early radio is a frequent frame of reference for Keillor's public radio programs "A Prairie Home Companion" and "The American Radio Company," with their monologues, songs, dramatic sketches, and parodies of soap operas, detective programs, and commercials. Too, Garrison Keillor's novel *WLT: A Radio Romance*, especially in its opening chapters, is a lively recreation of radio's freewheeling pioneer days.[3] Keillor's fun begins with his title; he reasons that, if the pioneering Sears station in Chicago can claim the call letters WLS, "World's Largest Store," then a Minneapolis restaurant family might call its station WLT, for "With Lettuce and Tomato." The subtitle might be justified by the book's assorted amours, but Keillor also pursues "romance" in its traditional literary sense: an evocation of something lost, greatly valued in latter-day reflection.

NOTES

1. "Modern Living: Rip Van Ranger," *Time* 103 (April 29, 1974); 71, 73.
2. *Vic and Sade: The Best Radio Plays of Paul Rhymer,* edited by Mary Frances Rhymer. New York: Seabury Press, 1976.
3. New York: Viking-Penguin, 1991.

13

Drama Anthologies

Early listeners often say that they unconsciously stared at the radio dial, lit by a small bulb inside the receiver's cabinet. The orange or yellow illumination often held the eye as the radio tale transported the imagination elsewhere. Through the radio's modest glow, the drama anthologies of the 1930s and 1940s sought to simulate the footlights or spotlights of the legitimate theater and the klieg lights of the Hollywood sound stage. Often scheduled for the most desirable evening hours and half hours ("prime time," in contemporary television terms), these were among the most expensive programs being produced, and they aimed to achieve elegance for the ear. These radio versions of films, Broadway plays, novels, short stories, and original scripts sometimes suggested heirloom silverware, at other times tinsel.

In its elaborate weekly opening, which tracked the arrival of Mr. First Nighter (the listener's connoisseur stand-in) just before Act One curtain time, "The First Nighter Program" explicitly evoked the street noises and the rush of the Times Square theater district, while the shorter-lived "The Mercury Theatre on the Air," with its emphasis on adapting literary classics, simulated the world of the repertory company. "The Lux Radio Theatre" was first produced in New York in 1934, when the telephone company's main network sending lines ran only from east to west, but within two years the program's relocation to Hollywood became technically and financially viable.[1] With the change of origination point, the program adapted fewer and fewer Broadway plays. Hour-long versions of recent films became the norm, the screen leads usually reprising their roles for the Lux microphones. Film director Cecil B. DeMille became the longtime host of this best-remembered anthology series, and each Monday evening (at 9:00 in the East) much of the listening nation heard the movie capital's triumphant proclamation "Lux presents . . . Hollywood!"

"People complain that television's golden hours of drama are over, pointing to 'Philco Playhouse,' 'The Armstrong Circle Theatre,' and 'Playhouse 90' as examples," Owens Pomeroy reflects;

But do they remember when radio gave us "The Columbia Workshop," "The Mercury Theatre," "The Lux Radio Theatre," "The Screen Guild Players," "Family Theatre," "Grand Central Station," "Helen Hayes Theatre," and so many other dramas? Do you remember "Roses and Drums" or "The War of the Worlds"? Were you listening when Spencer Tracy and Pat O'Brien did "What Price Glory?" or Loretta Young and Orson Welles starred in "Jane Eyre"? That was when Lux presented Hollywood with "Ladies and gentlemen, your producer, Mr. Cecil B. DeMille." Name any star of stage, screen, and radio who didn't appear on the Lux program, and you have a better memory than I have.

Roger Rollin also finds a significant difference in the star quality of yesterday's radio dramas and today's television productions: "Nowadays, really major movie stars never appear on television except on talk shows or the rare sitcom cameo. Only actors on their way up—or down—perform on the tube. But back in the days of radio, major stars—the Cary Grants and Gary Coopers, the Carole Lombards and Joan Crawfords—regularly performed in radio versions of their latest movie or in 'a script written for radio.' [On 'The Lux Radio Theatre'] the female stars often extolled Lux soap as the secret of their fabled beauty." Corinne Sawyer depended on the Lux program for its steady parade of stars: "Their voices were often highly identifiable—as was DeMille's soft voice."

Roger Koonce found the Lux program "thrilling. The program began with a dramatic roll of the kettle drums, big music, and an announcer that sounded like God." In Texas during the 1940s, Malcolm Usrey says, "Only a serious emergency kept us from hearing 'The Lux Radio Theatre.' As the small town where we lived had no movie theatre, those Monday night programs helped us keep up to date on Hollywood films." In contrast, the Hollywood prominence in that program's best-remembered seasons brought a crisis in the home where Dr. Ralph R. Doty grew up: "My parents had a bit of an internal moral dilemma about 'The Lux Radio Theatre.' Because we were raised in a religious fundamentalist home, we were not allowed to go to movies. Thus, my only window to the movies was through the Lux program. I can recall my parents internally struggling with whether I should be able to listen to a movie I couldn't see in a theater. They ultimately allowed me to listen to the program, probably rationalizing that because the radio was suitable for all their favorite programs, it therefore should be suitable for audio portrayals of movies."

As with other highly popular programs of the era, the Lux presentation's format remains in memory more fully than individual offerings do. Corinne Sawyer illustrates:

I remember only one particular "Lux Theatre," though I listened every week without fail. I had a ruptured eardrum and was condemned to stay home in bed while my parents, my visiting cousin, and my little sister went to see a movie I'd yearned to see myself: the three Barrymores (Lionel, John, and Ethel) in *Rasputin*. The baby sitter (Mother never let us stay alone till we were in our mid-teens) was down in the living room, and I was aching away in the bedroom feeling awfully sorry for myself. Then "The Lux Radio Theatre" came on, and I listened, enchanted, to Signe Hasso and Gary Cooper recreating their screen roles from *The Adventures of Marco Polo*. When my sister got home, I told her loftily that I'd had the better deal . . . it was a wonderful broadcast! . . . and maybe that's true. Who knows?

Corinne Sawyer also knew "The First Nighter Program" from the days of its first host: "I remember way back when Don Ameche was 'Mr. First Nighter,' who introduced (and occasionally appeared in) a radio drama each week, the signature of which was the sounds of city auto traffic, then of a taxi drawing up to a curb, the door is opened and the theater doorman (I guess) says, 'Good evening, Mr. First Nighter'. . . then something like 'Right this way, your seat is waiting. . . .' All that was way over my head. I didn't even know what a 'first nighter' was! But I never missed the broadcast. I missed Ameche for a long time when he was replaced by Macdonald Carey" and others.

Owens Pomeroy discovered the same program later in its long run. Among the anthology dramas, he says,

I guess "The First Nighter" was my favorite, with Barbara Luddy and Les Tremayne, starring in the Little Theatre Off Times Square. Our seats were always third row center, and there was always an usher to inform us, "Smoking in the downstairs and outer lobby only, please." Whatever the adventure or love story on the stage that evening, we built the sets in our own "mind's eye" and we could see the action just the way we wanted it to take place. Was Barbara Luddy tall and blond or a short brunette? She was what you wanted her to be just by using your imagination. And that dulcet voice never once let you down.

The program fit perfectly into Elly Truebenbach's world:

Milwaukee summers could be as hot and humid as the winters were cold and frosty. Sometimes I would be sent to the ice cream store for a pint of vanilla so my dad could make black cows with root beer he had made himself. Or, after a scorching hot day, a late evening thunderstorm would bring out every goose bump on my body. I would wrap up in a blanket on the floor behind the screen door and watch the drops falling under the street lights. Usually this was also a good time to listen to 'First Nighter' from 'the little theatre off Times Square.' I got to know the names of all the famous actors and actresses from this program and had a pretty good collection of movie star pictures—autographed![2]

"The Mercury Theatre on the Air," an offshoot of the WPA theater work of John Houseman and Orson Welles in the mid- to late 1930s, adapted Bram Stoker's *Dracula* for its first broadcast on CBS in the summer of 1938, and that should have been a warning. Hour-long versions of works by Dickens, Shakespeare, Chesterton, Conan Doyle, Tarkington, and Verne followed, and in the fall the program was shifted to Sunday evenings opposite NBC's highly popular Edgar Bergen. Concerned by the ratings gap between Bergen's program and theirs, Welles and his associates updated H. G. Wells's *The War of the Worlds* on October 30, 1938 as a way of saying "boo" for Halloween (according to host Orson Welles's closing comments) to a nation growing nervous about European events being reported in newspapers and, more and more, in radio eyewitness accounts. On the morning after that "Mercury Theatre" broadcast, Welles, seeming abjectly innocent and wide-eyed about the panic induced by his ostensible joke, gave an impressive performance before the newspaper reporters.

"At the time of the uproar concerning 'The War of the Worlds'," Constance Lackey says, "I was living in Nutley, New Jersey. Luckily, we were listening to Charlie McCarthy and so didn't go crazy waiting for our doom at the hands of funny-looking little men. For years I kept all the clippings [about the broadcast] I could find, but somehow they have disappeared." Grover's Mill, New Jersey, was, after all, the Martians' landing site in the broadcast's resetting of the story, and this proximity was enough to alarm fifteen-year-old Dottie Zungoli and her friends, who were vacationing at Somers Point in that state: "'Oh, my God, come in and hear this,' one of the friends said from the cottage. 'These things are landing, and they're getting closer to the radio station,' and [quoting now from the broadcast] 'I don't know how much longer we can go on'." Dottie Zungoli confides, "We were all shaking in our boots. I said, 'I don't want to die here; I want to go home to my mother,' and she [the hostess, a friend of Dottie's mother] said, 'Well, how can I take you home? The roads are all full of those horrible things.' Finally, Payton [the host] had the sense to change the station and see that the other stations were not carrying it."

Other listeners were not so quick to get their radio bearings, and in many places the panic was very dangerous or, in retrospect, very comic. Holly Self Drummond's mother was hosting the church ladies that evening:

The setting was my Mama's and my Mamie's late-1800s parlor. Refreshments were being served to ladies of the First Baptist Church, Ninety Six, South Carolina, after concluding a rather lengthy Women's Missionary Union Bible Study. The French doors were opened to an adjoining hallway in order, hopefully, to relax to radio station WKKO's music—maybe Guy Lombardo—when suddenly, "We interrupt this program to bring you the following: Martians have landed on Washington, D.C."—sirens squealed, ambulances were everywhere, while the police were called out in full force to shoot upon sight these little men from Mars. Immediately, these little old W.M.U. ladies, seated in Mama's and Mamie's parlor, prayed fervently for protection—and especially for my big brother, who was serving his internship in a hospital in Palmerton, Pennsylvania. Pistol shots could be heard louder and more frequently. Of course the sandwiches and stickies were left behind when the broadcast informed us the men from Mars were headed south. It was only later when we learned that prayers had been answered and that radio had brought us an Orson Welles production.

At the mention of that broadcast, AARP representative Roger McNeill sighs, and his eyes focus on the middle distance. "I missed it," he says in a tone of longtime privation, "and all the kids were talking about it at school the next day. But my father was very strict about bedtime. No exceptions."

Scripted radio naturally assumed the privilege of simulating places as well as events. It should not be surprising, then, that the atmospheric evocation of the Manhattan theater district on "The First Nighter Program" was created in the NBC Chicago studios, while "Death Valley Days," redolent of California history, originated from NBC in New York beginning in 1930. (It later shifted from NBC Red to the Blue network, and it was heard on CBS from 1941 to 1945.) The series was often praised for its educational value and historical accuracy, and Bill Buri remembers that the narrator, known as the Old Ranger and played by a succession of actors, "had the greatest voice." He especially remembers an episode called "She Burns Green," the title reflecting the fact that borax, when placed in fire, produces a green flame. (Not incidentally, the program's sponsor was the Pacific Coast Borax Company, which packaged its product under a number of labels, including 20 Mule Team Borax and Boraxo.) In this anthology of desert and mining camp tales, Bill Buri finds evidence for his opinion that radio was "much more [imaginatively] interactive than TV. I could *see* the desert when The Lone Ranger and Tonto would be riding away in the sunset. I could see it; I could smell it. On 'Death Valley Days' it was very similar. The desert was a palpable thing. You had to concentrate on it."

While most of the big-name showcase radio anthologies were scheduled for evening listening, radio plays were also offered on Sunday afternoons and Saturday late mornings (to early afternoon). Originally an evening program, "Grand Central Station" is best remembered as a human-interest entertainment to accompany Saturday lunch. Tracing the lives of those who pass through New York's huge railway terminal, this anthology had one of radio's most elaborate standard openings, rivaling that of "The First Nighter Program" for length and evocative power. The announcer feverishly traced the path of the "shining rails" leading into Manhattan; the plunging of the engine is suggested in the rapid narration of its passing; the arrival of the passenger train is confirmed as the opening announcement dovetails with the conductor's cry, "GRAND CEN-TRAL STA-SHUN!" The listener was made to feel that an episode in the life of any passenger so magnificently arrived was worthy of tracing, at least for half an hour. Marshall Ramsey, Jr. was impressed by the blazoning articulation of the title "'Grand Central Station,' said long and dramatically, and the words about 'people passing' through that terminus and tales of their lives." In truth, most listeners remember the opening much more readily than they recall the tales that followed.

Another long-running (1941-1954) Saturday lunch hour anthology was "The Armstrong Theatre of Today," which prefigured early network television's "The Armstrong Circle Theatre." Harry Durham names "The Armstrong Theatre of Today" as his favorite program during his young adult years. One episode particularly impressed him:

I believe the title was "The Ugliest Man on Earth." At least that was the subject, if not the exact title. The story chronicled the life of a man whose physical appearance was so unattractive that people reacted negatively toward him. He had a hard time with any sort of personal relationship because other people were bothered by his appearance.

Then one day he happened to meet a blind girl, who was moving into his apartment building. He helped her as she was moving in, and she, unlike all others, responded to him in a warm and friendly way. Their relationship continued to develop, and soon they fell in love. For the ugliest man in the world, it seemed to be the perfect arrangement. She cared for him because of who he was, and she was not distracted by the way he looked. They got married. He was happier than he had ever been in his life. Then, one day, a mutual friend of theirs, a doctor, read about a new operation that he believed might restore the girl's sight. But of course there was a risk, and the doctor said he would not even mention it to the girl unless her husband agreed that he should. The ugliest man in the world panicked. He felt that he stood to lose everything if his wife regained her sight. And yet, he truly loved her and wanted her to have a full life as well.

I'm sure you can finish this story. The husband agreed to tell the wife, who was eager to try the operation. When the bandages came off the girl's eyes, she looked at her husband and called his name, saying she would recognize his sweet face anywhere.

That story seems to me to be a perfect example of how radio is particularly well suited to certain kinds of presentations. Everyone has his or her own concept of "ugly" or "beautiful." Radio lets the listener fill in the outline with colors and textures from his or her own experience. In many ways, I believe listening to radio drama is almost as personal as reading a book. Good radio drama has strong emotional appeal.

NOTES

1. The story of the networks' "Round Robin" relay system and its technical problems is amusingly told in veteran radio actress Mary Jane Higby's autobiography *Tune In Tomorrow* (New York: Cowles, 1968); especially pp. 20-22.

2. A fine illustration of radio's leaving some details to the listener's perception occurs in Owens Pomeroy's and Elly Truebenbach's differing treatments of their references to the playhouse. For one, it is the proper name of the imagined theatre, analogous to the wedding chapel best know as The Little Church Around the Corner. For the other, it is a generic reference to a showcase in the theatre district.

14

Crime and Terror Programs

The very titles of some nighttime (and Sunday late afternoon) programs threatened nightmares, almost guaranteed them: "Lights Out!," "Suspense," "Escape," "The Witch's Tale," "Inner Sanctum Mysteries" (sounds claustrophobic), "The Whistler" (in the dark, for certain), "The Mysterious Traveler" (dark tunnel ahead). "Escape"? How narrow an escape? Beyond the titles were the hosts' promises of "a tale well calculated to keep you in . . . Sus-PENSE" and the intent "to *thrill* you a little and *chill* you a little." The final Mutual network run of "I Love a Mystery" was aired at 10 p.m. Eastern time (a late hour for most schoolchildren on weeknights), and the opening organ glissando sweeping into Sibelius's *Valse Triste* seemed to pull the listener into a vortex of darkness and danger. The signature music of "The Mysterious Traveler" and "The Shadow" suggested the throbbing of a fearful or a guilty heart, while the "Suspense" theme music found no steady pulse; against minor chords the orchestra bells chimed in irregular soundings, abruptly cut off by a burst of timpani strokes. And those sound effects: creaking, squeaking, scuffing, moaning, ripping, pulsing, humming, throbbing . . . .

Beyond the horror anthologies were the police procedural and detective programs, many of them direct adaptations from pulp novels, monthly magazines, and comic books. Spanning the range from "Official Detective" and "The FBI in Peace and War" to margin-of-the-law private eyes of the Raymond Chandler-Dashiell Hammett hard-boiled school, these programs contributed an underworld patois to radio language, and they raised the decibel level: cry of protest . . . bam-bam . . . groan . . . clatter of fallen object (often a slow gun) on floor . . . thud of body . . . cruel laugh of departing gunman. In these familiar action sequences, moans and pauses could be invoked ad libitum, depending on the instincts of the actors, the director, and the sponsors. (Gun silencers, on the other hand, had limited usefulness in the radio crime arsenal).

Drawn to these programs like the proverbial moth to a flame, the child listener often finished hearing them with knees knocking and teeth chattering, and adult listeners traced headaches and nightmares to one tense half-hour program or an evening's sequence of radio thrillers. In some homes, then, crime and horror programs were strictly rationed or entirely forbidden, and in other settings, the family listened together for mutual assurance. "One of my fondest memories of radio drama was a show called 'Devil's Roost'," Max Salathiel says; "I used to listen to it with my folks, and it gave me nightmares!" Dottie Zungoli reports that she and her mother used to get into their beds and listen to "Inner Sanctum" and, she says, "I could hardly move, it was so frightening." Harry Durham adds, "Up in my room, I had a small radio which my brother had built into one of the wall cabinets next to my bed. Nothing was more deliciously scary than snuggling down in my bed with the lights out and listening to 'Suspense' or 'Inner Sanctum.'"

"I was not allowed to listen to scary stories [alone] at all," Gordon Kelley remembers.

This meant I never knew that "The Hermit's Cave" was on the air at 11:00 on Saturday nights. However, listening to "Inner Sanctum Mysteries" was a family affair. We turned the lights out, and my sister and I cuddled up to my mother while we shivered and shook through each episode. Some of the episodes I remember were broadcast on WFBM (CBS) on Tuesday nights at 8:00, and we always listened. The stories were scary, but the family made them less so, and I did not go to bed frightened most of the time. The most memorable thing about this was we always had hot, fresh popcorn in a large pan to make the listening more enjoyable. I do remember the weird host Raymond and his gruesome laugh, and I cherish the times I have gotten to visit with him [actor Raymond Edward Johnson] at several recent radio conventions. His voice is still very distinctive.

By contrast, Elly Truebenbach remembers, "As a child I loved them all, even the really scary ones. We lived in a large house with the bedrooms upstairs, far away from the family gathered in the living room. When my *mean* older sisters were sitting with me, we would listen to these programs and then they would make me put myself to bed even though I was scared to death of the dark."

John Butler was a highly discriminating childhood listener who offers these reflections on the radio horror genre:

"Scary" programs seemed to work so much better on radio than they have on television—mostly, I guess, because the spooky details were left to the imagination. The old haunted house on radio was more familiar (and hence scarier) because it was based on your concept of a house—*your* house—and the same was probably true about most of the small details of any horror story setting on radio. You got to see the details on television, [but] they were the director's details, and not so familiar (and thus scary) to you.

"Lights Out" was by all odds the scariest of the radio dramas to my mind; the very name "Arch Oboler" [the best-remembered of its writers] even sounded sinister (it still does—try it: *ARCH OBOLER!*) The story about the chicken heart that keeps growing (and *beating!*) until it engulfs the world ["Chicken Heart," starring Boris Karloff] is one that I particularly remember. By comparison, "Inner Sanctum" (with squeaking door and "Raymond"—whose last name was, apparently, "Yourhost") seemed pretty tame—but still pretty scary!

"Inner Sanctum Mysteries" was, nonetheless, a general favorite from its 1941 beginning to its 1952 demise. Charles Jennett associates the program with the World War II days when he was living with his grandparents in eastern Texas ("where you don't see many sights except prairies"). His grandparents, he remembers, had a large floor-mounted radio.

But the one I remember most was a very large desk model—I believe a Philco. The children were allowed to stay up and listen to "Inner Sanctum" on it. This was a scary program, made even more so because it was on after dark. In Texas, every window in the house would be open to catch any cooling breeze. Grandmother had a very large rose bush that climbed the side of her house and onto the windowscreen. "Inner Sanctum" started with a creaking door and got scarier every minute. As the show continued, the wind would cause the rose bush to scratch against the screen; imagination did the rest.

Having written more than half a dozen mystery novels set in a California retirement center, Corinne Holt Sawyer has found that she prefers to work within the polite restraints of the English "cozy" style: dead or quite badly bruised bodies are allowed, but only a suggestive minimum of flowing blood and scrambled human flesh, please. Perhaps her preference for this reasonably genteel form of storytelling began in her Midwestern childhood, when, one autumn evening, "Lights Out" offered a test of radiophonic terror:

Horror shows were wonderfully effective on the radio. Your imagination could create scenes of greater impact than any TV set can show you. "Inner Sanctum," ushered in by the sound of a creaking door and the host's unmistakable voice, was a prime example. Mother didn't especially like us to listen to it—or to other shows of the "horror" genre. But by the time I was in high school, she usually didn't try to regulate my listening.

One October evening my mom and dad had gone outside into the yard to rake leaves, a job I abhorred, and I was allowed to stay inside. Probably they expected me to do my homework, but I turned on the radio, and there was an "Inner Sanctum." This evening it was a story starring Boris Karloff as a grave robber who was warned not to disturb the grave of a priest. The thief pays no attention, and digs up the grave during a thunderstorm (of course) and puts the body in a large gunny sack into his horse-drawn buggy, propped up like a passenger in the seat beside him. The thief whips the horse into a gallop and heads toward the distant town, where he'll sell the body, but something is happening as heaven's rain falls on the gunny sack and its gruesome burden. Between the roars of thunder you hear the sound of ripping cloth. . . . The sack is being rent apart. And in the flash of lightning the grave robber sees that his ghastly burden has miraculously come to life! The dead man is seeking his revenge . . . the rotting fingers close around the thief's neck . . . accompanied by more thunder, many gurgles, and a few screams . . . and all the while the horse, wildly galloping on and the buggy creaking. . . .

And I could listen no more. I burst from the house and out to the yard to help my parents with the raking! They were surprised, and I never told them why I volunteered to help! But the vivid qualities of radio drama had made it impossible for me to stay alone in a twilight house.

Jeanne Kenmore's family owned no radio in her youngest years ("Depression days," she explains), but at the age of fourteen she discovered radio drama at a summer church camp: "I heard for the first time 'Inner Sanctum,' a spooky show that came on very late. And 'The Whistler.' I can still hear the theme songs of those two shows." Two years later her absorption of radio fright programs created a brief crisis in her academic career:

I was a freshman at the University of Minnesota the year I was sixteen. In freshman English we had to write a theme every single week. One week I tried to imitate "Inner Sanctum" without explaining to the professor what I was doing. I wrote about riding the bus to college and knowing that everyone was looking at me. And on the streets there were eyes following me. Eyes, eyes, eyes. I thought I was pretty cool about it. Well, a week later the professor told me she had made an appointment for me at the Student Health Service. OK. I went. And it was to see a psychiatrist! The professor had thought I needed psychological help, but the psychiatrist and I had a great laugh and she took me out to lunch.

While many listeners report that they were figuratively "scared to death" by the terror dramas, Joan Bobbitt nearly died, literally, of "Inner Sanctum." About 1948, when she was three years old, she was eating peanuts one by one from the handful in her lap. At a particularly scary moment in the program, she swallowed a peanut, which "went the wrong way" down her windpipe. She began to turn blue and had to be rushed one hundred miles to New Orleans by ambulance for major throat surgery. "Boy, you were a lot of trouble," her mother commented years later.

At about the same time, Trina Nochisaki "became a suburban house-wife and soon after a mother, living in a small tract house in Connecticut . . . .[My] husband still talks about the night he got home as I was listening to ["Inner Sanctum Mysteries"] and [he] found me paralyzed with fright, cowering in the corner, certain that I was about to be killed or worse by whoever was trying to get in." John T. Schlamp, a quality assurance engineer living in New Jersey, also has a family story about "Inner Sanctum Mysteries":

My family—mother, father, brother, sister, and I—listened to our Philco console situated prominently in the living room. My father pretty much controlled the programming, but he enjoyed a wide variety of shows, so there was something for everyone. His main interest, however, was mystery, so we always heard "Lights Out," "Suspense," "Sherlock Holmes," and his favorite, "Inner Sanctum." My anecdote concerns "Inner Sanctum," broadcast in the New York City area in the fall of 1943 on WABC, the CBS outlet, on Saturday night at 8:30.

We were all in the living room, with only one small light on (for effect), listening, my brother and I head to head on the floor.

Unbeknownst to any of us, my father's brother was on his way to visit us, and when the story reached a particular point of horror, Uncle Bob burst through the front door, causing everyone in the room to scream out loud, completely bewildering him. It was a few minutes before we calmed down to explain the situation to him.

Norma Brown Hanrahan recalls the program concisely: "The summer evenings and 'Inner Sanctum' and we did turn off the lights. Internally generated pictures; better than television."

The chief rival of "Inner Sanctum Mysteries" in audience favor carried the firmly demanding title "Lights Out." Larry Lowery especially remembers "Lights Out" in its early fifteen-minute format during the 1930s: "As a primary-age youngster, I took my radio seriously. When a program said 'Lights Out,' I insisted it meant 'lights out,' and all the lights would be turned off throughout our home. It was eerie, sitting in the dark listening to some of the best-written radio tales. The dark, the tales, and the gathered family were a deeply rooted ritual."

"We loved the mystery stories," declares Doris Swehla. "I was scared practically spitless, but I wouldn't miss the thrill for anything!" With her family too, "Lights Out" was "a favorite, and I loved it when my dad would join the announcer in the opening line, 'Turn out your lights. Turn them out!' and he would turn out our lights, whisper these last words in my ear, and then sit beside me on the davenport so I wasn't really frightened." Of this and other programs she adds, "The bad guys were 'badder,' the good guys were 'gooder,' and the terror was more delicious because it came from our imagination rather than from the graphic bludgeoning and bleeding we see daily on our TV screens."

Between 1930 and 1955 radio was seldom without an adaptation of Sir Arthur Conan Doyle's Sherlock Holmes adventures. These programs were heard at one time or another on every national network except CBS, and the title part was essayed by William Gillette, Basil Rathbone (playing against Nigel Bruce's Watson), Tom Conway, and others. Al Fick remembers the classic early 1930s dramatizations well:

There was a Sherlock Holmes network program broadcast weekly from WGY in Schenectady, New York. The program came on after bedtime for schoolboys, but we enjoyed the adventures of Sherlock Holmes all the same. The bedroom where my brother and I slept was heated by a register in the floor which brought heat up from the dining room below, where the Zenette radio was located. Our parents sat in the adjacent living room, which meant the volume had to be turned up a bit in the dining room. We could hear quite nicely through the ceiling register. I remember only one [specific] program. It was *The Hound of the Baskervilles*, which scared me so much I listened only to portions, alternating between fascination and terror with the blankets pulled over my head. The sponsor was G. Washington Coffee Aces, a forerunner of today's instant coffee. I recall that it was packaged in small aluminum containers—perhaps those were mailed samples—looking a bit like a miniature shotgun shell with a crimped top.

Many another schoolchild would have been grateful for a heating system that funneled radio stories into the bedroom after the parentally prescribed hour for retiring.

Malcolm Usrey credits 1930s radio for encouraging his interest in classic books. For instance,

My introduction to Sherlock Holmes came with a radio production of *The Hound of the Baskervilles*. Giving me goose bumps and making me more afraid of the dark than ever, the Baskerville hound and the dark, foreboding setting of the story became as genuine to me as the scrub oak-covered low hills of our Texas farm. Hearing that production sent me to the library to get a copy of the Sherlock Holmes stories, which I read; but the printed version of *The Hound of the Baskervilles* was not nearly as alive as the radio version. A radio dramatization of a Poe story— perhaps "The Pit and the Pendulum"—left me emotionally drained and physically exhausted. A favorite of my sister was "Inner Sanctum," but it was so diabolically scary that I could not bear to listen to it.

Adapted from Walter Gibson's Street and Smith pulp magazine stories, "The Shadow" was a long-running radio classic of a different sort, the title character being played by a succession of actors, including Orson Welles, Bill Johnstone, and Bret Morrison. The narrator's opening statement, explaining that wealthy Lamont Cranston had learned in the orient how to "cloud men's minds" so that they "could not see him" and The Shadow's own closing caveat "The weed of crime bears bitter fruit; crime does not pay" are among the most familiar bywords from the era of radio drama, and many listeners puzzled over Lamont Cranston's precise relationship with "his friend and companion Margot Lane," the only person to share the secret of his alternate identity.

From "The Shadow" and similar programs Ann Chase discovered radio's evocative powers during her Depression-era childhood, when her father was often out of town and her mother, to increase the family income, had resumed her teaching career in the Baltimore schools. Her parents had arranged for a neighbor to provide meals for the children when illness or other necessity kept them at home in the middle of the day or during the late afternoon hours when their mother's required teacher-education course was in session. As Ann Chase recalls,

I became ill with I don't remember what, so it was decided that I should stay home alone with the radio and a tray of food sent over by our feeding neighbor. The plan sounded good until I was half finished with my nourishment.

I was sitting alone in the corner of the living room on what was lovingly called "The Big Chair." My tray was supported by each of its overstuffed arms. Silence reigned. Slowly, ever so slowly, the dark, creaky sound of a door opening caught my ear. Spooky drawn-out words entered the room: "Who knows what evil lurks in the hearts of men?" My tray flew into the air as I fled from our house to the warm shelter of our neighbor's, where all were calmly seated enjoying their meal. Germs mingled with health. Comfort was found among the well. Sound alone had provoked fear difficult to erase from memory.

Dorothy Stancliff says, "I used to sit in Dad's lap to listen to 'The Shadow.' The advertisement for Lava soap taught me to spell the word!"

(In those commercials, a deep-voiced chorus chanted 'L-A-V-A, L-A-V-A' behind the announcer's spiel.) On the other hand, Allen Hilborn had reached a higher rung on the educational ladder when he regularly heard the program in the late 1930s: "When I was in college, 'The Shadow' was our cult program, and dinner on Sunday evenings in our fraternity house was rescheduled so we could listen en masse." Patricia Day had a startling encounter with The Shadow one foggy morning when she stepped onto a dock at her parents' home in coastal Maine. Through the fog she heard an eerie, yet a familiar, laugh. Later she learned that the radio actor (probably Bret Morrison, but memory is uncertain on that point) had been visiting there with friends and had perhaps been asked to demonstrate radio's unfunniest laugh.

In suburban Birmingham on the evening of January 14, 1948, young Patrick O'Shee had the two-story house at 1130 Lakeview Crescent to himself. Anticipating the first broadcast of an episode called "Leiningen vs. the Ants" on CBS's reliable-for-thrills anthology series "Escape," Pat O'Shee knew how to make the best of a radio evening at home alone. Turning off every lamp and overhead fixture in the house, he readied himself close to the faint glow from the dial of his "brand-new, very modern-design Zenith AM." The episode's South American setting was established, and the action began. "By the time the army ants had gotten past the concrete wall, the moat, and the gasoline fire and were eating the flesh off Leiningen's bones as he watched, screaming, every light in this house was burning brightly, and comfortingly—more or less."

Police and investigative agency dramas such as "True Detective Mysteries," "Mr. District Attorney," "The FBI in Peace and War," "Official Detective" (featuring Detective Lieutenant Dan Britt in the stoically somber pursuit of lawbreakers), and the afternoon serial "Dick Tracy" gave a contemporary sternness to crime fighting on the radio. Gus Wentz dismisses the Sunday afternoon crime melodramas of his high school listening days as "cookie-cutter intrigues," but Ken Weigel revelled in the thrillers of any day and hour:

I remember clearly how crime programs rattled my larval sensibilities. The dark underside of homo sap. was revealed to me in crime and mystery shows like "Gangbusters," "Murder and Mr. Malone," "The Lineup," "Sam Spade," "The FBI in Peace and War," "Inner Sanctum," and "The Mysterious Traveler." These shows likewise introduced me to breezy women with cold hearts who could drink and four-flush with the best of men. This astonished me; I'd thought only men ran to seed. Ken Lynch, Frank Lovejoy, Mandel Kramer, Richard Kiley, Ralph Bell, and Peter Leeds were my favorite tough guys. There were *actors* in those days.

Lovejoy, Mason Adams, and Elliott Lewis were (still are) my favorite dramatic actors. These guys handled a microphone the way Sinatra handled a ballad. Just below them was an unsung talent menage of both sexes that could deliver the goods in whatever dialect, accent, tone, or attitude the script called for.

Owens Pomeroy, "plucking memory's strings," adds others to the list of radio crime fighters: "Van Heflin was that smooth sleuth Phillip Marlowe, and Richard Widmark was filling the columns as Front Page Farrell. There were so many heroes in those days: Bulldog Drummond, Ellery Queen, Martin Kane, Mr. Keen, Tracer of Lost Persons, and Mr. District Attorney, 'champion of truth, guardian of our fundamental right to life, liberty, and the pursuit of happiness.' "

In 1936 "G-Men" became "Gang Busters" (its title later often spelled as a single word), a very popular show that would pass from NBC to CBS to ABC during its lengthy existence. Each "Gang Busters" episode ended with a description of the "most wanted" criminal being sought at the time by the FBI or a major police department. Many of the featured fugitives had Italian names and Mediterranean facial features. Some law-abiding listeners made mental notes of identifying scars and "armed and considered dangerous" warnings, while others simply regarded this feature as a verification of the program's "realism." But the at-large-menace-to-society feature brought a special fear to Nancy Farmer (née Braccini), as her husband, Jim Farmer, reports: "Her father's physical appearance was that of the stereotypical Italian mobster, and every week she listened with dread as they described the latest 'most wanted' criminal. All too often that portrait, in her mind, meant Daddy could be in serious trouble! With tremendous insecurity, and confiding in no one, she would live the following days awaiting the 'paddy wagon' that never came" to take her father away.

"Gang Busters" had an ear-grabbing calling card. As Stanley C. Morrison recalls hearing it on Boston's WBZ in the 1940s, " 'Gang Busters' always started with the distinct sound of submachine gun fire, the 'Tommy-gun' (Thompson sub-machine gun). The 'G-Men' always won, the bad guys went to prison. Police car sirens were common. It was frightening." Norma Brown Hanrahan listened to the program with her older brother in 1938: "The opening shots and sirens scared me, and I would cover my head. So there *was* violence on radio." Ted Norrgard reports, "I remember very vividly going over to my neighbor's house to listen to 'Gangbusters' [because] my mother thought it was too violent for me. I believe I was about eight years old at the time. I suppose the fact that I was forbidden to listen made it all the more exciting." Roger Rollin recalls his mother's wariness:

One show my mother had decided reservations about was "Gangbusters," which began with a series of symbolic sound effects—the clank and tramp of chained feet, a police siren, and a burst of machine gun fire—and which was supposedly based on True Crime. She had decided it was entirely too thrilling for me at 10 p.m. on Saturday—until we discovered that it was listened to without fail by one of her elderly aunts, the very soul of decorum.

I was more into another crime show, "The FBI in Peace and War" because "G-Men" were more glamorous than mere cops and because J. Edgar Hoover was a national hero. I had no idea how much this show, many FBI movies, and even comic books were Hoover-encouraged propaganda. (Ironically, the program's theme was the march from *The Love for Three Oranges* by that commie, Serge Prokofiev.)

Historian Robert S. Lambert found "Gang Busters" especially vivid on one occasion in 1939, when he was twelve years old:

I suffered a broken arm in a playground accident . . . , and I was admitted to the Hackensack Hospital in New Jersey, encased in an upper-body cast, and assigned to a ward for adult males.

One day, when I had begun to feel better, I became aware that a policeman was present in the ward at all times. I learned from my parents during a visit that the occupant of the bed next to mine was the victim of a gunshot wound suffered while committing a crime. That night I lay in bed in the dark listening through earphones to the popular program "Gang Busters," very much aware that a "gangster" was near. Nothing happened, and after awhile I fell asleep. In time I even conversed occasionally with my neighbor until he was well enough to be discharged. And, boylike, I never confessed to him or my parents that his presence and "Gang Busters" had bothered me in the least.

Jeanne Kenmore's judgment is that "Gang Busters" and "The FBI in Peace and War" provided "innocent gore—no bad language, no descriptions of blood and guts, no beating of women or child abuse—just cops and robbers." Marshall Ramsey, Jr. was impressed by the authenticating presence of Colonel H. Norman Schwarzkopf (father of the Desert Storm military operation's commander "Stormin' Norman") as a "real life" interviewer of local or U.S. lawmen who figured in the weekly dramatizations of "actual cases."

Beginning as a fifteen-minute afternoon serial on West Coast NBC stations in 1939 (but never sounding like the "children's hour" series in tone or content), "I Love a Mystery" developed a small but avid following, listeners who were willing to endure a number of format and time changes, network shifts, and, indeed, an interruption lasting several years between the original NBC and CBS broadcasts of the early 1940s and the Mutual revival (1949-1952) of earlier scripts, performed by a largely new cast. Written by the prolific Carlton E. Morse, who accumulated many chapters and books in the "One Man's Family" saga at the same time, "I Love a Mystery" maintained the A-1 Detective Agency as its ostensible base of operations, but its characters were, in fact, existentialist adventurers who might appear anywhere that danger and excitement lurked. Most devotees feel that the serialized adventures, each running for several weeks, were superior to the episodes offered in the weekly half-hour format. Jack Packard, laconic Texan Doc Long, crisp Brit Reggie York, and their associates kept a quick pace through such sequences as "Bury Your Dead, Arizona," "The Thing That Cries in the Night," "The Girl in the Gilded Cage," and "The Stairway to the Sun."

Glen Resch best remembers "I Love a Mystery" as a dinner-hour serial that was difficult to turn away from: "6:15, Central Time. Been called to dinner several times now. I don't know how I engineered it, but I usually managed to catch most of that downright bloodcurdling adventure series. How did they do it, without today's acrylic-paint blood and slime? Yes, it's fun knowing today that Tony Randall [who was not yet famous for his stage and screen roles] and Barton Yarborough [who concurrently played a major role in 'One Man's Family'] were its sometime players, but don't think for a minute that that information is near as exciting as listening was, and never mind who the voices were. I was ten, and my place was with them, in the Den of the Vampires." Owens Pomeroy adds, "That famous trio of rugged characters, Jack, Doc, and Reggie, once proved to my complete satisfaction that they could emerge unscathed from a head-on automobile accident while the gang that was holding them hostage was wiped out. 'Simply a matter of knowing how to take precautionary measures,' said Doc. And I believed every word of it."

"This is still my favorite radio show," declares Bill Anthony, who listened to "I Love a Mystery" with his brother in Pittsburgh. Especially vivid in his memory is the adventure "The Thing That Cries in the Night," the tale of a murderously dysfunctional family living in the Gothic manse where blood flowed freely and madness reigned: "We were both petrified when the baby cried," he says. That disconcertingly floating cry came at many unexpected moments in the sequence, usually from a place that seemed impossible to pinpoint. But it was the business of Jack, Doc, and Reggie—their names always seeming to fall into that ritual order—to make the impossible doable.

Calling "I Love a Mystery" "one of the greatest adventure programs of all time," Elton Dorval says, "All of the stories were great, but the one that impressed me the most and one that I never forgot was entitled 'Temple of the Vampires.' What a disappointment in later years when I hoped to acquire the series for my tape collection. Quite a bit of the middle portion of the story was missing and so far has not been located. Enough of the beginning and ending has been saved, though, and makes great listening." Tom Fetters recalls the same sequence from the Mutual series: "I remember when I first heard one of the 'I Love a Mystery' shows in the 1950s. I was hooked instantly. Jack, Doc, and Reggie were in Central America in a temple full of vampires with no lights. How easy it was to turn off the lights in the [listening] room and live every moment as Jack and Doc pushed their way along the narrow path up along the walls of the temple as they heard the vampires swooping past. Suddenly Jack was gone, and Doc and I stood alone, together on the shelf, high above the floor, unable to see ahead or behind. A sinister laugh broke the silence. And we were told to tune in tomorrow!"

Among Larry Telles's listening choices in the late 1940s and early 1950s were two programs produced for West Coast audiences. "One of the detective shows I liked was 'Let George Do It,' heard over KFRC, a Mutual station at 610 KHZ. He seemed to get hit over the head a lot. Over on KPO, the NBC station, in 1950 was a woman detective program, 'Candy Matson, YUkon 2-8209,' which took place in San Francisco. It was nice to hear Candy investigating murders at some of the places I had really seen. I also remember [the full network's] Sam Spade, another great San Francisco-based detective, on KPO."

Larry Telles knew the popular network anthologies, too, and he confesses, "Several of the horror shows did scare me a little. 'Lights Out' was the best at horror, with 'The Mysterious Traveler' and 'Inner Sanctum' close behind. 'Suspense' had a lot of variety just like 'The Whistler.' I remember that 'The Whistler' was sponsored by Signal Oil Company. It moved from station to station here in the Bay Area. I tried to get my dad to buy that kind of gas for our family car. I thought it would be easier than getting him to drink Roma Wine, from the sponsor of 'Suspense'."

Now a major mover of the Old Time Radio Club in Lancaster, New York, Richard A. Olday grew up during the latter half of radio's golden age, but he especially remembers an occasion from the last year that CBS carried "Suspense" and "Yours Truly, Johnny Dollar." The second of those programs, dealing with the expense account adventures of a free-lance insurance investigator, had shifted from weekly self-contained half-hour stories to a five-nights-a-week serial format (1955-1960) and then to the weekly half-hour again in its last two seasons. Dick Olday says,

On a sunny summer Sunday afternoon in the early 1960s, I drove across the border with a few of my friends to a nearby beach. Since we were all in our late teens or early twenties at the time, we listened to rock and roll music on the way to the beach. However, on the way home around 6 p.m., I changed the station to Buffalo's WBEN. My friends were very upset with me for changing to a non-music station. As they began protesting, "Suspense" came on the air. Their protests continued for about two minutes and then it became very quiet! Yes, they had all become very engrossed in the story. When the story ended, I expected to hear "Turn the station," but instead the response was "What is coming on next?" What was next was "Yours Truly, Johnny Dollar." After that, my friends were "hooked," and whenever we were out together after that, they always wanted to know what was on that "other station." [Through taped copies of the program] I am still converting people to become "Johnny Dollar" fans to this day. The multi-part adventures starring Bob Bailey are the "bait" I use.

15

Music Programs

A sampling sweep across the dial in most cities today would suggest that "radio" is synonymous with two options for most listeners: popular music and talk. For operators of early radio stations, music was a convenient time-filler or a means of showcasing local talent. To many listeners, especially in homes where leisure-time activities had shifted locus from the parlor piano to the crystal set, the easy availability of radio music was itself sufficient reason to hope that broadcasting would grow and prosper. In the beginning, some stations owned only a few 78 r.p.m. records but saw no difficulty in airing them repeatedly, accumulating scuffy needle wear with each playing. Home record collections, on the other hand, might have included Paul Whiteman's band in its jazzy Victor release of "Mr. Radio Man" or Frank Bessinger's adoring "Radio Lady o' Mine" on the Perfect label.

As networks' and local stations' perceptions of listener tastes matured in the 1930s, certain portions of the broadcast week were committed to satisfying a range of musical tastes. The Metropolitan Opera broadcasts soon achieved institutional status on Saturday afternoons; Sundays meant symphonies, choirs, and organ recitals; Monday evenings showcased the light classics, operetta and musical comedy, and the concert band repertoire.[1] Meanwhile, the microphone, whether used in an auditorium or in the broadcasting studio, changed popular singing styles and techniques and led to the age of the romantic crooner and the "song stylist." From the beginning, radio was a major factor in the spread of country and gospel music and jazz beyond their regional sources. Music on the airwaves gave impetus to a subsidiary industry handling the royalty rights of composers and lyricists; ASCAP and Broadcast Music, Inc. gained considerable leverage in extracting performance fees from radio interests. At the same time, the instituting of program ratings services further encouraged radio's tendency to pursue overlapping mainstream tastes—ballads and dance bands for general consumption, swing for the youngsters, jazz for the up-to-date set, country music for traditionalists.

The early prominence of country music on the radio, even before the networks were established, was a major factor in the South's especially eager welcome of broadcasting. "The National Barn Dance" from Chicago's WLS and "The Grand Ole Opry" from Nashville's WSM established Saturday evenings as a time for country fiddlers, plaintive singers, and rural comedians. A neighbor's Atwater Kent receiver on which Paul Snow listened to the barn dance program picked up "a lot of static" in the early 1930s, but the program was nonetheless "a treat to dirt-poor country folk." In Juanita Capell's recollection, "On Saturday nights we all had to gather around and not make a sound while 'The Grand Ole Opry' was on. My dad just loved Uncle Dave Macon and all those banjo and fiddle players." Saturday nights marked a ritual for Ruby Fisher and her friends too: "When I was a teenager, living in the country, we didn't have a radio, so on Saturday night we teenagers would walk two or three country miles to a friend's home to listen to 'The Grand Ole Opry.' They didn't have chairs for everyone, so we sat on the floor, but we didn't mind. We enjoyed listening to Eddie Arnold, June Carter, 'Sara and Sally' (they were so funny), Jim Reeves, and many more."

Having moved from Mississippi to Chicago, George Robinson took full advantage of the opportunity to see his favorite performers in the WLS studio at 1230 Washington Boulevard: "A large plate glass window separated three or four rows of church pews from the performers, but remote speakers piped in what was going out over the air. Admission was free, and there was always room in the pews. We watched the Arkansas Woodcutter, the Hoosier Hotshots, Little Georgie Goebel, Roy Rogers, Jolly Joe Kelly, and Lulubelle and Skyland Scotty. Ernest Tubb came through one day and completely destroyed the mental picture I had formed earlier."

Genella Olker, by contrast, lived near country music's most prominent Southern shrine, but, she says, "I remember nothing of 'The Grand Ole Opry,' and none of us ever heard it, listened to it, or saw it in the Ryman Auditorium. It was just 'hillbilly music' to us." In Kathy Cunningham's family, musical taste was divided: "My mother hated country music, and as an older child and into my teens, I would sit in the car with Daddy and listen to 'the Opry'." During his high school years in Niagara Falls, New York, Richard Saunders found that none of his friends listened to the Nashville broadcast, "but for me, it was music from another world."

WSM, the "Opry's" originating station, had a cross-state rival in Knoxville's WNOX. In the 1930s Harriet Burt was fond of the latter's "'The Midday Merry-Go-Round,' where folks downtown for the day could wander in to meet Roy Acuff or maybe Johnny Cash or the Carter Family. I listened faithfully in front of our dome-shaped floor model, except on the days when an old Ford, with a ragged awning draped across a wooden frame from which swung some scales, rattled by with its load of onions, beans, and tomatoes."

A local country music program was a special attraction to Ruby Fisher: "My boy friend (now my husband of fifty years) played with a band called Modern Hillbillies at WAIM in Anderson, South Carolina. We would walk to the neighbor's home every Saturday to listen on their radio. He would usually dedicate a song to me. That really thrilled me."

In its Greenville, Mississippi days, George Robinson's family also knew the special pride of having one of its own perform on the air:

My dad was a Dixieland banjo player and was soon to become part of the migration that moved Dixieland up the Mississippi River to Chicago. By 1926 he had put together his first band, which he called the Moonlight Serenaders, long before Glenn Miller came up with his. Greenville had its own radio station, probably a five or ten watter, and they filled the air time with local talent. The Moonlight Serenaders would go down to the station, play a few songs, and ask for telephone requests. Their repertoire was limited, and my mother knew it from start to finish. To keep things from getting out of hand, she would sit by the phone and keep calling in requests for songs she was sure the boys in the band could play. We moved to Chicago in 1930. The Moonlight Serenaders drifted into town by ones and twos and would get together to play in the speak-easies and gin mills, but they never got back on the radio again.

By the time the elder George Robinson was organizing his Moonlight Serenaders, Harvey Rettberg had become an enthusiast for "the dance music (we called it Jazz) that covered the dial from 9 p.m. till the wee small hours. In particular, there was one orchestra that grew up with radio: the Coon-Sanders Original Nighthawks. They made the first broadcast by an organized dance band; they were first to broadcast on a coast-to-coast network; they were the first to be represented by Jules Stein, who developed the giant Music Corporation of America." Since the 1920s Harvey Rettberg has been an avid collector of recordings, photographs, and articles related to the pioneering radio bands.

Owens Pomeroy sees radio as central to the growth of popular music as he knew it in Baltimore in the 1930s and 1940s:

I wonder whatever became of the military servicemen during WWII, strangers to our city, on leave, heading for the nearest USO for an evening of dancing to the music of the big bands (broadcasting remote) and a little conversation to forget the fact that they were miles from home, their wives, their best girls . . . The sheet music department of the local 5 & 10¢ store, with the piano-playing salesperson, who would play your song you heard on the radio the night before, before each sale . . . The ice cream parlor in your neighborhood, where you congregated after school, with the Wurlitzer jukebox playing the latest hits of Miller, Dorsey, Goodman and the like, and the little eight-by-eight-foot dance floor in the back. (Sometimes a five cent Coke lasted all afternoon, much to the dismay of the matronly counter lady in her nice white uniform) . . . The "cool-off" rides on the streetcars during the summer, rides that ended at the local dance pavilion, where you danced all night to a new tune you heard on the radio the night before, or listened to the music piped by loudspeakers surrounding the park, as you and your date went for a boat ride on the moonlit lake . . . The radio stars who appeared at your local Bijou, "down-town." You were the first in line to see if they looked the same as you had imagined they would in your "theater of the mind." (If they were not the same, you closed your eyes while they performed, where the "magic and power" of radio took over) . . . And, finally, the radio sales and service stores that *always* had a radio program playing through a loudspeaker over the door, in hopes you would stop and listen and maybe—just maybe—come inside and see the newest radio models.

Raymond Ruland notes that WALR, the first radio station in Zanesville, Ohio in the mid-1930s, expanded its call letters into the slogan "We All Like Records," and, he comments, "they did have a lot of record shows. And about this time a small radio appeared on top of our refrigerator. This thing was turned on very softly in the morning and went on till bedtime."

Dance band remotes satisfied single listeners as well as cuddling couples. Ed Roper, who was a military college freshman in 1936, recalls, "Friday nights were very dull; we had to clean up our details room and our own room for inspection on Saturday morning. Most of the freshmen's radios were tuned to a Chicago station, and good music was coming from the Aragon-Trianon Room in Chicago. That was the only pleasant occurrence on Friday nights." Jeanne Kenmore discovered the band remotes after having her appendix out at the age of eighteen: "While recovering at home, I listened half the nights to the romantic music of the big bands coming from various hotel dining rooms with fascinating names, usually in New York. I daydreamed my way back to health. Some of the tunes: 'It Looks Like Rain in Cherry Blossom Lane, the sunshine of your smile's no longer there.' Or 'With the Wind and the Rain in Your Hair.' Music with lots of rhythm, of course: 'Alexander's Ragtime Band,' 'Put Another Nickle In, In the Nickelodeon' ['Music, Music, Music']. And the show tunes from Fred Astaire's movies. [Soon] I was in college, earning my way by playing the piano for a dancing studio twenty-five or more hours a week. To do that, I had to know the popular tunes, so the radio became vital to my earning possibilities." Alice Boyd Proudfoot adds, "During high school I slept with a radio practically under my pillow. 'Coming to you from Frank Daly's Meadowbrook on the Pompton Turnpike in Cedar Grove, New Jersey!': I thought it sounded like the most romantic place in the world. We have kids who live there now. The Meadowbrook is still there, having been used for a number of events in the past fifty years. Romantic it's *not*."

Big band remotes were significant in Tom Heathwood's Boston youth too:

Boston had several nightspots that featured the big band sound and the "swing" sound in the '30s and on into the '50s. The groups were a little scarce during the war years. The Hi-Hat was one of the most famous for the "real" thing and featured live remotes right into the '50s. Black jazz and swing musicians entertained countless thousands every year without a thought of a racial issue. Nowadays that is a racially charged danger zone. Some of the hotels had nightclubs on their roofs where big band sounds would fill the night and would make their way by network radio to every part of the country. But New York City cornered the market on Big Band remotes! "From the Green Room of the Hotel Edison in downtown New York ... NBC presents, for your listening pleasure, fifteen minutes of music in the Blue Barron style." "Symphony Sid" was the last big-band remote host I remember still doing his thing on the air in Boston well into the '50s.

For the most part, these music shows were unsponsored and were carried by the networks as late-night "fill" programs. Little did they ever expect that they would enjoy the popularity that they did. Restaurants, bars, and hotels would gladly pay a little extra to have a coast-to-coast audience hear a famous bandleader talk about how wonderful their place was, and hear the great live music. It was great for business. And it was fine for the band's bookings, too.

Still another popular music radio institution was "Your Hit Parade," which underwent many changes of format between 1935 and 1959. "Like everyone else," John Butler says, "I waited breathlessly every week for 'Your Hit Parade' to announce which song was (drum roll) *number one!*" Gus Wentz's family "used to keep a list of the 'Hit Parade' selections each

Saturday night." He says, "Sometimes I would be allowed, from my perch on the steps overlooking the radio, to write each choice in its place on the list as it was announced after yet another 'Lucky Strike Extra' had added to the suspense."

The years 1938 to 1942 were high school days for James L. Sender and his friends in Oak Park, Illinois. In those war-shadowed years, he says, "the radio tastes of my peers changed [from afternoon adventure serials] as we discovered girls and found that dancing with them at high school functions could be an exhilarating experience. We now listened to 'The Fitch Bandwagon'—'Laugh a while; / Let a song be your style. / Use Fitch Shampoo. / Don't despair; / Use your head, save your hair. / Use Fitch Shampoo'—'The Camel Caravan,' 'Kay Kyser's Kollege of Musical Knowledge,' 'Make-Believe Ballroom,' and the big bands playing from the Aragon and Trianon Ballrooms in Chicago. In those days it had to be big band all the way. On Sundays I even listened to Ralph Ginsberg and the Palmer House Quartet and was dutifully instructed in gracious waltzing by my grandmother."

"What better timing," Nelson Mallary exclaims, "than one should enter high school, enter the golden age of radio, enter the period of 'Your Hit Parade,' and enter the Big Band Era simultaneously . . . while living in Macon, Georgia." He continues,

In February 1935 I entered high school. (In Macon at that time high school began with the eighth grade.) April 20, 1935 marked the first radio broadcast of "Your Hit Parade," and the beginning of the swing band is popularly dated from the debut of the Benny Goodman orchestra on August 21, 1935. Who else in any other period grew up with such beautiful music, such wonderful dancing, and so much fun?

As I listened to the radio in the '30s, I would make a record of how the orchestras were introduced on the air ("Out of the night comes the music of TED WEEMS and his orchestra"), various titles the leaders were known by, and their theme songs ("Out of the Night" was Ted Weems's theme). As any good packrat would, I still have these records (some over fifty years old). Virtually all of us in those days were serious radio listeners—many of us documenting our listening with written records. Perhaps the habit of documentation came from the habit of preparing a sheet of paper with numbers one through fifteen written down in advance as we listened to "Your Hit Parade." Songs were played in random order, with Number 1 being played last on the program. Of course, any good reference book would provide the fifteen song titles, but what no book would provide is the *annotation*. Here is a sample:

"YOUR HIT PARADE"
February 15, 1936

"Red Sails in the Sunset" disappears after tying the record.

1. Alone
2. Moon Over Miami
3. Lights Out (Entered Hit Parade as #15 just 6 weeks ago). . . .
9. Beautiful Lady in Blue (Over 100,000 copies in 2 weeks). . . .

We often jotted down the big bands we heard on a single night. On "Monday, August 19th" (I didn't record the year) I heard: (1) Tommy Dorsey, (2) Benny Goodman, (3) Glenn Miller, (4) Artie Shaw, (5) Duke Ellington, (6) Glen Gray, (7) Dick Jergens, and (8) Woody Herman all *LIVE!* Don't you wish you'd been there?

We kept our own "hit parades," general and special. By this I mean we would write down the name of the song as we heard it, and every time we'd hear it again, we'd make a hash mark. One of these looks like this:

IMMORTALS

1. Moonglow
2. Moonlight Serenade /////////////////
3. Night and Day ////////
4. Time on My Hands /////////
5. Sweet Sue //
[and thirty further titles].

THIS . . . was music!
Then at around midnight December 31, 1945 the Big Band Era ended. And, at around midnight December 31, 1949 MUSIC ceased to be written . . . almost; to be replaced by "noise in music's clothing."
And oh what a tragedy was that, my countrymen.

As Billie B. Blocker knows from his World War II training camp, fox-hole, and Stalag VII-A experiences, "The Lucky Strike Hit Parade" (alter-nately called "Your Hit Parade" or "The Hit Parade") was many a draftee's or volunteer's measure of normalcy: "Lonely GIs all across the country and around the world listened to [it] in barracks, canteens, and service clubs. Next to a letter from Mom or the girlfriend, 'The Hit Parade' was the serviceman's best means of 'being' at home even if for a short hour once a week. The magic of radio was never better!" Conversely, being at the battle-front or in a prison camp meant losing track of, among many other things, that patterned weekly journey to popular music supremacy. Billie Blocker recalls the scene in a German POW camp in the spring of 1945. Before transportation arrived to remove the newly liberated men, "a radio was brought into the camp, and one small group . . . had their first opportunity in many months, years for some, to hear 'The Hit Parade.' " Earlier tunes were, as usual, played in a random order—number five, number nine, number four—, but anticipation grew as the playing order took a straighter path—number three, number two—toward the final revelation:

Now all eyes were on the little cloth-covered speaker compartment of the radio, so as to better hear the name of the top song of the week back home in America.

"And now, ladies and gentlemen, the top tune of the week," came the excited voice of the announcer. The liberated POWs were in another world. All thoughts of their barbed-wire-enclosed home . . . were now far away until the announcer continued his introduction of hit number one: "Here it is, the most popular tune in America, 'DON'T FENCE ME IN.' "

Ah, the magic of radio! Not only could it take you away; it could also bring you back.[2]

Other popular music showcases were available to younger listeners back home. Marshall Ramsey, Jr. was a loyal listener to "The Pause That Refreshes" with Frank Black and "The Coke Club" with Morton Downey. "Later on, during the war," he adds, the soft drink maker had "'The Coca Cola Spotlight' with various orchestras making visits to Army, Navy, and Marine bases." Dottie Zungoli says, "Dick Powell, when I was in my teens, was the idol of my whole life. My girlfriend Janie and I would run home so we could listen to Dick Powell every Friday night." Roger Rollin recalls live music shows "in late mid-afternoon—for example, one starring two very popular singers of the time, Gordon MacRae and Gisele MacKenzie (both of whom wound up doing a few movie musicals). Another starred a very 'romantic' (the word 'sexy' was unknown to me) French singer, whose name couldn't have been Jean Valjean but which was something like that. I envied his heavily accented crooning, which in those days of Charles Boyer I was sure would entrance girls, and I used to imitate it, singing his theme song, 'Falling in Love Again.' (I can still sing it, complete with French accent.)"

Often one song, made readily available in radio's audience-pleasing repetitions, crystallized a hope, a regret, or a need for emotional release. Wartime goodbyes were said as the radio crooned "We'll Meet Again" or "I'll Get By." George A. Walker, Jr. remembers that his father, a newspaper editor and publisher who "had a lot of ups and downs during the '40s that were certainly impacted by the war news," endured "many late nights, 'putting the paper to bed'," or holding the press "for the latest events or casu- alty lists." The Walker father and son, their work finally concluded, would frequently sit together, waiting for a Philadelphia station's next periodic playing (at midnight, 3 a.m., or 6 a.m.) of "The Blue Bird of Happiness," sung by tenor Jan Peerce. "Perhaps it gave us some peace of mind, some sanity amidst insanity and death," the son concluded. For Jeanette Caler, the "deepest" wartime emotion came on "the day they liberated Paris. The news reports were sketchy, but the local station immediately following the announcement played 'The Last Time I Saw Paris.' My heart leapt up in my throat and tears rolled down my cheeks. I was about thirteen years old, but old enough to truly feel joy for the people being freed."

In Atlanta, young Jim Fanning received his own small white Silvertone radio and "heard Bing Crosby sing 'White Christmas' on that one for the first time on Christmas Eve, 1943," while Maine native Harry Boothby was serving in the Pacific: "One of the most memorable moments for me was a radio program I heard aboard the U.S.S. *Howard Gilmore*. We were in the Marshall Islands with all its tropical beauty. The radio in the dining area played Bing Crosby's version of 'White Christmas.' It hit me how much I missed the snow and memories of home and my loved ones."

Raymond Ruland confesses that, during his World War II military ser- vice, one musical program was irresistible. "I was a radio operator on a patrol boat in the Greenland area for a short time," he explains. "At that time all naval craft monitored 500 kcs on the radio band; this was the dis- tress frequency. However, WOR in New York (650 kcs) had The Three Suns on every evening for a half hour from the Circus Bar of the Piccadilly Hotel. Since our ship had limited radio equipment, I had to retune from 500 kcs to 650 kcs for this half hour. Since I never did hear a distress call in about eight months, I didn't feel too guilty about this little deviation."

Glenn Miller and his band did many remote broadcasts, but he was also featured in regularly scheduled programs, including a series for Chester- field cigarettes from 1942-1944. "During that period I was caught up in the Glenn Miller fever, of course," says Susan Taylor. "Late in the afternoon when his nightly broadcast would come on, my friends and I would listen in my room, and when he'd say 'Everybody that smokes 'em likes 'em,' we'd light up a Chesterfield, and in a few minutes my mother's voice could be heard at the foot of the stairs!" Hal Higdon remembers another Miller series:

My all-time favorite memory concerns listening to broadcasts of the Glenn Miller band toward the end of the war, probably late 1944 or 1945. I was in a Boy Scout troop in seventh and eighth grades. We had troop meetings on Friday nights, and

I'd hurry home to hear the Miller broadcasts, which came on around 9:00 in the evening. I was just developing an interest in what was called swing music. I loved Miller's slick style featuring a syrupy saxophone section. Miller, of course, was killed in a plane crash toward the end of the war. I don't remember much about that. I just remember rushing home each Friday night to hear the broadcast. Later, in high school and college, when Tex Benecke hit town fronting the Miller band, or Ralph Flanagan, who was a clone of Miller, I would take dates to their dances at the Edgewater Beach or other dance halls. And, of course, I bought all the Miller records.

The Freddy Martin orchestra frequently supplied music for "The Fitch Bandwagon" and "The Jack Carson Show," and Pat O'Shee was fond of a comic routine within the band: "The weekly hilarity for me was provided by 'Mrs. Martin,' who lashed out at one of the band members, who would yell, 'NO, MRS. MARTIN! NOT THAT! NOT THE WHIP! YAAAAAAAGH!'" Genella Olker "was crazy about the Guy Lombardo program which came on the air just in time for Sunday dinner. I can remember often asking to be excused or to bring my radio into the dining room. Sometimes yes and sometimes not, but during the 1940s we listened mostly or only for music. I found I could read and listen at the same time. That helped, but I was not allowed to have it on while I did homework, and I realized there was no use in arguing about that." Having grown up in New Orleans, Jerry Reel remembers being bemused by a juxtaposition of tones in the programming of Jesuit-owned clear-channel station WWL: "We had 'The Rosary' at 5:00 and those marvelous hotel dance orchestras at midnight."

With the rise of crooners and big bands, the playing of their records became an increasingly specialized affair, presided over by the disc jockey. Between its 1935 beginning and the 1954 end of its run on New York's WNEW, Martin Block's "Make-Believe Ballroom" grew from fifteen minutes to an hour and a half and then to three and a half hours, six days a week. Fulton C. Hines says, "We never missed Martin Block's famous 'Make-Believe Ballroom' on Saturday mornings, later taken by William B. Williams." Marshall Ramsey, Jr. was a regular listener to "some great d.j. musical presentations" from New Orleans and Nashville: "Dick Martin had 'Moonglow with Martin' from the Roosevelt Hotel in New Orleans, and, as you can imagine, his theme was 'Moonglow.' WWL was a powerful station then, 50,000 watts. I remember picking it up when in the Navy in California. Then, from WLAC in Nashville, the d.j. Gene Noble had his program alternately sponsored by Randy's Record Shop of Gallatin, Tennessee, and Sterling Pilzner Beer. With the latter, Gene would open up by blowing through a straw into a glass of water (?) in imitation of foaming beer. His themes were alternately 'Gene's Boogie' by Krupa and 'Sewanee River Boogie' by Albert Ammons." In the late 1940s, Bob Poole's Chicago disc jockey program "Poole's Paradise" (using "Paradise" as its theme music) became a genial weekday afternoon feature on the Mutual network, as Marshall Ramsey further recalls.

"In the late '40s," Roger Rollin notes, some disc jockey programs shifted their appeal from general or adult listeners to the teen crowd; they "chatted up the young audience that the shows were aimed at. Of course, there had always been 'Your Hit Parade,' and even though we were not really a musical family, we did tune in on it regularly. But these new shows were different. They were local, and disc jockeys like Pittsburgh's Art Pallon became teen celebrities. And they played new releases before they had become 'hits,' so they were more musically adventurous than 'Your Hit Parade' (which became a TV show, which rock 'n' roll mercifully killed off)."

In time, disc jockeying encompassed a variety of music types beyond the mainstream proclaiming of "hits." Robert Cox remembers his reaction to a joke told by a country music disc jockey that he and his sister listened to: "The disc jockey said, 'I figured out why everybody's happy today. It's because school started back.' I fell out of my chair and was rolling around on the floor pretending to be having a heart attack at the disc jockey's remark. My sister was laughing at me. Then the disc jockey said, 'Well, ol' ticklebox fell plumb out of the chair there. Get back up and enjoy the program.' This came as quite a surprise to my sister and me. Could it be possible he could see into our living room somehow? No, he was miles away at the radio station. Someone there must have done the same thing I did at precisely the same time." Meanwhile, Lemie Lentz was discovering a new kind of music, previously labeled "race music," as she tuned in a Sumter, South Carolina, station and listened with her family's maid each afternoon as "Jivin' with Joe" came on the air with this greeting: "Dig that jive from fo' to five; this is Hattie Pratt's little baby boy Joseph L. Anderson . . . Jivin' with Joe."

While the family maid was teaching Lemie Lentz to "jitterbug" to this newly acceptable music on the back porch, Patricia Webster Stewart was becoming a regular listener to KRES-AM in St. Joseph, Missouri:

They had a contest to be a Junior Disc Jockey on a fifteen-minute program at 4:30 every weekday afternoon. The station's format was Top 40 78 r.p.m. records. Names were drawn from entries mailed in. I was thrilled to hear Pat Webster's name drawn.

I went to the station and was given four records to introduce. It was the custom to dedicate the songs to couples who considered each song "their" song. On Friday I heard that I had won that week. Of course, the prize was records, the only one of which I remember was Frankie Laine's "Mule Train." There was one problem in winning records. There was no record player in the Webster home. We continued to hear Frankie Laine on KRES-AM until we finally had the money to buy a record player. Years later, when I had to live through the music of the '60s and '70s of my seven children, I realized how my mother felt every time she had to hear Frankie Laine's whip cracking over the mule train. Three Dog Night couldn't compare to Frankie Laine.

In retrospect (and as a collector of Old Time Radio tapes) Ken Weigel sees something of a plot in radio's mid-century changes:

Had I been born ten years earlier and taken a personal interest in radio in the mid-'40s instead of the mid-'50s, I'd have a stock of Mortimer Snerd and Finnegan gags to regurgitate right about here, but it wasn't in the cards. I reached my teens in the mid-1950s, and by that time TV and rock-and-roll were elbowing radio, and disc jockeys were taking over the nighttime hours. I remember listening to "Dragnet," "Our Miss Brooks," "Dimension X," and "Gunsmoke," all respectable late-comers, but by then I was too preoccupied with Bill Haley, Fats Domino, Elvis, Jimmy Clanton, and a cute blond from across the tracks to pay much attention. My favorite station was KOMA in Oklahoma City, one of the early mega-watt rock 'n' roll stations. My favorite d.j. was the zany Hal Murray on KLIF in Dallas ("KLIF-klock time is 12 past 10"). Both KOMA and Dallas were a long haul due south, but they came in clear two or three times a week. Murray was unlike anything heard in the Midwest. He clowned, told jokes, and smashed records, one of the early d.j. gimmicks that eventually gave way to the one-record marathon and the giant single-cell amoeba that terrorized Denver. One night Murray told about how he dreamed he ate a bowl of Shredded Wheat and awoke to find his mattress gone—a switch of an old Fred Allen gag. (In Allen's version he dreams he's eating marshmallows and wakes to find his pillow gone.) In the years since Murray and KLIF I've caught up on OTR, and it turns out that disc jockeys began feeding on radio comedians' scraps even before the genre was officially passé. This is like going through a dying man's pockets. Murray was only one of the first to borrow. By my count, disc jockeys have lifted or switched roughly every gag told by Allen, Jack Benny, Red Skelton, Ed Gardner, Bob and Ray, Henry Morgan, Burns and Allen, Fibber McGee, Martha Raye, Jack Kirkwood, Abbott and Costello, Judy Canova, Bob Hope, Jerry Colonna, Joan Davis, Georgie Jessel, Amos 'n' Andy, Edgar Bergen, Goodman Ace, Stoopnagle and Budd, Eddie Cantor, and Fannie Brice, not to mention two by Squeakie the Mouse. And when they used them up, they started stealing from each other. If there had been any originality left in radio after OTR was run off the air, it wouldn't have become the banal medium it is today.

NOTES

1. These "high culture" programming patterns have been discussed in Chapter Eight, "Cultural, Educational, and Religious Programs."

2. Ironically, Bing Crosby's recording of "Don't Fence Me In" was a particular favorite of German POWs incarcerated in an Arizona camp, according to Johann Kremer, a "69-year-old . . . grizzled machinist from Cologne," whose recollections at a recent POW reunion were reported in Jack Fincher, "By Convention, the Enemy Never Did Without," *Smithsonian* 26, 3 (June 1995); 128.

16

Audience Participation, Amateur Talent, and Related Programs

To appear on the radio, to have one's voice or one's playing carried through an electronic labyrinth and beamed into the air—that was a highlight of many lives in broadcasting's early decades. To be a contestant or a man-in-the street interviewee could set the pulse pounding, and to hear one's relatives perform was a privileged excitement. Almost all voices seemed welcome at radio's beginning, and the format shifts of the post-World War II era increasingly mingled innocent voices with trained ones in quiz shows, talent searches, and similar programs. While some listeners preferred the polished and "cultivated" delivery of radio professionals, others could readily identify with the warts-and-all humanity of amateur performers and audience participation show guests.

Lois Robinson recalls the firm judgments passed by Major Edward Bowes in his network "Original Amateur Hour" beginning in the mid-1930s: "If a performer had talent, they'd get to finish, but part-way through a bad act, they'd 'get the gong,' and that would be the end of that." On the other hand, Jim Farmer sympathetically remembers a contestant on one of the many programs hosted by Horace Heidt:

I recall when that world of Amos and Andy, Edgar Bergen, and The Lone Ranger also housed a blind pianist whose name has evaporated with time. We "met" him on the Horace Heidt talent show. This weekly show included several novice performers all vying for a prize, which included a coveted return trip to compete in the next round of the contest. This blind man had our entire family enthralled as he continued to win, week in and week out. Our anticipation as the show entered the audience applause vote was not unlike the suspense of the seventh game of the

World Series. That performer with no name and no face was part of our life for many weeks. I err somewhat when I say "no face," because every member of our family knew *exactly* what he looked like!

Especially on Saturday mornings, local talent shows were broadcast from movie theaters in large cities and small ones. Marge R. Crowley was a veteran of these programs: "I used to sing on talent shows in Columbia and Camden (my home town), South Carolina. The winner would receive cash or coupons for food. During the '40s I spent a lot of my Saturday mornings singing on the radio, trying to win those prizes. And I did win a few!"

In the late 1930s and early 1940s, Doris Swehla's family "matched wits with the contestants" on "Dr. I.Q." and "Kay Kyser's Kollege of Musical Knowledge." "Of course we didn't get the prizes," she adds, "but we competed as if we could." N.D. Mallary, Jr. liked "Information Please" and "Dr. I.Q.," and he appropriated bits of the latter program as private jokes with Groucho Marxian overtones. Hosted by Lew Valentine, then by Jimmy McClain, and then by Valentine again, "Dr. I.Q., the Mental Banker" toured from city to city, usually originating from movie houses where the host's assistants roamed the aisles, carrying microphones and tapping contestants. Of this ritual Nelson Mallary recalls,

Many of the repeated phrases on "Dr. I.Q." "entered" my personal vocabulary permanently. I adopted them, and I *still* use them. The roving assistant would call out, "I have a lady right here in the balcony, Doctor." [This declaration, leeringly parodied, appealed to the lurid imaginations of 1940s schoolboys]. More frequently (on the first floor) he said simply, "I have a lady, Doctor." To this good day, whenever the situation can support it, I say, "I have a lady, Doctor." Nobody knows what I'm talking about. Some think I am referring to an absent female physician. Others think I am somehow, and for some reason, announcing the gender of my own physician. Most don't even try to decipher it. Only once in my life has someone snapped and said, "That's Dr. I.Q."

Dr. I.Q. never tried to persuade his contestants to put the silver dollars they had already won at risk (by taking on another question) but rather always asked, "You have (e.g.) eight. Would you like to try for nine?" (or however much the next question was worth). Whenever I ask someone if they want "x + 1" of anything, I use the same timing and intonation.

Roger Koonce is confident that Ralph Edwards and Art Linkletter deserve recognition as the most popular hosts of 1940s audience participation shows: "Edwards, prior to bringing 'This Is Your Life' to life, was the host of 'Truth or Consequences.' There he would select some poor soul from the audience and send him off on a wild goose chase, letting the audience in on the secret by chortling, 'Aren't we devils?' " Although Art Baker was the original host of "People Are Funny," most listeners will join Roger Koonce in remembering Art Linkletter as the mischievous emcee of the program, "cast much in the same mold" as Ralph Edwards's show.

From the mid-1930s onward, schoolchildren found ways to "be on the air," at least in imagination. Larry Lowery, who especially admired the sound effects on "I Love a Mystery," "Inner Sanctum," "The Jack Benny Show," and others, created his own program:

In upper elementary school, radio's influence led me into a two-month school project—the writing of a radio script which utilized lots of sound effects. Although I was the author of the script, I also insisted on doing the sound effects—BBs in a balloon for thunder, crinkling cellophane for fire, and inverted cups for hoofbeats. It was a great opportunity to be inventive. I made sure there was a part for everyone in the class, and we did a performance in the school auditorium for parents. Too bad there were no tape recorders in those days. But maybe the memory is better than a recording that retains the details, the inconsistencies, the faux pas.

Roger Rollin, quoted elsewhere as an admirer of many types of radio performers and programs, had his innings on the "live" side of the microphone:

Early in my high school years I had a chance to become a "radio personality" myself—if on the smallest possible scale. A school chum became involved in a fifteen-minute show—"The American Junior Red Cross on the Air"—that aired locally every Saturday morning on Pittsburgh station KQV and asked if I were interested in performing. Was I! For years I had been listening to radio and thinking, "If only I could do that!" Here was my Big Chance.

Wednesdays after school we took a trolley downtown, where we met with a few other kids, were assigned parts, and read through our scripts several times. Most of the scripts were mini-dramas with some educational or health thrust to them, and I had the impression that they were written by someone at Red Cross national headquarters. However, one of our best scripts, a kind of comic dream sequence in rhyme, was written by a kid, a fellow performer. We even "toured" with it, putting on benefit readings at various local venues. Inspired by my friend's success, I tried to write some scripts myself—I remember one was based on a journey to Yucatan, about which I'd lately been reading—, but none of them, I think, was actually produced.

After about a year the thrill of "being on the radio" wore off (I think my mother was the only person to actually listen to "The American Junior Red Cross on the Air"), and I dropped out for more boyish pursuits like neighborhood Saturday morning football or baseball. In any case, I had found that my image of the glamorous life of the radio studio had been overdrawn, at least as far as KQV in Pittsburgh was concerned. We performed in small, bare rooms, with the only person visible being an engineer in a glass booth who gave us hand signals. Glamorous personalities were conspicuous by their absence.

In Susan Taylor's extended South Carolina family there was much interest in a weekly radio quarter of an hour:

The first major radio happening was in the 1930s when my aunt took her large family to New York and "put them on the radio." They were an enormously talented musical family, and their entrance into broadcasting was a family "sketch," as they were then called, combining drama with songs on WJZ [and carried on NBC beginning in 1932]. It was called "The Vass Family" and was about a typical Southern family of that era with four daughters and a son. One of my cousins wrote the script, and I remember the excitement of Saturday mornings, gathering around the small cone-shaped radio to hear them, sometimes (usually) through sputtering static. They later appeared on radio variety shows with their gentle Southern folk songs.

"The Vass Family," variously featuring Fran, Sally, Emily, Louise ("Weezy"), and Virginia ("Jitchy"), ended its run on the Blue network in 1941.

Born on a Central Oklahoma farm in 1935, Max Salathiel counts himself "extremely lucky" in that his family was made up of singers and musicians. "Two of my uncles were professional musicians and performed on the radio in Oklahoma City six days a week," he says, "and my Aunt Gerry was with a vocal group, The Smart Set, on "The Al Pierce Show" from Hollywood every Saturday and later on "The Alan Young Show." My uncles moved to California in 1941 and went on to perform nationally. One of my uncles, Merl Lindsay, had his own Western swing band and appeared in movies with Jimmy Wakely, and my other uncle, Doyle Salathiel, joined Lionel Hampton's orchestra and became a top jazz guitarist, working with many stars."

By his mid-teens Tom Heathwood was a radio veteran, having become a "Junior Announcer" on a Boston station in the mid-1940s; he adds that he "was also the 'studio rat' as the unpaid runner for coffee, sandwiches, cigarettes, etc., for the announcers and engineers." After several months he "began to be 'rewarded' with announcing and production 'tips,' copies of scripts, ABC network correspondence, a chance for more 'on the air' work, and perhaps most treasured of all, used broadcast discs of local and ABC shows," which he now recycles in his vintage radio programming.

Looking back to those apprenticeship days, Tom Heathwood recalls how various kinds of remote broadcasts seemed to invite technical problems:

When I was doing a Sunday morning shift at WKOX-AM in Framingham, Massachusetts, I introduced the minister who was about to deliver his weekly sermon. At the appropriate hour of 10 a.m. I flipped the key, and he began his talk. I flipped another key and cut him off the control room monitor. Then I picked up one of my favorite C & W records of the day, "Movin' On" by Hank Snow, put it on the turntable, and sat back and began to enjoy one of Hank's big hits. Within a minute the five-line telephone was lit up—people calling in indignation that I should be playing such a song and drowning out the Good Reverend who was speaking that day on how to insure a better path to Heaven. To say that I was embarrassed would be putting it mildly. The incident was so anxiety-producing I was barely able to do the live introduction to the transcribed Sunday feature "Puck, the Comic Weekly."

Bill Sherman and Nelson Bragg were still doing Man in the Street shows in the Boston area when I was a junior apprentice. From them I learned the art of interviewing people who had nothing to say. Frequently they would literally grab people on the sidewalk and coerce them into talking on the radio. Sometimes this was a big mistake because these people had no opinion about anything and were often so frightened that they became mute. Try to talk your way out of an "interview" when the other person won't talk. I think that's why the Man in the Street came back inside!

No matter where you lived, there were remotes. Everything from the Dog Show to the World's Fair, the Hog-Calling Contest to the Christmas High School Choir and Orchestra Pageant. The radio remote was a thing of very special interest. It was REAL!

In its first thirty years, then, radio strained at both ends of the representational spectrum. In some types of program, especially informational ones and those sponsored by toney clients, radio professionalism was expressed in a polished, sometimes "too-perfect" manner of delivery; a mere station break or a timecheck might assume a tone of oracular revelation. Although H. V. Kaltenborn, Elmer Davis, and H. R. Baukhage exhibited clear regional or ethnic speech characteristics in their newscasts, the "neutral" midwestern speaking style was thought to be a great advantage to would-be announcers, and the networks assembled thick pronunciation guides for on-air personnel. Compiled by James F. Bender and first issued for public sale in 1943, *The NBC Handbook of Pronunciation* manifested the network's care and authority in matters of "General American speech."[1] "Proper" radio speech became something of a fetish for some network executives, and announcing school enrollees were drilled in subtleties of intonation and articulation.

On the other hand, radio's entertainment programs were inheritors of vaudeville and minstrel traditions, where ethnic speech patterns were not only tolerated but were essential. The brogues of sportscasters and of many musical performers further illustrated the variety of American speech. If Titus Moody, Mortimer Snerd, George "Kingfish" Stevens, Tonto, the Old Wrangler, the Old Timer, Charlie Chan, and Mrs. Nussbaum represented varying degrees of exaggeration, then the guests in radio's quizzes, man-in-the-street interviews, talent searches, and other audience participation programs kept the medium reasonably honest. Even when these programs were not the most amusing, the most informative, or the most uplifting fare available, they constituted a mirror in which the audience could dwell.

NOTE

1. New York: Crowell, 1943. The quoted phrase is from the Preface to the third edition (1964), revised by Thomas Lee Crowell, Jr. (p. vii).

17

Radio Travels: Memory, Time, and Place

Fifty years ago, moviegoers were dazzled by the RKO Radio Pictures screen logo, a colossal transmission tower, its legs spanning a plaster of Paris globe and its top beaming lightning-bolt sound signals. The German language offers an evocative word for this radio phenomenon: *"Rundfunk"*— "round-spark," an expanding circle of airborne energy like a ripple in a celestial pool. Theoretically, as the popular explainers of science and technology have often said, the space traveler of 2000+ should be able to pursue those ever-expanding radio signals, to chuckle again at what the Kingfish says to Amos, to catch up with the lost episodes of "I Love a Mystery," to hear Edward R. Murrow say (as if he were still standing on a London rooftop during an air raid) "This . . . is London," or to find Mr. Keen still tracing lost persons among the nebulae and the darting asteroids.

On a less cosmic scale, U. S. programming has passed across many national borders, carried by transcriptions or by powerful signals, by the entertainment and information purposes of Armed Forces Radio, and by the memories of American expatriates, business travelers, military and diplomatic personnel, exchange students, and others. By comparison and contrast, immigrants to the United States have helped to define the distinctive qualities and the spreading influence of American broadcasting. Today, Old Time Radio collectors pursue their memories (genuine or ersatz) of favored programs through transcription disc, cassette, and reel-to-reel holdings, while radio clubs and historical societies continue the work of preserving and detailing the record of radio's early decades. Radio newsletters, conventions (usually featuring program re-creations and appearances by veteran broadcasters), and tape exchanges preserve much of what is essentially a transient enterprise.

A seasoned radio listener by the time he entered college in 1948, Roger Rollin knew that the medium and his relationship to it were rapidly changing. "After graduation," he says, "I enlisted in the Army and for three years heard almost no radio, except Soviet military transmissions. I was stationed in Austria and Germany for a year and a half and on occasion was able to listen to the Armed Forces Radio Network. With American news readers and disc jockeys, AFR was like a burger at the PX — a little bit of America in what seemed a far-off place." Later, his military service completed and his academic career underway, Roger Rollin made still further discoveries:

In 1965 I took my wife, son, and daughter to England for a year's sabbatical leave. Our landlord provided a radio, but no TV, so for about fourteen months BBC radio was our mainstay. We tuned in in the morning while I was lighting the coal fire in the dining room (which became our living room also) and seldom turned it off. It was endlessly fascinating. We never got tired of the variety of U.K. accents, most of which were hilariously mocked on comedy programs like "I'm Sorry, I'll Read That Again." We loved quiz shows like "My Word" and "My Music" (which are still being recycled on National Public Radio), the news (although we lived in Oxford, our local news was for The Southeast), and even the weather (which tended at best to feature "sunny spells"). The BBC spoiled us. After we returned to the States, we could hear nothing like it — until National Public Radio came into our listening lives.

By the time George A. Walker, Jr. entered the service in the mid-1940s, he had developed a "longstanding romance, if you will, with that box," and he carried his affection for radio through his military career: "I have spent a lot of time at sea on USN hydrographic survey vessels, and getting close enough to land to pick up a radio broadcast, in any language, was always a big highlight. Adequate shortwave radios were not always available. Tuning in to the BBC was always a real treat. One of my smaller but bigger pleasures of life is to be on the beach with a book and a radio tuned to the public broadcasting network or to music of my era, and I have even been known to pop a beer or two after the sun is well over the yard arm."

During the 1950s, Dr. Jeanne Kenmore made several trips to England for summer visits with her pen pals of the 1940s, and she found that radio's representation of the United States, particularly on The Voice of America, had raised many "pointed questions" in her hosts:

Have you no problems in the USA? No poverty, no racial problems, no scandals? Why is everything presented in a 100% positive vein?

Why do Americans think they invented everything from electric lights to democracy, from poetry to mountains . . . ?

Why do Americans think that they have the best country — for EVERYTHING? Best education, best hospitals, best films, best . . . ?

What is the point of The Voice of America? To beg people to move there? To brag? To look down on other places? To get people to vote with the USA in the United Nations?

Of her six-year stay in Germany, Jeanne Kenmore says, "As you know, the USA has a lot of service people there. Two radio stations broadcast *by* them *for* themselves. To fill the hours, old radio shows were played every evening from 7 p.m. on. You can imagine that I listened nostalgically. The old cellar safe of Benny, the closet of McGee, the 'true' stories of the FBI. What a way to relive parts of one's youth!" Mixed with the nostalgia of Armed Forces Radio offerings were fresh perspectives offered at many points on the dial: "The best music program was a half hour of jazz on Sunday from Moscow! Alistair Cooke's thirteen-minute broadcast [from America for the BBC], heard at 1 a.m. South India time, was the best — and only — presentation of two or even three sides of any question. From 1955 to 1987, I listened to him from many countries, setting my alarm clock when necessary so that I could catch him in the middle of the night. He loved America, but he was able to talk about the underbelly of problems. You should have heard him on Nixon! Or Reagan! Or Christmas in Vermont with his daughter. Ah. . . . !"

The radio habit is still with Jeanne Kenmore:

During my late teens and my years as a young adult, the radio provided our views of the world: news, humor, drama, music, the people of the world, past and present.

Today I listen to news or classical music in my car. But after it is dark, my small short wave radio can pick up music from Moscow, politics from the Philippines, debates from South Africa, opera from Vienna, drama from Stockholm, and so on. Since I know several languages, I can visit all around the world by turning two knobs. TV gives breathtaking visual presentations, but radio allows one to use imagination. I don't need TV to enjoy *Macbeth*, *A Doll's House*, or discussions between the Prime Minister and someone from the Labour Party, or to understand reports of a mine disaster in Italy or an earthquake in Guatemala.

That is a long radio journey from her first acquaintance with the medium (detailed earlier in this book), when she sat for hours on the porch of a

Minneapolis duplex during the Depression and listened to the neighbors'
radio because there was none in her own home.

In his mid-nineteenth-century optimism for a growing America, Walt
Whitman graciously welcomed immigrants from all nations, seeing them
as the best "ambassadors" of their homelands and as further contributors to
the diversity of American life. In the mid-twentieth century and beyond,
circumstances of marriage, war, and opportunity have brought a new infu-
sion of "visitors," many of whom have become naturalized citizens. In
some ways their homelands had prepared them for the experience of listening to radio in the United States; in other ways, American commercial radio was a shock. Three representative accounts, useful in their compari-
sons and contrasts, follow.

Describing herself as "a seventy-year-old female, only four feet, ten
inches tall" who "can still run a mile in nine minutes, although only five
years ago I could do it in seven minutes," Joyce Holgate DeMille lives in
the plantations-and-roses city of Thomasville, Georgia, but she first knew
radio in England during the era when Americans were listening to Rudy
Vallee, Graham McNamee, and the daily adventures of Amos 'n' Andy:

Weekdays in the '30s seem to have been occupied with school, homework, taking
the dog for walks or playing outside. . . . So weekends stand out in my memory of
radio — especially listening to "In Town Tonight" (BBC) on Saturday evenings
while sitting round the open fireplace with the family (five of us altogether, including parents) and eating Saturday Night Assortment, candies individually
wrapped in a box. The introductory music lingers in my memory, written by a
well-known British composer (Eric Coates, I think it was) and interrupted by a
stentorian voice repeating "In town tonight," followed by "Halt" in a loud dictato-
rial tone, and the London traffic noise came to a sudden stop. This program became a special favorite during the war years when comedians like little Arthur
Askey became famous for his imitations of a London bus conductor and made the
phrase "Oi thank yew" in his inimitable cockney accent a part of everyday language.

On Sundays while eating family dinner at 1 p.m. we listened to Mr. Middleton
talk on gardening, we teenagers having to keep silent, but sometimes even we
found him interesting, each having our own little vegetable plot. Also, of course,
there was Alistair Cooke with his "Letter from America." Then I remember my
father and grandfather listening to soccer matches on Saturday afternoons.

We listened to Dickens's "A Christmas Carol" while decorating the tree on
Christmas Eve with real candles in the early '30s. (We celebrated the twelve days
of Christmas in England in those days — before this it was Advent in the Church
of England.) This may be my very first recollection of radio, this and "The Children's

Hour" at 5 o'clock, introduced by the haunting melody of "The Teddy Bears' Picnic."

On Christmas Day everybody stopped what they were doing to listen to the King's speech. (Now it would be the Queen, of course.)

We lived in a small town between the then-active Croydon airdrome and London. In early September 1940, we watched part of the Battle of Britain while painting the house. (Needless to say, my father made us go inside as German pilots were parachuting down in nearby gardens.) Listening to war news as we sat in front of the fireplace on winter evenings, hooking a large rug, even [helped by] my father, who was then an air raid warden and would often have to leave; we each working on a corner of the rug while hearing bombs and/or anti-aircraft flak as background noise.

Then by 1942 I was working in the BBC Overseas Department in Broadcasting House in London, where "This Is London" news was broadcast in forty-eight languages from below-ground studios to underground peoples in countries occupied by the Germans. I was secretary in the Norwegian Section, where I helped write programs into which the Norwegian writers and announcers who had escaped from Norway interspersed code messages informing underground workers in Norway about the dropping of radios and so on. Of course, I was not told what or where the messages were. (I had received letters on rice paper mentioning places and people by the pet names I had given them. A child in Norway wrote with a plea to wish the then King Haakon of Norway a happy birthday. So I sent the letter on to him, telling him that I could translate the names if he wished. So he sent for me in audience. I remember how proud I was but had been told to walk casually from a bus or taxi some distance away so as not to bring attention to myself because of spies and not to tell anyone where I was going.)

After the war I listened to Riks Krinkasting, the State-run radio in Norway. Then later, in Germany in 1949 I listened to the Armed Forces network news (AFN), especially to a fast-talking Canadian announcer whom I tried to take down in shorthand in order to be able to qualify as a court reporter for the USAF at Rhein-Main, Frankfurt, where my new GI husband was stationed. Of course there were no commercials on AFN radio, but later, Stateside, I recall my husband listening to football games and getting very excited and unapproachable during same, while I was constantly amazed at the ever-occurring commercials.

Now a retired textiles executive living in the United States, Siegfried Poser remembers the crystal sets built by relatives and friends in Germany during the late 1920s, but since his father was "opposed to radio," the household did not own a receiver until a console set was bought in 1939. Siegfried Poser's wife, Ingrid, dates her first radio recollections from a few years later than his. Both fondly recall the distinctive prewar musical signatures of the major German broadcasting stations, particularly those of Hamburg and Leipzig, the latter celebrating its historic association with J. S. Bach, cantor and organist of the Leipzig Cathedral, by adopting the sequence of notes that (in German notation) "spell out" B-A-C-H. They also remember that historical drama was impressively presented on German radio in the 1930s, the life of Frederick the Great being a favored subject. News summaries were given every hour on the hour, and from 6 to 7 p.m a comprehensive program of news and commentary was offered. Fancy program guides were published in that era.

Sports events drew great interest in Germany as well as in the United States in the 1920s and 1930s, and Siegfried Poser remembers crowding into a small apartment "with ten other guys" to hear the quickly decided 1938 Max Schmeling-Joe Louis bout from Yankee Stadium, carried live at 3 a.m. German time. "The damned thing was over before we all got settled," he comments, and the Posers recall that the boxing contest had prompted restaurants and sidewalk cafes to stay open all night so that customers might listen to the fight and, they hoped, celebrate the victory that did not come.

Mornings were devoted to educational and scientific programs, and German stations did their part in the national physical fitness movement that coincided with Ingrid Poser's childhood during the 1930s. Every morning brought gymnastics programs as well as children's sing-alongs, and even young children participated in these activities, directed by the radio voices received in the typical kitchen or living room. In her home, the first radio was a large brown Gothic-style set made from walnut. Through that instrument Ingrid Poser was especially eager to hear the "Leipzig Children's Hour," which blended games, readings of fairy tales, and gymnastic exercises at 3:00 each afternoon, and the bedtime story offered by the *Sandmännchen* (Little Sandman) brought a contented ending to each day. On the other hand, she and her sister were frightened when the intense voices of Adolf Hitler and Joseph Goebbels entered their playroom through broadcast speeches and rallies.

At the beginning of World War II, a fine Telefunken set cost about 550 Deutschmarks, while most families were satisfied with medium-priced radios in the 150- to 200-marks range (equivalent to $80 or $90 in U.S. funds). When Joseph Goebbels became Hitler's information minister, he directed that a "people's radio," receiving only the medium-wave band, be produced to sell at the equivalent of $15 in U. S. currency. The Posers remember it as a small, inelegant black box, a woven grille covering the speaker, with a circular dial on the bottom. The people for whom the "people's radio" was intended soon began to refer to this modest receiving instrument privately as *Göbbels Schnauze* ("Goebbels's Snout").

Under the Nazi government, listening to foreign broadcasts was illegal — in fact, a capital offense — but many families took their chances. Siegfried Poser recalls the day, probably in 1940, when a heavy knock came on the front door while the family was listening to the BBC; his mother fainted in fear when she heard the rapping. The visitor proved to be only an uncle who had been drafted into the German army and had come to say "goodbye." The Posers' listening to forbidden frequencies remained undetected by the authorities.

In those early war years, too, programs were often interrupted by a thundering passage from Franz Liszt's symphonic poem *Les Preludes* or by portentious orchestral phrases from Wagnerian opera, used as bridges to announcements of German battlefield victories. As the months passed, Siegfried Poser wryly notes, the victory announcements and their sonorous introductions "got rarer and rarer. Then they ceased altogether." (Ironically, children in the United States during those years would have recognized the same heroic-sounding Lisztian music as a bridge to the mid-program commercial on "The Lone Ranger" three times a week; they knew that the Masked Man was well on his way to tracking down the bad guys at that juncture. But the definitions of "good guys" and "bad guys" were very different in the two countries then.)

In his early teens, Siegfried Poser was often taken out of school and assigned to potato picking, but "I always got home for the radio concerts." After the war he came to the United States, and he was startled to find that the symphonic radio concerts were sponsored here: "Some very fine Brahms and then a cigarette commercial." He found it jarring, but he proved adaptable to this and other American ways, as he established permanent residence here.

Maurice A. Howe, a native of Australia and a psychologist by training, is a part-time visiting lecturer at the University of Massachusetts at Amherst, and he operates the exchange organization Education Australia. His youthful radio fare included an Australian rebroadcast of the U.S. aviation adventure series "Howie Wing," begun on CBS in 1938, and an adaptation of "The Lux Radio Theatre," the scripts being performed by Australian actors, according to John O'Hara, Director of the Australian Film, Television, and Radio School. Here is Maurice Howe's account of how radio, including elements of United States broadcasting, came into his family during his younger years:

"Phillips is your best buy, Fran. I can let you have this one for 24 pounds — I'm practically losing money at that price, but seeing you are my sister and all . . . ."

"Yeah, yeah. I'm sure you're not losing money, but what is it about the Phillips that's so good?"

"Well, check the cabinet for a start. This is not just a radio. This is a piece of furniture you'd be proud to have in your lounge room. And then, it can get short wave as well as local stations. All you have to do is to turn this knob. Here, I'll show you."

Uncle Noel clicked the knob, and we all listened to a series of screeches and whistles and occasional ditt-ditt-ditts of Morse code. Once or twice we heard foreign voices, and then there was a snatch of some oriental music. Finally, a voice in British English announced that this was the Overseas Service of the BBC, and we all listened with rapt attention to a minute or two of the news.

My mother had decided that it was time to enter the twentieth century and that purchasing a radio was one tangible way to do this. Of course, it was no coincidence that her brother, uncle Noel, was an electrician and had a shop just two blocks away, and that his latest entrepreneurial venture was radio. He used to drop in for tea several times a week and was very willing to share his enthusiasm for this latest marvel. They were selling well, and uncle Noel predicted that within ten years every home in Australia would have one. So we bought the Phillips, and listening to radio quickly became part of our daily routine.

The evening was the best time. "Howie Wing" came on at 6:30, followed by "Dad and Dave" at 6:45, and then there was the news at 7.

I used to like to lie on the carpet in front of the radio with my head practically inside it, listening to every word. You had to get it right because what happened during that half hour was the main topic of conversation at school the next day, and you would be really out of it if you couldn't respond with, "Yeah. And then there was that part where Dave had a date with Mabel and he couldn't get the old Ford to start afterwards and they had to walk five miles home, and Dave was late for the milking."

The story didn't ever go anywhere much — just a never-ending string of incidents — crises and funny situations — punctuated by theme music (from a popular song of the day about "Winding back / To that old-fashioned shack" on the Gundagai road) and advertisements for Bonnington's Irish Moss, "made from Pectoral Oxymel of Karageen, a rare seaweed, found off the west coast of Ireland. Up North [sounds of blizzard and coughing], where lives depend on it [more blizzard sounds], they take Bonnington's Irish Moss."

These were my special programs, but there was something on the radio for everyone. My parents listened to the news, which was my signal to go off and do my homework, and then on Sunday nights there was "The Lux Radio Theatre," and we all listened to that.

I don't remember exactly when it was, but at some stage Bogey and Bacall became regular Sunday night listening, as they cruised around the Caribbean and had weekly scrapes with bad guys and talked to us about life, in their inimitable fashion. Usually these episodes were studded with crooks who always spoke in

German accents, and heavy-handed cops and coast guards who made it difficult for Bogey by arresting him or taking away his passport.

We've come a long way since then. There were those who predicted that radio, like Bogey, would have died years ago. But they were wrong. The cabinets, shapes, sizes of radio have all changed radically, and so too has its place in our lives. But few of us would be without radio as we drive to work or to a favorite vacation spot. Music is the predominant fare in our car these days, but then again, there is nothing quite like listening to the news. Maybe things haven't changed all that much. Seems like my parents voted for the radio news as number one, all those years ago.

In the United States today, nostalgia rebroadcasts satisfy some listeners' wishes to hear their early favorites again. "We have Old Time Radio shows still playing in the Chicago area every day," says Thomas Fetters. "One of my big thrills was solving a Dick Tracy code given at the end of a show, using simple alphabet substitution (and a bit of deduction) and calling up to go live on the air with the solution. What a thrill to actually break a Dick Tracy code on the air some forty years after the show originally aired!"

In Hobbs, New Mexico, Frank Bell discovered about 1990 that he had become "irritated with local radio because of its being only rock, goat roper, or synthetic synthesized music. I went down to the local library to see what they had for loan and found the same thing, but there was one 'Amos 'n' Andy' tape and a few Big Band tapes, and I was again hooked. Shortly thereafter I bought several OTR shows, then started trading. Now my catalog lists over 3,500 of those same shows I listened to as a lonesome kid living in the country back in Tennessee. I particularly like OTR when I am working alone or am on the road."

Bob Morgan rediscovered familiar programs about 1975, when he was a letter carrier in Atlanta. "One day I had a package for a patron of mine and noticed that it had a return label about old time radio programs," he says. "The company was Radiola in Sandy Hook, Connecticut. When I delivered the package, I asked if that was what it was, and from there we developed a conversation. He agreed to make a copy of two 'Lum and Abner' shows for me later on." After that inquiry Bob Morgan purchased a number of radio comedy records, then accumulated more and more tape copies of "Amos 'n' Andy" and "Lum and Abner" episodes, which he purchased or traded though a widening network of sellers and collectors. "Anytime I want to enjoy a good laugh," he adds, "all I need to do is put on an 'Amos 'n' Andy' program. Anytime I want to know what is happening down in Pine Ridge at the Jot 'Em Down Store, all I have to do is put on a 'Lum and Abner' tape."

Ken Weigel has pursued less specialized tape collecting in his desire to catch up on some delights that he had missed and to recapture moments that he had heard:

I began collecting OTR about fifteen years ago. With diligence, and at times greed bordering on avarice, I've built a small trove of some 5,000 hours — enough to acquaint myself with some of the shows that left the air before the stork dropped me off, and to rediscover many old favorites. I've found that the most enjoyable time to listen to them is bedtime. I suppose I should mention that this late-night listening has cured me of insomnia. It would be criminal of me not to remind OTR fans that there really is no need to toss and turn or stare up at the ceiling. If you think about it, after you toss, you usually turn, so you end up right back where you started, and there's no point in that. As for the ceiling, there's nothing up there to stare at. With my method, one minute Raymond from "Inner Sanctum" is stepping through the creaking door and telling a sick joke, and the next you're out-snoring Bickerson himself.

It works, at least, in Van Nuys, California. In San Lorenzo, Larry Telles expresses his link to his radio past through a collection of antique radios, carefully maintained.

Titus Moody, the crotchety New England farmer played by Parker Fennelly on "The Fred Allen Show," once dismissed radio as "furniture that talks." But, as the Southern Senator Beauregard Claghorn, another habitué of Allen's Alley, was wont to say, "That's a joke, son!" As the broadcast television era begins to yield to a new entertainment and information era of cable, home satellite dishes, and CD-ROM, it is possible to see radio's real contribution as the first electronic medium to enter the home and the workplace. For the first time, inhabitants of lonely prairie towns and sleepy Southern villages were placed, by sound carried at the speed of light, on equal footing with city folk in their access to the news, gossip, music, and dramatic entertainment of the day — indeed, of the moment. Vintage radio was everyman's Scheherazade, and everyman's and everywoman's child, adept at tuning, could draw many times 1,001 nights' worth of magic from it.

Thus the power of the medium that does all the voices and plays all the tunes — or at least did, well within living memory.

18

Staying Tuned: Contemporary Sources for Old-Time Radio

Vintage radio produced more than thirty years' worth of broadcasts on several national and regional networks and on hundreds of local stations. The written and the electronically preserved record of that enormous output is necessarily scattered and incomplete. However, anyone wanting to become acquainted with programs from radio's earliest decades might profitably take one or more directions: reading from (and beyond) the small shelf of standard radio histories and reference volumes; subscribing to the academic journals, the newsletters, or the nostalgia publications centered on or frequently featuring broadcast material; joining one of the national, regional, or local radio clubs; attending the national Old Time Radio conventions held annually in Los Angeles, Cincinnati, Newark, and elsewhere. Many radio clubs have large lending libraries of tapes and print materials, and many commercial packagers offer cassettes for retail sale, with best remembered series titles often being readily available in record stores, chain restaurants, and tourist shopping outlets. Radio rebroadcasts may be heard weekly or daily on AM or FM stations and through cable systems in some areas. The following paragraphs survey several means of pursuing vintage radio interests.

Erik Barnouw's three-volume *A History of Broadcasting in the United States* stands as the most comprehensive narrative of radio's development. The first installment, published in 1966 under the title *A Tower in Babel*, traces the medium's pioneering days to 1933, while *The Golden Web*, issued in 1968, details the following twenty years of radio (and television) history, and *The Image Empire* covers the period between 1953 and its

1970 publication date. Harrison Summers' *A Thirty-Year History of Programs Carried on National Radio Networks in the United States, 1926-1956*, published in 1958, is a valuable shelfmate to the Barnouw volumes. Susan Douglas, in her 1987 study, *Inventing American Broadcasting, 1899 - 1922*, provides a fascinating chronicle of the early technological and entrepreneurial developments leading to programmed broadcasting. Tom Lewis's *Empire of the Air: The Men Who Made Radio* (1991) is the companion book to the public television film of the same title by Ken Burns. This account sees the development of radio through the careers of inventor-manufacturer Lee De Forest, FM innovator Edwin H. Armstrong, and RCA founder David Sarnoff.

Usefully placing radio within the context of American popular culture, J. Fred MacDonald draws details from fan magazines, *Billboard* articles and advertisements, and reports from early program ratings services to create a fresh perspective in his *Don't Touch That Dial: Radio Programming in American Life, 1920-1960*, published in 1979. Jim Harmon taps his longstanding enthusiasm for radio and Western film heroes to provide cross-media syntheses in *Radio Mystery and Adventure and Its Appearances in Film, Television, and Other Media* (1992) and in the lamentably out-of-print *The Great Radio Heroes* (1967).

Although radio is famously a medium of the imagination, some devotees will want to see what its performers and other movers looked like. Irving Settel's 1960 book *A Pictorial History of Radio* more than adequately fulfills its title's promise. Well-stocked libraries or used book shops will perhaps be able to supply Robert Campbell's *The Golden Years of Broadcasting* (1976), an illustrated celebration of the National Broadcasting Company's first fifty years. The Smithsonian Institution Press has issued the exhibition catalog *On the Air: Pioneers of American Broadcasting* as a record of the joint presentation in 1988 and 1989 of the National Portrait Gallery in Washington and the Museum of Broadcasting in New York.

Vintage radio sets are worthy of picturing too, as David and Betty Johnson demonstrate in their *Guide to Old Radios: Pointers, Pictures, and Prices* (1989), which balances an informative text with a generous number of (largely black and white) illustrations. Those interested in handsome color photographs of Deco bakelite and similar types of radio receivers from the 1930s and 1940s will want to seek out *Radios: The Golden Age* (1987) and *Radios Redux: Listening in Style* (1991), both written by Philip Collins and illustrated from his collection. The Vestal Press in Vestal, New York, has reprinted a variety of catalogs showing antique radios and designating their model numbers and features. Morgan E. McMahon's collectors' guides to vintage radios have been reissued by Antique Electronic Supply, 688 W. First Street, Tempe, AZ 85281.

Thomas DeLong's *The Mighty Music Box* (1980) tells of radio's and the phonograph's roles in the evolution of American musical tastes. Arthur Frank Wertheim's *Radio Comedy* (1979) is a well-balanced survey of a major broadcast genre, and veteran soap opera actress Mary Jane Higby's *Tune In Tomorrow* (1968) is a lively insider's account of adventures not only in the sudsy serial trade but also in the technical developments and the managerial machinations that accompanied the growth of the major networks. The essay collection *Speaking of Soap Operas*, edited by Robert C. Allen (1985), offers a variety of analyses. No radio enthusiast should leave unread James Thurber's classic essay "Soapland" (collected in *The Beast in Me and Other Animals*, 1948), and Brock Brower's "A Lament for Old-Time Radio" in the April 1960 issue of *Esquire* is a model of nostalgic evocation. Biographies and autobiographies of leading radio personalities abound, in and out of print.

New editions are due (and, in both cases, have been promised) of two highly useful reference volumes, both alphabetically arranged by program titles. John Dunning's 1976 book *Tune In Yesterday: The Ultimate Encyclopedia of Old-Time Radio, 1925 - 1976* offers entries, a single paragraph to several pages in length, on all major programs and many less well known ones. Dunning's discussions include details of casts, sponsors, premiere and ending dates, network or local station originations, and representative story lines. Frank Buxton and Bill Owen provide succinct listings of casts, opening lines and catch phrases, networks, series beginning dates, and (for most listings) thumbnail descriptions of programs in their *The Big Broadcast, 1920 - 1950*, published in 1972 as an expanded version of the same authors' 1966 effort *Radio's Golden Age*.

Subscribers to the bimonthly *Hello Again* will attest that the publication and its editor constitute a veritable clearinghouse of Old-Time Radio activity today. Jay A. Hickerson (Box 4321, Hamden, CT 06514) is the organizer of an annual convention in Newark, New Jersey, and his newsletter ($15.00 per year, in January 1996) keeps its readers well informed of recently published books, articles, catalogs, and program logs and of newly discovered and newly circulated recordings. *Hello Again* is, in effect, a bulletin board for individuals and clubs involved in every aspect of Old-Time Radio, and it is a guide to Mr. Hickerson's own useful reference publications. Chief among those is *The Ultimate History of Network Radio Programming and Guide to All Circulating Shows* (1992), with supplements issued annually. Not a narrative chronicle, this volume devotes most of its pages to the listing of all programs known to be available in taped copies from a variety of sources. The early pages of *The Ultimate History* provide names and addresses of log preparers, radio publications, clubs, and tape dealers and hobbyist traders. Lists of program sponsors and their products and of band remote broadcast locations are also included. Any inquiry sent to Mr. Hickerson or to collectors listed in his publications (and to the organizations discussed below) should be accompanied by a stamped, self-addressed envelope.

While especially active radio clubs are centered in Buffalo, Cincinnati, Denver, Washington, D.C., and other cities, two organizations merit mention as "national" membership groups. The North American Radio Archives maintains reel-to-reel, cassette, and print materials libraries and issues both the quarterly *NARA News* and the occasional publication *Through the Horn*. These NARA journals offer feature articles, columns and other personal commentary, and reprints of newspaper and magazine articles. The rental cassette library contains about 20,000 programs, with 50,000 further programs (from NBC) expected to be added in 1995. The NARA membership director is Janis DeMoss, 134 Vincewood Drive, Nicholasville, KY 40356. The membership rate in January 1996 is $20.00 per year by check payable to "NARA."

The Society to Preserve and Encourage Radio Drama, Variety, and Comedy holds monthly meetings and annual conventions in the Los Angeles area, but many of its activities draw national participation. For this reason SPERDVAC was the subject of an article by Leonard Maltin in the March 1987 issue of *Smithsonian*. As Maltin points out, the blind brothers John and Larry Gassman are significant figures in this organization, and their influence has made SPERDVAC especially sensitive to the needs of sight-impaired persons. For instance, the monthly *SPERDVAC Radiogram* is available to blind members in audiocassette form. Currently boasting a paid membership of over 1,600, this organization maintains general and archives libraries (some portions of which are occasionally declared "closed by earthquake") as well as a printed materials collection. The full membership rate (in January 1996) is $25.00 for the first year (when the new member will receive a complete listing of loan holdings) and $15.00 for renewals. Annual subscriptions to the *Radiogram* only may be had for $15.00. Membership and subscription checks may be directed to Carrolyn Rawski, P.O. Box 2236, Chino Valley, AZ 86323-2236. The general information and official business address is P.O. Box 7177, Van Nuys, CA 91409-7177.

The Journal of Radio Studies was begun in 1992 in recognition of radio's having taken a back seat to television in mass communications studies.

Noting that "radio is deeply rooted in the American life style and culture," the founding editors have opened their pages to "new opportunities for scholarship, whether critical, descriptive, empirical, philosophical, or comparative." Subscriptions are $15.00 for each annual issue, obtainable from Martin P. LoMonaco, Managing Editor; Department of Communications; Nassau Community College; Garden City, NY 11530-6793. Inquiries about editorial matters may be addressed to Frank J. Chorba, Editor; Communications Department; Washburn University; Topeka, KS 66621. Dr. Chorba is also the chairperson of the Radio-Interest Area of the Popular Culture Association of America, whose annual meetings occur each spring in a variety of cities.

Many nostalgia and collector publications feature articles, anecdotal items, and listings concerned with radio listening memories, premiums, antique radio sets, and so on. The colorful bimonthly *Reminisce* attractively showcases its readers' radio memories with variable frequency. The January-February 1995 issue, being reasonably typical, contains a one-page article on "Inner Sanctum," a three-page feature on a variety of listeners' recollections, one single-paragraph radio anecdote, and two articles on bands and singers often heard on the air. Toy collector, auction survey, and other publications provide information and current market prices for adventure series premiums, Charlie McCarthy memorabilia, and other radio-related collectibles.

Rebroadcasts of vintage programs may be heard in many cities. In some locations, especially on the West Coast, these presentations include interviews with the stars, directors, or writers of the programs being heard. Individual station schedules are too highly variable to allow listing here. Available by satellite and carried on some FM stations and cable systems is the Yesterday USA Superstation, a service of Bill Bragg's National Museum of Communications in Richardson, Texas. On some college radio stations and in cities where retiree populations are strong (Hendersonville, North Carolina, and a number of California communities, for instance), radio drama enthusiasts continue to produce new scripts and fresh performances of previously produced ones. Thus, although one might have to search a bit for it, there is a tantalizing bit of "old" radio on the air in "new" radio times.

Such vessels.

Such wine.

Bibliography

A. BOOKS AND ARTICLES

Allen, Robert C. *Speaking of Soap Operas*. Chapel Hill and London: The University of North Carolina Press, 1985.

Barnouw. Erik. *A Tower in Babel: A History of Broadcasting in the United States to 1933*. New York: Oxford University Press, 1966.

——————. *The Golden Web: A History of Broadcasting in the United States, 1933-1953*. New York: Oxford University Press, 1968.

——————. *The Image Empire: A History of Broadcasting in the United States Since 1953*. New York: Oxford University Press, 1970.

Bender, James F. *The NBC Handbook of Pronunciation*, 3d ed., revised by Thomas Lee Crowell, Jr. New York: Crowell, 1943.

Billy Whiskers and the Radio. Akron and New York: Saalfield, 1927.

Boyce, Mary Louise. "Letters," *Washington Post*, 15 January 1937; 8.

Brower, Brock. "A Lament for Old-Time Radio." *Esquire* 53 (April 1960); 148-150.

Brown, Richard. [untitled item]. In Ron Alexander, "Metropolitan Diary," *New York Times*, 17 February 1994; 18.

Buxton, Frank, and Bill Owen. *The Big Broadcast, 1920-1950* [Revised edition of *Radio's Golden Age*]. New York: Viking, 1972.

Campbell, Robert. *The Golden Years of Broadcasting: A Celebration of the First Fifty Years of Radio and TV on NBC*. New York: Scribner, 1976.

Collins, Philip. *Radios: The Golden Age*. San Francisco: Chronicle Books, 1987.

——————. *Radios Redux: Listening in Style*. San Francisco: Chronicle Books, 1991.

[Correll, Charles J., and Freeman F. Gosden]. *All About Amos 'n' Andy and Their Creators Correll and Gosden*. New York: Rand McNally, 1929.

DeLong, Thomas A. *The Mighty Music Box: The Golden Age of Musical Radio.* Los Angeles: Amber Crest Books, 1980.

Douglas, Susan. *Inventing American Broadcasting: 1899-1922.* Baltimore and London: The Johns Hopkins University Press, 1987.

Dunning, John. *Tune In Yesterday: The Ultimate Encyclopedia of Old-Time Radio, 1925-1976.* Englewood Cliffs, N. J.: Prentice-Hall, 1976.

Fincher, Jack. "By Convention, the Enemy Within Never Did Without," *Smithsonian*, 26, 3 (June 1995); 126-143.

Goldberg, Vicki. "Photography View: Setting the Standards for War Pictures," *New York Times*, June 5, 1994; 34H.

Hall, Jacquelyn Dowd, James Leloudis, Robert Korstad, Mary Murphy, Lu Ann Jones, and Christopher B. Daly. *Like a Family: The Making of a Southern Cotton Mill World.* Chapel Hill and London: The University of North Carolina Press, 1987.

Harmon, Jim. *The Great Radio Heroes.* New York: Ace Books, 1967.
————. *Radio Mystery and Adventure and Its Appearances in Film, Television, and Other Media.* Jefferson, N. C., and London: McFarland and Company, 1992.

Hickerson, Jay. *The Ultimate History of Network Radio Programming and Guide to All Circulating Shows*, second edition. Hamden, CT: Jay Hickerson, 1992 [with Supplements].

Higby, Mary Jane. *Tune In Tomorrow.* New York: Cowles, 1968.

Johnson, David and Betty. *Guide to Old Radios: Pointers, Pictures, and Prices.* Radnor, PA: Wallace-Homestead, 1989.

J. W. W., "Excerpts from Our Letters," *Washington Post*, January 31, 1937, Features section; 9B.

Keillor, Garrison. *WLT: A Radio Romance.* New York: Viking-Penguin, 1991.

Koch, Howard. *The Panic Broadcast: The Whole Story of the Night the Martians Landed.* New York: Avon Books, 1970.

Lewis, Tom. *Empire of the Air: The Men Who Made Radio.* New York: HarperCollins, 1991.

MacDonald, J. Fred. *Don't Touch That Dial: Radio Programming in American Life, 1920-1960.* Chicago: Nelson-Hall, 1979.

Maltin, Leonard. "They're Tuned In to the 'Thrilling Days of Yesteryear,'" *Smithsonian*, 17, 12 (March 1987); 70-79.

"Modern Living: Rip Van Ranger," *Time*, 103 (April 29, 1974); 71, 73.

National Broadcasting Company. *The Fourth Chime.* n.p.: NBC, 1944.

National Portrait Gallery/The Museum of Broadcasting. *On the Air: Pioneers of American Broadcasting.* Washington, D. C.: Smithsonian Institution Press, 1988.

Opt, Susan K. "The Development of Rural Wired Radio Systems in Upstate South Carolina," *Journal of Radio Studies*, 1 (1992); 71-81.

Rhymer, Mary Frances, ed. *Vic and Sade: The Best Radio Plays of Paul Rhymer.* New York: Seabury Press, 1976.

Sampson, Emma Speed. *Miss Minerva Broadcasts Billy.* Chicago: Reilly and Lee, 1925.

Settel, Irving. *A Pictorial History of Radio.* New York: Bonanza Books, 1960.

Smith, Mickey. *Pharmacy and Medicine on the Air.* Metuchen, NJ: Scarecrow Press, 1989.

———. *Reflections of Pharmacy in Old-Time Radio.* Madison, WI: American Institute of the History of Pharmacy, 1986.

Streeter, Ed. *Daily Except Sundays, or, What Every Commuter Should Know.* New York: Simon and Schuster, 1938.

Summers, Harrison B., ed. *A Thirty-Year History of Programs Carried on National Radio Networks in the United States, 1926-1956.* Columbus: The Ohio State University Press, 1958.

Thurber, James. "Soapland." In *The Beast in Me and Other Animals.* New York: Harcourt Brace, 1948.

Voss, Frederick S. *Reporting the War: The Journalistic Coverage of World War II.* Washington, D.C.: Smithsonian Institution Press, 1994.

Wertheim, Arthur Frank. *Radio Comedy.* New York: Oxford University Press, 1979.

Wilson, Evan. "About the South," *Atlanta Journal-Constitution*, June 5, 1994; 2M.

B. RADIO PERIODICALS

Hello Again, 1970-present, bimonthly
The Illustrated Press, 1975-present, monthly
The Journal of Radio Studies, 1992-present, annual
NARA News, 1973-present, quarterly
Radio Amateur News, 1919-1920, monthly
Radio Digest—Illustrated , 1922-1933, weekly
Radio Guide, 1931-1943, monthly (later *Movie and Radio Guide*)
Radio Mirror, 1933-1939, monthly (continues until 1961 under several name changes, including *Radio and Television Mirror* and *TV Radio Mirror*)
Radio Recall, 1984-present (began as *When Radio Was King*)
SPERDVAC Radiogram, 1974-present, monthly

Contributor Index

Abercrombie, Barbara, 128-29
Anthony, Bill, 21, 167
Ausburn, Florence Ward, 7

Baker, Doris, 13
Bell, Frank W., 48, 199
Black, Janie Lyle, 8-9
Blocker, Billie B., 63, 177-78
Bobbitt, Joan, 161
Boomgaarden, Darrell E., 124-26
Boothby, Harry, 9-10, 70, 179
Bowers, Ann C., 130
Browne, Wilton M., 70
Buri, Bill, 11, 18, 41, 50, 65-66, 68-69,
    80, 91, 100, 115, 141, 153
Burt, Harriet, 49, 77, 131, 141, 142,
    173
Butler, John, 80, 89-90, 106, 108, 159,
    175

Caler, Jeanette, 15, 179
Capell, Juanita, 15-16, 40, 172
Cartwright, George, 51
Caskey, Claire, 80, 82
Caskey, Martha, 137, 144
Chase, Ann, 20, 163

Chastain, V. T., 16
Chastine, Kathy, 105
Cody, John V., 115, 138
Cox, Robert, 104, 124, 181
Crowley, Margie R., 50, 186
Cunningham, Kathy, 72, 172

Day, Frank L., 129
Day, Patricia, 164
DeMille, Joyce H., 194-95
Dorval, Elton, 33, 112, 116, 121, 131,
    167
Doty, Ralph R., 43-44, 150
Dowis, Fred M., 9
Drummond, Holly Self, 153
Dukes, William E., Sr., 55
Dunnells, Merrill, 10
Durham, Harry, 28, 130, 154, 158

Edmonds, Ellen L., 17, 72, 75, 76, 94
Edwards, Laura H., 52

Fanning, Jim, 27, 39, 76, 86, 110, 130,
    142, 179
Farmer, Jim, 41, 165, 185
Farmer, Nancy, 165

Fetters, Thomas, 71, 117, 143, 168,
  199
Fick, Al, 162
Fisher, Ruby, 104, 172, 173
Franklin, Barbara Lyon, 29, 94, 147
French, Jack, 110, 121, 132

Garrett, Paul, 28, 32
Garrison, Lois, 42, 62, 80
Glazner, Robert B., 53

Hanrahan, Norma Brown, 47, 75, 130,
  161, 165
Harmon, Jim, 19, 111
Harper, Tony, 45
Harris, Joe, 53
Heathwood, Tom, 133, 145, 175,
  188-89
Higdon, Hal, 42, 119, 121, 140, 179
Hilborn, Allen, 6, 42, 63, 164
Hines, Fulton C., 103, 119, 128, 180
Hinkley, H. K., 27, 142
Holtzclaw, Marion, 127
Howe, Maurice, 197-99
Hunter, Marjorie, 50, 84

Ice, L. William, 138
Idol, John, 29, 73, 76, 108

Jennett, Charles, 159
Jennings, Jack, 69
Jones, Joe, 11, 16
Juzek, Chuck, 114

Keepers, Walter M., Jr., 110
Kelley, Gordon, 22, 64, 76, 126, 158
Kenmore, Jeanne, 20, 70, 89, 93, 130,
  140, 142,160, 166, 174, 192-93
Kirkpatrick, Margaret, 68, 71, 73-75,
  91, 103, 109, 120
Kobler, Jane, 46, 50, 119
Koonce, Roger, 116, 122, 140, 146,
  150, 186-87

Lackey, Constance S., 103-105, 144,
  152
Lambert, Robert S., 166
Lemon, Rodman, 9
Lentz, Zelime, 30, 95, 97, l0l, 181
Looper, Paul E., 9
Lowery, Larry, 161, 187
Lyons, Owen, Jr., 12, 81

MacDonald, Bill, 123
Mallary, Nelson D., Jr., 10, 69, 91,
  137, 140-41, 176, 186
Marcaccio, Rose, 41, 104
Matthews, Percy M., 62, 81, 109
McCrackan, Mary Lee, 4, 16, 62, 64,
  76, 139
McKaughan, Rachel P., 17
McNeill, Roger, 153
Mebane, Bell, 6
Messer, Ruth F., 43
Meyerson, Chick, 40
Morgan, Bob, 31, 83, 199
Morrison, Stanley C., 147, 165

Nault, Raymond, 48
Newman, Tom H., 47, 73
Nochisaki, Trina, 17, 144, 161
Norrgard, Carol, 109
Norrgard, Ted, 64, 165

O'Donnell, Mike, 92
Olday, Richard A., 168
Olker, Genella, 44, 73, 172, 180
O'Shee, Patrick, Jr., 34-35, 48, 71, 91,
  116, 140-44, 146, 164, 180

Parks, Erma H., 45
Pomeroy, Owens L., 89, 102, 114,
  123, 138, 141, 146, 151, 155 n. 2,
  165, 167, 174
Poser, Ingrid and Siegfried, 195-97
Proudfoot, Alice Boyd, 6, 175

Raines, Frank, 39, 122
Ramsey, Marshall, Jr., 36, 98, 139, 142, 154, 166, 178, 180-81
Reel, Jerry, 180
Resch, Glen, 30, 72, 74, 89, 119, 146, 167
Rettberg, Harvey, 173
Roach, Pat, 72, 83
Robinson, George, 7, 42, 144, 172, 173
Robinson, Lois, 7, 18, 93, 185
Rollin, Roger, 37, 61, 65-66, 94, 99, 102, 109, 114, 120, 131, 132, 140, 143, 144, 147, 150, 165, 178, 187, 192
Roman, James M., 82
Roper, Ed, 51, 174
Ruland, Raymond, 12, 174, 179

Saffan, Stella, 68
Salathiel, Max, 21, 105, 158, 188
Saunders, Richard, 36, 173
Sawyer, Corinne Holt, 11, 98, 111, 118-19, 137, 139, 141, 150-51, 159
Sayles, Ron, 118
Schlamp, John T., 161
Seabrooke, Brenda, 35, 65, 122
Sender, James L., 50, 65, 74, 95, 112, 114, 120, 176
Simms, John B., 40, 45, 65, 71
Smith, Mickey, 145
Snell, Absalom W., 19, 74, 81, 84, 92
Snow, Paul F., 17, 54, 172
Stallings, Gloria, 71
Stancliff, Dorothy, 73, 104, 163
Steinmetz, Philip Humason, 6, 93, 129, 139
Stewart, Patricia Webster, 181
Sutherland, Frances N., 53
Swehla, Doris, 64, 83, 101, 105, 115, 120, 130, 136, 162, 186

Taylor, Susan, 49, 102, 179, 188
Telles, Larry, 31, 37, 75, 116, 168, 200
Thomason, Evelyn B., 16, 115
Tidwell, Helen J., 19
Trively, Maxine, 5, 81, 104, 105
Truebenbach, Elly, 30, 71, 83, 92, 95, 99, 103, 109, 151, 155 n. 2, 158
Tucker, Charles Wilson, 55-57

Ulbrich, Holley, 84
Usrey, Malcolm, 21, 44, 90, 103, 150, 162

Walker, George A., Jr., 18, 47, 50, 73, 74, 84, 94, 178, 192
Waller, Joan, 20, 22 n, 114
Waller, Robert A., 19, 83, 108, 114
Webb, Hubert, 7
Weigel, Ken, 44, 100, 101, 117, 132, 136, 164, 182, 200
Wentz, B. A. "Gus," 17, 45, 74, 91, 94, 164, 175
Whaley, Gray, 83, 122
Whitworth, Helen Hunt Holmes, 4
Williams, Ellen Messer, 34

Youse, Paul M., 45

General Index

Ace, Goodman and Jane, 119, 146
"The Aldrich Family," 49, 146
Allen, Fred, 141
"The American Junior Red Cross on the Air," 187-88
"America's Town Meeting of the Air," 93
"Amos 'n' Andy," 27, 42, 51, 138-39
André, Pierre, 113, 115
Antennas, 12, 19-20, 32
"Archie Andrews," 132
Armed Forces Radio, 75, 192-93, 195
"The Armstrong Theatre of Today," 154
Australian radio, 197-99

Bailey, Jack, 100-101
Barnard, Arlyn E., 129
Baseball broadcasts, 12, 31, 83-84; studio simulations, 82; World Series, 9, 79, 81
Basketball broadcasts, 84
Benny, Jack, 37, 72, 91, 139-41
Bentley, Julian, 74
Bergen, Edgar, 40, 88, 137, 141-42
Birthday greetings, 131

"Blondie," 136
"Bob and Ray," 27, 147
Boxing broadcasts, 46-47, 80; Billy Conn, 41; Jack Dempsey, 9, 80; Joe Louis, 41, 80, 196; Max Schmeling, 80-81, 196
"The Breakfast Club," 19, 99-100
"Britain to America," 93-94
British radio (BBC), 192, 194-95
"Buck Rogers," 109, 118
"Burns and Allen," 146
Byrd, Adm. Richard E., 62

Caniff, Milton, 121
Cantor, Eddie, 88, 137-38
"Can You Top This?," 41
"Captain Midnight," 111, 116, 120
Carney, "Uncle Don," 128-29
"Chandu the Magician," 118
Christmas programs, 49, 92
Classical and semi-classical music, 89-91
Commentators. See names of specific broadcasters.
Conn, Billy, 41
Connor, Eugene "Bull," 82

Cooke, Alistair, 193-94
Coughlin, Father, 95
Crosby, Bing, 179

Dance band remotes, 174-76
"The Dayton Reporter," 98-99
D-Day bulletins, 74
"Death Valley Days," 153-54
Dempsey, Jack, 9, 80
"The Devil Bird," 120
"The Devil's Roost," 158
Disc jockeys, 181-83; classical, 90
"Dr. I. Q.," 186

"Easy Aces," 119, 146
Edgar Bergen-Charlie McCarthy
    programs, 40, 88, 137, 141-42
Edison, Thomas A., 61-62
Election reports, 16, 61-62, 76;
    KDKA's pioneering, 3, 61
Elliott, Bob, 27, 147
"Escape," 164

"The Farm and Home Hour," 51
"The FBI in Peace and War," 166
Federal Communications
    Commission, 40, 87
"Fibber McGee and Molly," 27, 135,
    143-44; closet effect, 50
"The First Nighter Program," 149,
    151-52
Fitzgerald, Ed and Pegeen, 100
Football broadcasts, 84
The Fourth Chime (NBC), 66-67
Freeman, Dr. Douglas Southall,
    64-65

"Gang Busters," 165-66
George F. Cran Company, 26
German radio, 195-97
Godfrey, Arthur, 76, 99-100
Gosden, Freeman, 123, 139
Goulding, Ray, 27, 147

"Grand Central Station," 154
"The Grand Ole Opry," 52-53, 55,
    172-73
"The Great Gildersleeve," 36-37,
    144-46
Grapevine radio, 52-55, 57 n. 4

Heatter, Gabriel, 65
Heidt, Horace, 185-86
Hershfield, Harry, 41
Hickerson, Jay, 203-4
Hope, Bob, 142-43
"The Hour of Charm," 90-91
"The House of Mystery," 132

"I Love a Mystery," 31, 166-68
"Inner Sanctum Mysteries," 158-61

"Jack Armstrong," 111, 119-20
"The Jack Benny Show," 36, 72,
    139-41
Jordan, Jim and Marian. *See* "Fibber
    McGee and Molly"
"Jones and Hare," 136-37
Journal of Radio Studies, 204-5
"J.W.W., Bethesda, Md.," 87-88

Kaltenborn, H. V., 63-65, 122
KDKA, election returns (1920), 3, 61;
    listener joke on, 5; reception, 4, 12
Keillor, Garrison, 148
Kelley, "Jolly Joe," 131

"Let's Pretend," 129-30
"Lights Out," 159-62
*Like a Family: The Making of a
    Southern Cotton Mill World*, 52
"The Lincoln Highway," 133
"Little Orphan Annie," 11, 115,
    119-20
"The Lone Ranger," 108, 122-25,
    197; music, 112-13; premiums,
    116-17

"Lone Wolf Tribe," 120
Louis, Joe, 41, 47, 80, 196
"Lum and Abner," 199
"The Lux Radio Theatre," 149-51, 197-98

Mack, Nila, 129-30
"Make-Believe Ballroom," 180
Man-in-the-street interviews, 189
"Ma Perkins," 105-6
"The Marlin Hurt and Beulah Show," 147
Martin, Freddy, 180
Mayer, Dr. Walter, 95
McNamee, Graham, 79
McNeill, Don, 19, 99-100
"The Mercury Theatre on the Air," 152
Metropolitan Opera broadcasts, 43, 91
"The Midday Merry-Go-Round," 173
Miller, Glenn, 179-80
"Moon River," 91-92
Morgan, Henry, 146-47
Morrison, Herbert, 64
Morse, Carlton E., 103, 166-67; *See also* "One Man's Family"
Murray, Hal, 182
"Myrt and Marge," 49, 50, 105

NARA (North American Radio Archives), 204
NBC news division, 66-68
NBC Symphony, 35, 89-90
"No School Today," 132

Oboler, Arch, 159
Old Time Radio, organizations, 203-4; tape collecting, 199-200
"One Man's Family," 103, 105
"Our Miss Brooks," 147

Pearl Harbor attack, 34, 70-72
Penner, Joe, 137

Poetry recitations, 91-92
Premiums, children's serial, 114-17
Propaganda broadcasts, 74

"Queen for a Day," 100-101
Quiz programs, 186-87

Radio Digest—Illustrated, 3-4, 33
"Radio fixer," 55-57
REA (Rural Electrification Administration), 15, 19, 30, 48
Reception difficulties, 5, 11, 18, 19 28-29; in car, 125
Remote broadcasts, 189
Remote control radio, 20-21
"Rendezvous with Destiny," 67-68
"Reveille with Beverly," 75
"The Romance of Helen Trent," 106
Roosevelt, Franklin D., 67-69; death and funeral reports, 76; war declaration, 72-73

Schmeling, Max, 80-81, 196
"The Shadow," 64, 163-64
Shepherd, Jean, 147-48
Sherlock Holmes dramatizations, 18, 162-63
"The Singing Story Lady," 130-31
Skelton, Red, 143
"Sky King," 113
Smith, Kate, 100, 104
Soap operas, 101-6
"Songs of Hope and Comfort," 45
Songs, popular, 174-75, 178-79; *See also* "Your Hit Parade"
Sound effects, 82, 136; crime programs, 165-66, 157-58; McGee's closet, 144
SPERDVAC (Society to Preserve and Encourage Radio Drama, Variety, and Comedy), 204
Stern, Bill, 79

St. John, Robert, 65
Streeter, Ed, 22 n. 1
Sunday comics readings, 128-29
"Suspense," 169-69

"Terry and the Pirates," 121
Thomas, Lowell, 50, 63, 65
The Three Suns, 179
"The Tom Mix Ralston Straight-
    Shooters," 112, 114
Turner, Roscoe, 120-21

"Uncle Wiggily," 128

Vallee, Rudy, 137
"The Vass Family," 188
"Vic and Sade," 104, 148
V-J Day reports, 75
The Voice of America, 192-93

"The War of the Worlds," 152-53
Welles, Orson, 152-53
West Coast programming, 27
West, Mae, 40
Wicker, Ireene, 130-31
Winchell, Walter, 65-66
"Wolf Paw," 120
World Series, 9, 79, 81

"Young Widder Brown," 105
"Your Hit Parade," 42, 175-78
"Yours Truly, Johnny Dollar," 168-69

(

About the Author

RAY BARFIELD is Professor of English at Clemson University. He has authored numerous articles, conference papers, and reference book entries on radio, cartoons, children's books, and 1920s fads. He is co-author of a business communications handbook.